First published in 2012

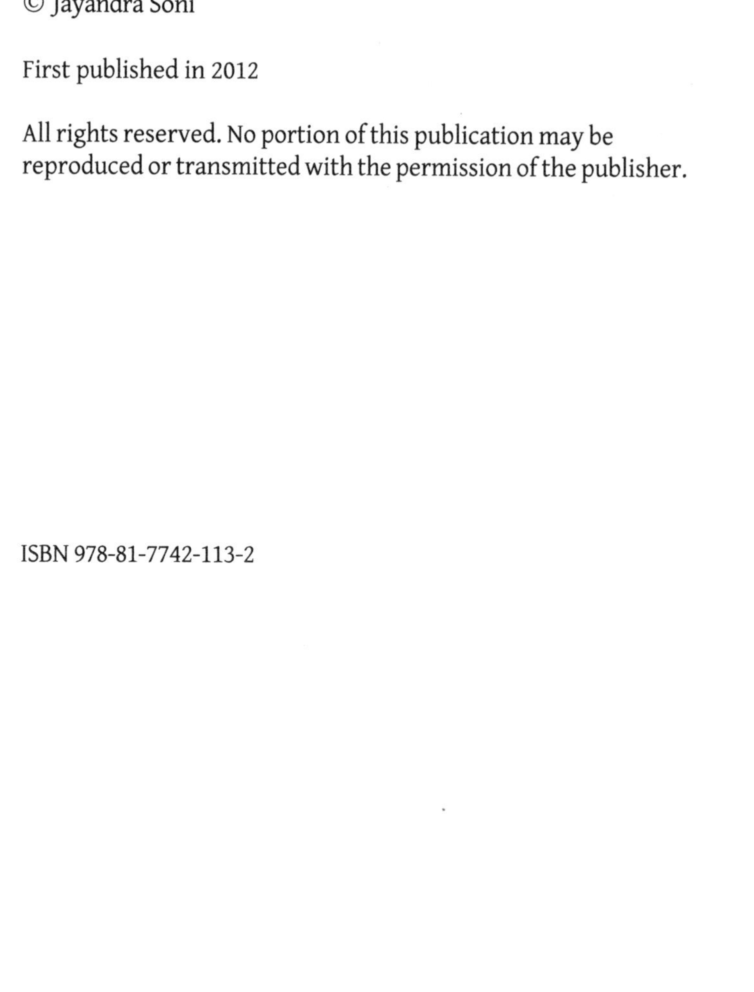

ISBN 978-81-7742-113-2

Published by Aditya Prakashan, 2/18, Ansari Road, New Delhi – 110002.

email: contact@adityaprakashan.com
website: www.adityaprakashan.com

Printed at Salasar Imaging Systems, C-7/5, Lawrence Road Indl. Area, Delhi – 110 035.

Dedicated to the memory of Muni Jambuvijayajī (1923–2009), respectfully and affectionately called 'Sahebjī' by all of us who were privileged to have known this learned and generous scholar-monk.

Contents

Contributors

Nalini Balbir

Nalini Balbir is professor of Indology at Sorbonne-Nouvelle, Paris where she teaches. Her research areas include Jain studies (literatures, religion, etc.), manuscriptology, Pali and Prakrit lexicography. She is currently the content director of the Jainpedia project (www.jainpedia.org).

Université Paris-3 Sorbonne-Nouvelle
UFR Langues, Littératures, Cultures et Sociétés étrangères
Département Etudes arabes, hébraïques, indiennes et iraniennes
13, rue de Santeuil
F-75230 Paris Cedex 05
France. nalini.balbir@wanadoo.fr

Christine Chojnacki

Christine Chojnacki is professor of Indian languages and culture at the university of Lyon 3 in Lyon,France. She has specialised on Jaina Studies, in particular medieval Jain literature in Prakrit and Sanskrit from 8–17th centuries. In 2008 she published (Marburg: Indica and Tibetica) a translation and study of Uddyotana's *Kuvalayamālā* written in 779.

Faculté des Langues
Université Lyon 3
8, cours Albert Thomas
F-69008 Lyon
France christine.chojnacki@univ-lyon3.fr

Anne Clavel

Anne Clavel's main research work is in the field of Jaina philosophy. She concentrates on Sanskrit and Prakrit texts dealing with epistemology and logic. Her PhD was on theory of knowledge of the Jaina thinker Akalaṅka.

16 rue Fabrot
F-13100 Aix-en-Provence
France anne.clavel@club-internet.fr

Anna Aurelia Esposito

Anna Aurelia Esposito is assistant professor at the University of Würzburg, Germany. Her main fields of research are Sanskrit drama, Prakrit studies and Jain narrative literature.

Universität Würzburg
Lehrstuhl für Indologie / Südasienkunde
Philosophiegebäude, Zi. 8U6

Am Hubland
D-97074 Würzburg
Germany anna.esposito@mail.uni-wuerzburg.de

Shin Fujinaga

Shin Fujinaga is professor and has published a great deal on Jainism in general, and particularly on the history of cosmology.

Department of General Education
Miyakonojo National College of Technology
Tadeike 614-9, Mimata, Miyazaki
889-1914 Japan fujinaga@cc.miyakonojo-nct.ac.jp

Julia Hegewald

Julia Hegewald is Professor of Oriental Art History at the University of Bonn. Her research interests are Jaina art and architecture, Jaina culture in south India, water architecture and re-use theory.

University of Bonn
Institut fuer Orient- und Asienwissenschaften (IOA)
Abt. fuer Asiatische und Islamische Kunstgeschichte
Adenauerallee 10, D-53113 Bonn,
Germany julia.hegewald@uni-bonn.de

Basile Leclère

Basile Leclère currently teaches Indian civilization and literature the University of Lyon 3. His particular areas of interest are Jainism, Indian medieval theatre and medieval history.

Faculté des Langues
Université Lyon 3
8, cours Albert Thomas
F-69008 LYON
FRANCE Basile-Raphael.Leclere@ac-lyon.fr

Bhikkhu Pāsādika

Bhikkhu Pāsādika was the Honorary Professor in the Dept. of Indology and Tibetology, Philipp's University Marburg where he taught various themes on Buddhist studies. He is currently concentrating on early Mahāyana literature.

Helisossteig 4, D-34454 Bad Arolsen
Germany pasadika@t-online.de

Sreeramula Rajeswara Sarma

Sreeramula Rajeswara Sarma was formerly Professor of Sanskrit, Aligarh Muslim University. His field of research includes the history of mathematics, astronomy and astronomical instruments in India. He is currently preparing a descriptive catalogue of the latter.

Hoehenstrasse 28
D-40227 Duesseldorf
Germany sr@sarma.de

Jayandra Soni

Jayandra Soni is a lecturer whose research is mainly concerned with Indian philosophy in general and, for some years now, particularly Jaina philosophy.

Department of Indology and Tibetology
Philipps-Universität Marburg
Deutschhausstr. 12
D-35037 Marburg
Germany soni@staff.uni-marburg.de

Himal Trikha

Himal Trikha's research interests are in epistemology, history of Indian philosophy and Jaina philosophy. He is now doing post-doctoral work in his field.

Institute for South Asian, Tibetan and Buddhist Studies
Vienna University
Uni-Campus AAKH
Spitalgasse 2, Hof 2.1
A-1090 Vienna
Austria himal.trikha@univie.ac.at

Introduction

DOT, the *Deutsche Orientalistentag*, is the German Oriental Studies Congress which, as the homepage (http://www.dot2010.de/) says, takes place every three years. It is the most prominent conference of Oriental Studies in Germany convened by the *Deutsche Morgenländische Gesellschaft* (DMG). Researchers and academics from various disciplines of Asian, African and Middle Eastern Studies participate. It is open to all researchers and is not subject to membership in the DMG. The 31st DOT was held in Marburg, Germany, from 20th to 24th September 2010.

The panel 'Jaina Studies' was organised for the section 'Indology and South Asian Studies'. The following description of the panel was announced so as to accommodate as many scholars, and a wide range of specialisations, as possible: 'The aim of the panel is to bring together scholars working in the various fields of Jainism. The panel invites participants to contribute a paper on any field within the area, for example, Jaina philosophy, religion, literature, history, canonical texts. Themes dealing with contemporary Jainism are also welcome'.

For the Newsletter of the Centre of Jaina Studies, SOAS (London), March 2011, Issue 6, Luitgard Soni reported on the panel: 'Jaina Studies Panel at the 31st Deutscher Orientalistentag (DOT)', pp. 20–21. It is reproduced here (without the photographs), with thanks to Peter Flügel for the permission to do so, with minor changes to suit this publication.

The DMG, German Oriental Studies Society, held its 31st Conference of Oriental Studies in Marburg (Germany) from 20–24 September 2010. In the extensive frame of the most prominent conference of Oriental Studies in Germany, in the section "Indology and South Asian Studies" a panel on Jaina Studies was organised by Jayandra Soni, Department of Indology and Tibetology, University of Marburg on Thursday, 23rd September 2010. It was the first Jaina panel ever held at DOT (*Deutscher Orientalistentag*) and, thanks to the response of Jaina scholars, it was the biggest within the section. Twelve participants from Austria, England, France, Japan and Germany presented papers on various fields of Jainism. A friendly autumn sun shone on that day and it was *pūrṇimā*.

Sreeramula Rajeswara Sarma (Aligarh University) started the day with a fascinating introduction to the *Dravyaparīkṣā* by

Ṭhakkura Pherū, a Jain Assayer at the court of the Khaljī Sultāns in Delhi in the first quarter of the fourteenth century. Of his six works in Apabhraṃśa verse on diverse scientific subjects, Sarma presented an exemplifying account of the *Dravyaparīkṣā* which deals with the examination of the metal content (*dravya*) in coins, a then very important technique for pricing coins. The text is unique and very important for the research on realia.

Nalini Balbir (Sorbonne Nouvelle) presented her investigation of the case of Mantri Karmacandra of the seventeenth century. His activities for the promotion of Jainism, which are traceable from various sources, shed light on the patterns of relations between political power and the Jaina community in a given historical setting. Balbir gave an encompassing analysis of the various sources, texts and their authors and drew a multifaceted picture of the functions and the sphere of influence of this Jaina politician. Title: Genealogical Discourse and Jain Sectarian Promotion. *Mantri Karmacandra-Vaṃśāvalī-Prabandha* and the Kharataragaccha.

Bhikku Pasadika (University of Marburg) offered a detailed textual analysis of the Buddhist *Kālāmasutta* with relevant parallel passages from the *Sāḷhasutta*, especially those related to the beginnings of the Jaina *syādvāda*, or regarded as being a Buddhist parallel to it. He showed that the content of the *Kālāmasutta* is indeed epistemological as well as ethical. The famous "know for yourselves" and the avoidance of the ten grounds that should not be gone by for ascertaining a statement's reliability, as well as the four kinds of confidence (*assāsa*), were linked to the non-committal attitude of the intellectually non-violent position of *anekāntavāda*.

Himal Trikha (University of Vienna) expounded the composition of the chapter on Vaiśeṣika in Vidyānandin's *Satyaśāsanaparīkṣā* by analysing the arguments Vidyānandin uses in discussing Vaiśeṣika doctrines. Many of these arguments are found in other philosophical treatises, corresponding to them even literally. Trika's intricate investigation into the integration of these passages in the context of the argument elucidated various realms of composition, which in turn made it possible to see the links to other philosophical works of the Jainas and to appreciate Vidyānandin's specific achievement in the discourse.

Jayandra Soni (University of Marburg) revisited Jaina epistemology and paid special attention to erroneous cognition which may occur not only in sensory but also scriptural knowledge and clairvoyance. Drawing from *sūtras* of the *Tattvārthasūtra* and two of its commentaries, he developed a concise picture of the Jaina theory of error within Jaina epistemology. The term *upayoga* in its application as *darśana* and *jñāna* emerged as a key concept in this context.

Anne Clavel (University of Lyon) introduced the intriguing question of whether *syādvāda* is true only from a certain point of view and explored a possible answer from several philosophical texts by Akalaṅka and others in the course of which the term *añjasā* (besides *paramārthataḥ* and *ekāntena*) was given special attention. The clear cut analysis of the significant passages concerned showed that there are meta-statements which escape the *syādvāda* and that the sevenfold predication draws its validity through perfect cognition, that is omniscience.

The afternoon session, usually subdued by the low energy after lunch, started nevertheless very enjoyably with Julia Hegewald's (University of Bonn) expert examination of the sources of Jaina *havelī* temples in northern India. In word and picture one could follow how the structure and style of the courtyard house-temples developed over the centuries from the initially open courtyard into a roof-covered construction, creating multi-storied halls and spaces, which suit the Jaina ritual requirement.

The next two presentations by Christine Chojnacki and Basile Leclère (both of the Unversity of Lyon) focussed on the *Vibudhānanda* play in Śīlāṅka's novel *Caupannamahapurisacariya* and interpreted it as an innovative form in Jaina literature. Chojnacki, after summarizing the plot, analysing its structure and placing it in the context of the novel, elaborated the interesting peculiarity of inserting a dramatic text in a narrative one. This led to questions about the interaction between drama and narrative, its function, use and performance practices. The discussion about the genre was taken up by Leclère, elicited by the fact that the *Vibudhānanda* is a rare example of a tragic play. The use of dramatic genre depicting sad events and sorrow in human existence might, for Buddhists and Jainas, better serve their doctrinal tenets and their transmission to the audience.

Anna Aurelia Esposito (University of Würzburg) reflected on the relation between the *Bṛhatkathā* and Saṅghadāsa's *Vasudevahiṇḍī* by first giving a survey of the complex story and then pointing out the way in which Guṇāḍhya's material is intertwined with the world history and value system of the Jainas.

Shin Fujinaga (Miyakonojo Kosen) introduced Jinabhadra, whose life and work is fairly reliably datable and thus represents a definite figure for historical references with regard to Jaina philosophy and philosophers. His *Bṛhatsaṃgrahaṇī* indicates the reception of ideas contained in the *Āgamas*. Malayagiri's commentary on it is also rich in quotations from different sources and thus the two works represent an important field of research.

Peter Flügel (SOAS), as the last speaker, rounded up the day by drawing attention to a surprisingly rich and colourful area of social and literary activity: 'Praising the Living, Remembering the Dead. The Sociology of the Jaina Festschrift', was unfolded with numerous examples of this genre from different gacchas and other Jaina groupings, whose householders, monks, nuns and institutions were bestowed with volumes of praise and felicitation. Flügel's lively talk was a fitting end to the panel. One got the impression that all the participants enjoyed the stimulating presentations and discussions. [End of the report.]

These twelve presentations were held in four groups of three each, and filled the day most profitably. Each group was made up of themes somehow related to one another, for example Trikha, Soni and Clavel dealt largely with philosophical aspects of Jainism. It was therefore decided to publish the articles in same sequence as was presented in the panel.

A few words of thanks are appropriate here. First of all, thanks go to the participants for responding to the call for papers of the panel and for making it a most enjoyable success with their presence and presentations, as the report also evinces.

Special thanks are due to Mr Aditya Goel of Biblia Impex for spontaneously accepting to publish this volume in his series when he was approached, and for the pleasure of working with him for it.

Jérôme Petit (Bibliothèque nationale de France, Paris) kindly prepared the Genealogical Tree at the end of Balbir's paper. Thanks are due to him not only for this but also for making available the PDF version of it used here.

My colleague Stanislav Jager very kindly agreed to have a glance at the completed manuscript with a critical eye and I thank him very much for his keen observations.

J. Soni
Marburg, Germany, May 2011.

A Jain Assayer at the Sulṭān's Mint. Ṭhakkura Pherū and his *Dravyaparīkṣā*

Sreeramula Rajeswara Sarma

Abstract

Of the rich contributions made by the Jains to the intellectual history of India, an important but not so well explored aspect is their role as mediators between the Islamic and Sanskrit traditions of learning. One such mediator is Ṭhakkura Pherū who held a high office at the court of the Khaljī Sulṭāns of Delhi in the first quarter of the fourteenth century. Pherū composed several works on different scientific subjects in Apabhraṃśa verse. The most significant of these is the *Dravyaparīkṣā*, which deals with the techniques of refining precious metals and of determining their fineness, and provides the name, provenance, weight, metal content, and exchange value in terms of the Khaljī currency, of some 260 coin types issued by various kingdoms of north India from the twelfth to the early fourteenth centuries. The present paper discusses the contents of this work and explains its importance for the monetary history of the period.

Keywords: ᶜAlā' al-Dīn Muḥammad Khaljī, assay, currency exchange, *Dravyaparīkṣā*, *Gaṇitasārakaumudī*, Jains, Kannāṇā, Khaljī Sulṭāns, Pherū, Quṭb al-Dīn Mubārak Shāh, test sticks, touchstone, *varṇa*

1.0 Pherū's Life

Of the rich contributions made by the Jains to the intellectual history of India, an important but not so well explored aspect is their role as mediators between the Islamic and Sanskrit traditions of learning. I have discussed elsewhere how the Jains were in the forefront of preparing manuals in Sanskrit to teach the Persian language[1] and how the Jain monk Mahendra Sūri wrote the very first Sanskrit manual on the construction and use of the astrolabe, the Islamic astronomical instrument *par excellence.*[2] Ṭhakkura Pherū, who held a high office at the treasury of the Khaljī Sulṭāns of Delhi in the first quarter of the fourteenth century and who wrote on diverse scientific

---

[1] Sarma 1996 and 2002.

[2] Impressed by the versatile functions of the astrolabe, Mahendra Sūri, a pupil of Madana Sūri of Bhṛgupura, gave the astrolabe a Sanskrit name *yantra-rāja* and composed under this title a manual at the Delhi court of Fīrūz Shāh Tughluq in 1370; cf. Sūri 1936. About the end of the fifteenth century, another Jain scholar, Muni Megharatna, pupil of Vinayasundara of the Vaṭagaccha, wrote a small manual entitled *Usturalāva-yantra* in 38 stanzas. See Sarma 1999 and 2000.

and technical subjects in Apabhraṃśa verse is a mediator in several respects: mediator between Sanskrit and Islamic traditions of learning, mediator between the elite Sanskrit and popular Apabhraṃśa, and also mediator between the *śāstra* and commerce.

Pherū is known to the academic world though seven works: *Kharataragaccha-yugapradhāna-catuḥpadikā* (composed in AD 1291) which contains a eulogy of the pontiffs of the Kharatara sect, *Jyotiṣasāra* on astronomy and astrology (1315), *Vāstusāra* on architecture and iconography (1315), *Ratnaparīkṣā* on gemmology (1315), *Dhātūtpatti* (n.d.) on metals and perfumery articles, *Gaṇitasārakaumudī* (n.d., but before 1318) on mathematics, and *Dravyaparīkṣā* (1318) on assay and exchange of coins.[3] Pherū mentions frequently that he is from a town called Kannāṇā or Kannāṇa-pura, which survives today as Kaliyana at 28°33′ N; 76°12′ E in the Bhiwani district of the Haryana state.[4]

Pherū was born in the Śrīmāla caste and was a member of the Kharatara sect of the Śvetāmbara Jains. His father was Ṭhakkura Candra, and his grandfather Kalaśa had the title *siṭṭhi* (Sanskrit: *śreṣṭhin*), "merchant-banker". Pherū mentions a son Hemapāla and a younger brother without name. It is probable that Pherū was born sometime in the second half of the thirteenth century, perhaps around 1270, and was brought up and educated at Kannāṇā. His education was wide-ranging. Besides the Jain religious texts, he also studied several Sanskrit and Prakrit texts on astronomy, astrology, mathematics and architecture. His writings, moreover, reveal his practical experience in the trade of gems and perfumery articles, and in assay and money exchange.

---

[3] The well known Jain savants Agar Chand Nahata (Bikaner) and his nephew Bhanwar Lal Nahata (Kolkata) discovered, around the year 1946, a manuscript containing all the seven works in a Jain Library in Kolkata. The manuscript was copied in 1347, i.e., during Pherū's lifetime or immediately thereafter. The Nahatas published the seven works in 1961; cf. Nahata in the bibliography. Later some of these works were published separately, the details of which will be given below at the appropriate places.

[4] For a detailed account of Pherū's life and works, see Sarma 1984, pp. 1–20.

When the Delhi Sultanate was established towards the end of the twelfth century, the Sulṭāns did not begin fresh coinage with Arabic legends. Instead, they adapted the fabric of existing Chauhan coinage and added their respective names in Nāgarī script. Because banking and minting in the Gujarat-Rajasthan-Delhi region was largely controlled by the Jains,[5] their cooperation was sought by the Sulṭāns for conducting banking and minting operations. Especially the Jains of the Śrīmāla clan, to which Pherū belonged, were known for their expertise in minting and banking.

In the *Lekhapaddhati*, a collection of model documents from the early medieval Gujarat, the coins used in various public and private transactions are often described as *śrī-śrīmālīya-khara-ṭaṃkaśālā-hata-triparīkṣita*, implying that the coins were struck (*hata*) in a mint (*ṭaṃkaśālā*) belonging either to the city of Śrīmāla (modern Bhinmal, 25° 0′ N; 72° 15′ E, in the state of Rajasthan) or to persons belonging to the Śrīmāla clan, and that these coins were tested three times (*triparīkṣita*) for their metal content, or more precisely for the content of silver or gold. It is not clear what *khara* in this expression denotes. It is possible that it refers to the *kharatara-gaccha* of Śvetāmbara Jains. Then the expression would mean that coins were produced at a mint maintained by Śrīmāla Jains of the Kharatara sect, to which Pherū also belonged. After minting the coins, these were tested three times to ensure that they had the correct weight and contained the correct amount of gold or silver, which determines the intrinsic value of the coin. The fact that this expression occurs in as many as twelve documents shows that this must have been a standard formula in early medieval Gujarat to express the genuineness of a particular coin.[6] Owing to these commercial and monetary reasons, the Jains had good relations at the Delhi court. Several of them were also employed there.

Coming from a family of merchant-bankers, Pherū found a ready appointment at the treasury of the Khaljī Sulṭāns of Delhi. It is not known precisely when he entered the services of the Sulṭāns, but it must have been several years before 1315,

---

[5] See Deyell 1990, p. 247.

[6] See Strauch 2002, pp. 139, 171, 174, 177, 180 et passim.

because in this year he completed the *Ratnaparīkṣā,* where he states that he was employed at the treasury of ᶜAlā' al-Dīn Khalijī. Pherū continued the service under ᶜAlā' al-Dīn's successors, Shihāb al-Dīn ᶜUmar (r. 1316) and Quṭb al-Dīn Mubārak Shāh (r. 1316–1320) and possibly also under Ghiyās al-Dīn Tughluq (r. 1320–1325). In 1318 Pherū occupied a high position at the mint of Quṭb al-Dīn. The *Dravyaparīkṣā,* which Pherū completed in that year, was based on his experience at the Delhi mint.

V. S. Agrawala wrote that Pherū was the mint master at Delhi,[7] and since then everybody has been repeating it. However, there is no clear evidence to support this view. At the beginning of the *Dravyaparīkṣā*, Pherū merely states that he was "employed at the Delhi mint" (*siri ḍhilliya ṭaṃkasāla kajjaṭhiye*). He does not say that he was the head of the Delhi mint, as Agrawala supposes. As we shall see below, the coinage of ᶜAlā' al-Dīn Khaljī and his successors whom Pherū had served contain several imperial and religious titles in Arabic which the monarchs assumed. In the reign of Quṭb al-Dīn Mubārak, the range of coinage was substantially increased; in addition to the circular fabric of coins, a new square fabric was introduced. More important still, in his coinage Quṭb al-Dīn dispensed with the nominal allegiance shown to the Caliph depicted in the coinage of his predecessors (e.g., *yamīn al-khilāfa,* "the right hand of the Caliphate) and assumed himself the titles of "Caliph, the Lord of the two Worlds" (*khalīfa rabb al-'alamīn*), the "Most High Imām" (*al-imām al-a'zam*) and similar grandiloquent titles. It is naturally the responsibility of the mint master to see that these religious titles in Arabic are correctly reproduced on the coinage. Such responsibility would certainly not have been conferred upon a non-Muslim.

Moreover, had Pherū been the mint master, the *Dravyaparīkṣā* would have contained some information on the process of minting which is totally absent in the *Dravyaparīkṣā*. What this work contains are brief descriptions of the techniques of assay and purification of precious metals and a detailed account of exchange of coins. These, as Pherū himself says,

---

[7] See Agrawala, 1951–1952, p. 321: *ṭhakkura pherū alāuddīn khaljī ke dillī kī taṃkasāl ke adhyakṣa the*; this is repeated in his subsequent publications.

were written down for the sake of his brother and son, who may have been embarking on a career as assayers and money-exchangers. Thus, the *Dravyaparīkṣā* is primarily a manual on assay and money exchange. It would be safer, therefore, to assume that Pherū was the assayer or the assay master at the Delhi mint under Sulṭān Quṭb al-Dīn Mubārak.

1.1 Pherū's Writings

Pherū's scientific writings in Apabhraṃśa differ from the earlier or contemporary Sanskrit scientific texts, not merely in language, but in several other respects. Sanskrit scientific writings, like other Sanskrit writings, are normative in nature, and avoid any spatial or temporal reference.

This will be clear, for example, from the metrology, or the units of measurement, employed in mathematical texts. Whether it is Āryabhaṭa writing in Kusumapura in Bihar towards the end of the fifth century, or Bhāskara I in Valabhī in Gujarat in the first half of the seventh century, or Bhāskara II in Maharashtra in the middle of the twelfth century, they all use what is called the Māgadha-māna, "the [units of] measurement of Magadha". Not so in the case of Pherū's writings, which allow us to reconstruct the metrology employed in the Delhi-Haryana region in the first half of the fourteenth century.

Moreover, Sanskrit writers generally state that they had studied all the works of the *purvācāryas*, and are giving merely a summary of their past writings. Thus, they lay greater emphasis on their *śāstra-jñāna*. Pherū also mentions the *śāstras* he has read, but lays stress on his practical experience, stating often *niyadiṭṭhiye daṭṭhuṃ*, "having seen with own eyes" or *paccakkhaṃ aṇubhūyaṃ*, "having experienced directly".

Four of Pherū's works show valuable traces of Pherū's direct experience and thus are rich in contemporary data. The *Dhātūtpatti*[8] deals briefly with the extraction and purification of metals like brass (*pittali*), copper (*tambaya*) and lead (*sīsaya*); and in greater detail with perfumery articles like camphor, aloe-wood, sandal, musk, saffron, their places of occurrence,

---

[8] See Nahata 1961, III, pp. 39–44 (text only) and Nahata 1976 (text with Hindi translation).

properties, varieties and, most importantly, their prices. It is possible that Pherū's family was engaged in the trade of metals and perfumery articles, along with gems.[9]

On gems Pherū wrote a small work with the title *Ratna-parīkṣā*[10] on the basis of the Sanskrit works by Buddhabhaṭṭa, Bṛhaspati and others, and more importantly on the basis of his practical knowledge. He states that he has "directly experienced the examination of gems by experts" (*paccakkhaṃ aṇubhūyaṃ maṃḍaliya-parikkiyaṃ*) "during the victorious reign of ᶜAlā' al-Dīn, ... after having seen with his own eyes the vast ocean-like collection of gems in his treasury" (*allāvadīṇa-kalikāla-cakkavaṭṭissa kosamajjhatthaṃ / rayaṇāyaru-vva rayaṇuc-cayaṃ ca niyadiṭṭhiye daṭṭhuṃ*). His family must have been in the gem trade, and Pherū may have been trained by the senior members of the family. Above all, he had the opportunity to see in the treasury of ᶜAlā' al-Dīn Khaljī a vast collection of gems. Pherū must have been an expert gemmologist and a high official in the treasury; otherwise, he would not have had access to ᶜAlā' al-Dīn's gem collection.

His book on gemmology follows the traditional pattern of the Sanskrit texts. What is new here is a very detailed tariff of prices of different kinds of gems, which increases exponentially according as the weight increases. It is certain that this tariff of prices is contemporary, that is, valid for the Delhi region in the first quarter of the fourteenth century.

The *Gaṇitasārakaumudī*[11] is not dated, but there are reasons to believe that it must have been composed much earlier than 1318 when Pherū wrote the last known work *Dravyaparīkṣā*. With 311 stanzas distributed in five chapters, it is the largest of his seven works. It is not only the first full-fledged mathematical text in Apabhraṃśa, but it also extends the range of mathematics beyond the traditional framework of the earlier

---

[9] On the perfumery trade, cf. McHugh 2008, pp. 306 ff.

[10] See Nahata 1961, III, pp. 1–16 (text only) and Nahata n.d. (text with Hindi translation); Sarma 1984.

[11] Nahata 1961, IV, pp. 41-74; SaKHYa 2009.

Sanskrit texts, and includes diverse topics from the daily life where numbers play a role.

The first three chapters are structured like the Sanskrit mathematical texts and treat traditional topics like fundamental operations, fractions, series, proportion, plane and solid geometry and so on. What Pherū had learnt from his own experience and from that of his contemporaries is presented as supplementary material in the fourth and fifth chapters. The supplementary material includes mechanical shortcuts in commercial arithmetic, mathematical riddles, rules for converting dates from the Vikrama era to Hijrī era and vice versa, and classification and construction of magic squares. These topics were not touched upon in any mathematical text before.

The section of solid geometry provides rules for calculating the volumes of domes (*gomaṃṭa,* from Persian *gumbad*), minarets (*munāraya,* from Persian *mīnār*), arches (*tāka,* from Persian *tāq*) and similar innovations in architecture introduced by the Sulṭāns of Delhi. The references to the arch and dome are particularly interesting, because just about the same time when Pherū was composing his *Gaṇitasārakaumudī,* the true arch and the true dome were employed successfully for the first time in the ᶜAlā' ī Darwāza, the gateway erected by ᶜAlā' al-Dīn in 1311 as part of his extension plans to the Quwwāt al-Islām mosque, which contains the Quṭb Minār.

Finally, there is a highly interesting section listing the average yield of several kinds of grains and pulses per *bīghā,* the proportions of different products derived from sugar cane juice, and the amount of ghee that can be obtained from milk. This valuable data has naturally attracted the attention of economic historians.[12]

Thus, Ṭhakkura Pherū's *Gaṇitasārakaumudī* throws valuable light on the development and popularization of mathematics in northern India in the early fourteenth century and also on the economic conditions of that period, especially in the Delhi-Haryana-Rajasthan region, as no other mathematical work does.

---

[12] Cf. Habib, 1982.

2.0 The *Dravyaparīkṣā*

Chronologically the last and in content the most unique is the *Dravyaparīkṣā* (henceforth DP)[13] which Pherū composed in 1318.[14] It consists of 149 *gāthās.* As in other works, here also the title of the work is in Sanskrit; within the text there are many section headings, colophons and sub-colophons which are in a kind of mixed Sanskrit. Thus, *iti svarṇa vivahāraṃ, vivaraṇaṃ jantreṇāha, iti draṃmamudrāḥ,* etc. There occur also some technical terms taken from the Persian, like *cāsanī* or *cāsanikā,* which will be discussed below.

But it is the main language of the text, Apabhraṃśa, which causes serious problems in understanding. When I came across Pherū's works for the first time many years ago, I was impressed that he wrote on so many scientific topics in the popular Apabhraṃśa, and in my youthful enthusiasm wrote a paper with the title "Popularisation of Science in the fourteenth century".[15] But when one begins to study the texts closely the Apabhraṃśa verses with the elision of many consonants and with the frequent elongation of vowels for metrical

---

[13] Nahata 1961, III, pp. 17–38 (text only); Nahata 1976 (text with Hindi translation). The Nahatas were keen that the renowned scholar Vasudev Sharan Agrawala should translate and annotate especially the work on numismatics. Agrawala too recognized the uniqueness of the *Dravyaparīkṣā,* but could not fulfill the wishes of the Nahatas completely. He published a partial English translation of *gāthās* 51–139; see Agrawala 1966 (reprint 1969). An English translation of the entire text is still a desideratum; it should clearly explain the chemical and metallurgical processes described in the *gāthās* 1–50 and contain a thorough analysis of the coin catalogue (in *gāthās* 51–149), comparing Pherū's data with the actual specimens and their modern assays.

[14] In the concluding verse of the DP, Pherū mentions that he has expounded the subject briefly for the sake of his son and brother in the year 1375 of the Vikrama era; cf. DP 149: *evvaṃ davvaparikkhaṃ disimittaṃ caṃdatanaya phereṇa | bhaṇiya suyabaṃdhavatthe teraha paṇhattare varise ||* .

[15] Sarma 1986. Curiously enough, this paper turned out to be very popular; it was printed three times in Kolkata! It was reprinted in *Jain Journal,* 21.3 (January 1987), pp. 86–95; and again in Ganesh Lalwani, *Jainanthology: An Anthology of Articles selected from Jain Journal of last 25 Years,* Jain Bhavan, Calcutta 1991, pp. 146–156.

purposes[16] proves to be an inadequate medium for scientific communication. When the subject is somewhat known, one can with some effort restore the consonants and draw some sense out of the text. Even then with undifferentiated case endings it is often difficult to know which is the multiplier and which is the multiplicand. But when the subject is new, it is often difficult to derive any sense out of the brief verses. When my Japanese friends and I were working on the *Gaṇita-sārakaumudī*, the mathematics was not difficult to understand, but when the subject is the calculation of the area of cloth required to cover various types of tents, our collective linguistic and mathematical expertise failed to cope with it. We looked at the pictures of tents in the Mughal miniatures of the seventeenth century; we talked to contemporary tent makers of the twentieth century, but all in vain. Pherū's discussion of tents is certainly valuable for the cultural history of the fourteenth century, but the correct apprehension remains still elusive.[17]

Similar problems occur also in the DP. However, there is a useful innovation in this book. Since the data provided in the metrical *gāthās* is numerical, Pherū adds after each block of text a table where he presents the same material in numerals in a visually more appealing manner.

As stated earlier, Pherū was the assay master at the mint of Quṭb al-Dīn Mubārak Shāh, and he composed the DP for his younger brother and son on the basis of his direct experience at the Delhi mint (*siriḍhilliya taṃkasāla kajjaṭhie / aṇubhūya karivi...*).[18] The term *dravya-parīkṣā* means the examination of

---

[16] Pherū even modifies his own name for metrical reasons as "phira" in 4ab: *taṃ bhaṇaï kalasanaṃdaṇa caṃdasuo phira [a]ṇubhāya taṇayatthe* and as "phera" in 149ab: *evvaṃ davvaparikkhaṃ disimittaṃ caṃdataṇaya phereṇa.*

[17] SaKHYa 2009, pp. 28–29, 36, 77–78, 86, 189.

[18] DP 2–3: *je nāṇā muddāiṃ siri ḍhilliya ṭaṃkasāla kajjaṭhiye | aṇubhūya karivi pattiu vanhi muhe jaha payāu ghiyaṃ || taṃ bhaṇaï kalasanaṃdaṇa caṃdasuo phira 'ṇubhāya taṇayatthe | tiha mullu tullu davvo nāmaṃ ṭhāmaṃ muṇaṃti jahā ||* "[Pherū] who is employed (*kajjaṭhiye*) in the mint (*ṭaṃkasālā*) at the glorious Delhi and thus has direct experience of various types of coins (*muddā*), just as clarified butter [is obtained] after melting [the butter] on the fire, even so after having [melted the coins and] understood (*karivi pattitu*) [their metal content]; Pherū, son of Canda, son of Kalasa, describes them (i.e., the coins)

the metal content (*dravya*) in the coins. As there was no official rate of exchange at that time for different currencies, the official or private money exchangers priced a coin on the basis of its metal content, for example, by ascertaining the amount of pure gold or pure silver in a particular coin. Such a determination of the metal content in artefacts is called assay.

Since the coins issued by several kingdoms in different periods of time continued to be in circulation, it was necessary to determine their intrinsic value by assay and to fix their exchange rate in terms of the local currency. Pherū calls this money exchange *nāṇavaṭṭa* (Sanskrit: *nāṇaka-vartana*). From this is derived the term *nāṇavaṭī* in the sense of money exchangers. The word survives still as a surname in Gujarat. How important this profession was can be seen by the number of related surnames like Parekh/Parikh (from Sanskrit *parīkṣaka*) or Potdar/Poddar[19] (from the Persian *fotah-dār*).[20]

The DP can be divided into two parts. The first part, consisting of 50 stanzas, deals with the techniques of assaying and thus provides the necessary technical background for currency exchange, while the second part, in 99 verses, offers valuable data on 260 coin types, which include not only the coins issued by the Khaljī Sulṭāns, but also by various kingdoms in northern India in the twelfth, thirteenth and early fourteenth centuries. This detailed listing of coins greatly adds to our numismatic knowledge, which is based on the limited number of extant coins preserved in museums and private collections. The uniqueness of this text cannot be overemphasized; there has not been such a text before or afterwards in India, in fact anywhere else in the medieval world. In this respect, Pherū's DP is comparable to the equally unique *De Re Metallica* of Georgius Agricola (1494–1555).[21]

---

for the sake of his brother and son so that they know the price (*mullu*), weight (*tullu*), metal content (*davvo*), name (*nāma*) and the place of issue (*ṭhāma*)".

[19] Wilson 1855, s.v.

[20] Assayers and money-exchangers were also designated by the Persian term ṣarrāf which was anglicized as "shroff". On the importance of this profession, cf. Mehta 1991, pp. 66–67 et passim.

[21] The original Latin version was published posthumously in Basel in 1556. For an excellent English translation, cf. Hoover 1912. It may be noted

John S. Deyell evaluates the DP in these words: "It [sc. the DP] concerns the contemporary coinage issued under his direction, discussing denominations, metrology and metal content. In addition, Pheru undertook a thorough survey of the various Indian and foreign coins which were tendered at the mint for melting and re-minting. The author, being well informed, was able to supplement the usual banker's nick-names for different coins with his observations on the political and geographic origin of the coins encountered. In this the *Dravya Parīkshā* provides the key to many obscure early medieval coinage series."[22]

2.1 Assay by Touchstone (*Varṇamālikā*)

The metallurgical process of assay or measuring the degree of fineness of precious metals was mainly of two types: with the touchstone (*nikaṣa* or *kaṣa*)[23] or by fire assay. Gold or any other metal, when rubbed against the rough surface of the touchstone, leaves on it a streak of very fine powder which shows a more consistent colouration than the same mineral in a massive form. Thus, the colour of the streak is a more accurate index of the quality of the mineral than its surface colour. There are reports of skilled jewellers being able to estimate the fineness of gold just by the feel of the piece between the fingers[24] or just by one look at the streak on the touchstone. However, the general practice is to prepare a series of gold pieces with descending degrees of fineness for the sake of comparison. The gold to be tested is rubbed on the touchstone and the streak thus produced is compared with the streaks of reference gold pieces.

I have discussed elsewhere the history of testing gold by the touchstone in India.[25] Kauṭilya was the first to mention

---

that Herbert Clark Hoover became subsequently the 31st President of the United States (1929–1933). For a German translation, see Schiffner 1928.

[22] Deyell 1990, p. 253.

[23] Sanskrit lexica list *śāṇa* as a synonym of *kaṣa* (*Amarakoṣa*, p. 348: *śāṇas tu nikaṣaḥ kaṣaḥ*, comm. *tṛīṇi suvarṇaparīkṣā-pāṣāṇasya*), but the actual usage shows that the former is a grinding stone and not a touchstone.

[24] See Thomas 1891, pp. 181–182.

[25] On the history of the assay by touchstone in India, see Sarma 1983.

this method of testing the purity of gold in the *Suvarṇādhyakṣa-prakaraṇa* of his *Arthaśāstra*, where he measures the gold in a scale of 1 to 16 *varṇas*.[26] The term *varṇa* denotes the colour of streak as well as the degree of purity or fineness. For easy handling, the reference gold pieces were cast in an elongated shape like pencils.[27] Such test sticks are called *varṇa-śalākās, suvarṇa-śalākās, parīkṣā-śalākās* or just *śalākās*. The series of gold pieces with regularly descending degree of fineness is known as *varṇamālikā*.

The preparation of the reference or test sticks involves the calculation of the proportions of gold and base metals in each stick. Starting from Śrīdhara's *Pāṭīgaṇita* of the ninth century, Sanskrit mathematical texts contain a small section called the "Mathematics of Gold" (*suvarṇa-gaṇita*) where they teach how to calculate the proportions of gold and base metal in an alloy of a certain degree of fineness or how to exchange certain amount of gold of fineness x against gold of fineness y, and similar problems.[28] These texts show the prevalence of gold assay by the touchstone. They also show that the fineness of gold was measured in a scale of 1 to 16 at least up to the twelfth century.

But in Pherū's time, the purity of gold was not measured any more on the scale 1 to 16, but on a new scale of 1 to 12. This new scale is akin to the modern scale of 1 to 24 carats, but it has not been possible to find out why this change occurred. It does not seem to have been borrowed from Persia because, according to Abū al-Faḍl, there they used a decimal scale of 1 to 10. And this new scale of 1 to 12 prevailed later on at the court of Akbar also, as Abū al-Faḍl reports.[29] In Pherū's

---

[26] *Arthaśāstra* 2.13.15–16.

[27] According to Abū al-Faḍl, in the Mughal period, the standard gold pieces were made in the shape of small balls and mounted on brass needles; cf. Blochmann 1873, pp. 18–38.

[28] The DP also has a small section (*gāthās* 38–41) dealing with the "mathematics of gold" (*svarṇa-vivahāra*); a mathematical problem of gold occurs also in Pherū's *Gaṇitasārakaumudī* 1.69; cf. SaKHYa 2009, pp. 14 (text) and 55 (translation).

[29] Blochmann 1873, p. 18: "The highest degree of purity is called in Persia *dahdahí*, but they do not know above ten degrees of fineness; whilst in India it is called *bárahabání*, as they have *twelve* degrees."

Apabhraṃśa, the term *varṇa* became *vannī,* and the purest gold was described as *vārahi vannī,* "that which has twelve *varṇas*".[30]

Pherū envisages a series of 48 test sticks, each less by a quarter *vannī* than the previous stick. For producing these, a mixture of 23 parts silver and 77 parts copper, which is called *rīsa,* is added to pure gold in different proportions.[31] Thus,

47 parts pure gold + 1 part mixture produces gold of 11 ¾ *vannī*

46 parts pure gold + 2 parts mixture produces gold of 11 ½ *vannī* and so on. [32]

It is not known how silver was graded before Pherū's time, but Pherū grades it on a scale of 1 to 20, purest silver being called 20-*visuvā* silver. For producing the reference sticks to test the purity of silver, the pure silver is degraded by the addition of a mixture (*rīsa*) consisting of 4 parts pure copper and 16 parts pure brass.[33] Pherū does not say how many test sticks are prepared for testing the fineness of silver, but it is reasonable to presume that at least one stick is made for each *visuvā.* Thus, a series of 20 sticks may have been prepared for measuring the fineness of silver on the scale of 1–20.[34]

2.2 Assay by Fire (*cāsaṇiya*)

The second method of assaying the purity of gold or silver is by melting it by fire. This is also known as the loss of weight method. One takes a sample of the gold or silver, weighs it, melts it at a high temperature to remove the impurities, and then weighs again. Pherū calls this process of assay by melting

---

[30] DP 38.

[31] DP 36–37.

[32] In his *De Re Metallica* Agricola describes the process of assay by the test sticks and even provides a woodcut depicting these test sticks. He grades the fineness in the scale of 1 to 24 and therefore his illustration shows a series of 24 sticks or needles, containing gradually increasing quantities of gold and regularly decreasing quantities of silver. Cf. Hoover 1912, pp. 253–256.

[33] DP 31–32.

[34] In his *Les six voyages,* the French jeweler Jean-Baptiste Tavernier (1605–1689) includes a sketch of 13 test-sticks used for testing the quality of silver in India; the sketch is reproduced in Petit 2008–2009, p. 148.

cāsaṇiya or *cāsanikā*. The word is from the Persian *chāshnī*. One who performs this task is called *chāshnīgīr.*[35]

The process is based on the principle that precious metals do not oxidize or react chemically and that they remain separate while the others form slags or other compounds. The metal to be melted is placed in a small cone-like vessel, which is surrounded by charcoal and heated. The vessel is called "cupel" (Sanskrit *mūṣā*[36]) and the whole process is also known as cupellation. According to Pherū, the cupel is made by moistening bone ashes and molding the moist substance into the desired shape. This is done so that the impurities in the metal to be melted are absorbed by the ashes.[37] Pherū's prescriptions for this are as follows:

> Take one part each of dry *Palāśa* (*Butea frondosa*) wood, wild cow's dung and goat's bones and burn them together. Strain the ashes. With one and a quarter *sers* (= 270 g) [of these ashes] form a cup (*gaha*) [in which place the metal to be melted]. Blowing gently with a blow-pipe (*vaṃkanālī*), melt it with one and a quarter man (= 11kg 3 g) of charcoals of the *Dhava* tree (*Grislea tomentosa* or *Anogeissus latifolia*)."[38]

This basic procedure of assay is followed in the DP by more elaborate processes of the purification of gold and silver and of extracting silver from lead. These are similar to the basic

---

[35] F. Steingass, *A Comprehensive Persian-English Dictionary,* s.v. explains chāshnī as "taste, taste by way of a sample, proof, trial, ... assay" and *chāsh-nīgīr* as "a taster to a prince, a cup bearer, a carver." In India, however, both the words were associated with the assay of gold and silver in the mint, and they were used in this sense by Abū al-Faḍl in his *Ā'īn-i Akbarī*; cf. Blochmann 1873, p. 23. Since *chāshnī* involves heating and liquefying metals, it came to mean also the treacle formed in the course of producing sugar from sugarcane juice. This is the sense that prevails in modern Hindi today.

[36] In Sanskrit there is extensive literature on the process of cupellation, which has been competently studied by Deshpande 1996.

[37] According to Agricola the best material is the ashes obtained from the burnt horns of a deer; cf. Hoover 1912, pp. 228–229.

[38] DP 5-6: *sukkaṃ palāsakaṭṭhaṃ gomaya ārannagā ajā atthiṃ | kami tiya ige gi bhāyaṃ egaṭṭhaṃ dahiya taṃ rakkhaṃ || chāṇiya sera savāyaṃ vaṃdhi gahaṃ vaṃkanāli dhami mandaṃ | dhava aṃgāra savā maṇi sohiya uttaraï cāsaṇiyaṃ ||*

assay, but performed on a larger scale. The metal to be refined is melted with an excess of lead, which becomes oxidized and forms litharge and dissolves any base metals present, thus separating them from the silver or gold. The litharge soaks into the lining but the precious metal is left on the surface. The more one repeats the process, the purer the metal becomes.[39] Thus, in order to achieve 100% pure gold, one has to melt the gold several times.[40]

The coins of various types which were in circulation were brought to the royal mint where they were melted and cast as pure gold or silver ingots. These ingots were either preserved as such in the treasury or used for minting new coinage. Therefore the knowledge of these processes is essential for officers of the treasury. Pherū's account is the earliest to be found in India. Three hundred years later, Abū al-Faḍl gives a more detailed account in his *Ā'īn-i Akbarī* in connection with the description of the imperial mint.[41]

2.3 The Basic Monetary and Weight Units

Before I discuss the coins and their parameters described by Pherū, it is necessary to briefly explain the monitory and weight units prevalent at Delhi at the time when the DP was written. The standard coin of this period is the silver *Ṭaṃkā* with a weight of one *tolā*. On the basis of the extant specimens, numismatists have estimated that the *tolā* of this period is

---

[39] Wulff 1966, p. 13: "The cupellation process that separates the precious from the base metals with the aid of lead added to the melt and subsequent oxidization of both lead and base metals must have been known for a long time, since most gold and silver objects of antiquity show a high degree of purity."

[40] Abū al-Faḍl boasts that at Akbar's mint the process of refining gold was so highly developed that ᶜAlā' al-Dīn's *dīnār* type of coin which was supposed to be purest gold at 12 *vannī*, turned out to be just 10 ½ *vannī* when tested by the advanced methods at Akbar's mint; cf. Blochmann 1873, p. 12.

[41] Blochmann 1873, pp. 18–38. The most detailed description of the processes of assay and purification of not just gold and silver, but a range of other minerals is given by Georgius Agricola in his *De re metallica*. Here he approaches the subject not as treasury official, but as a mining engineer, with elaborate woodcut illustrations. Cf. Hoover 1912, Books VII–XI.

roughly equal to 11.003 grams.[42] This silver *Ṭaṃkā* was equal in value to 60 *dammas* (Sanskrit *dramma*). The *damma*, popularly known as *gānī*, was a coin made of billon, i.e. an alloy of silver and copper, and weighed 1 *māṣā* (1/12 *tolā* = 0.917 g). There were eight different denominations of *damma* or *gānī* coins, viz., of 1, 2, 4, 6, 8, 12, 24 and 48 *gānīs*, which were designated respectively *iggānī, dugānī, caügānī, chagānī, aṭhagānī, bārahgānī, caübīsagānī, aḍtālīsagānī.* Pherū states that "in the treasury and in public transactions everywhere, the basis of accounting was *iggānī* or 1 *gānī*."[43] The lowest denomination is *visuvā* which has the value of one-twentieth of a *damma*. It is a copper coin, weighing 1 *māṣā* (0.917 g). The scheme of weights in the DP is as follows:

20 *visuvas* = 1 *java* (=0.057 g)
16 *javas* = 1 *māṣa* (=0.917 g)
4 *māṣas* = 1 *ṭaṃka* (=3.667 g)
3 *ṭaṃka* = 1 *tolā* (=11.003 g)

Here the weight unit *ṭaṃka* (approximately 3.667 g) has to be distinguished from the monetary unit *Ṭaṃka*, which weighs 1 *tola* or 11.003 g.

2.4 The Catalogue of Coins

The second part of the DP constitutes a kind of catalogue of coins. Here Pherū provides the name (*nāma*), provenance (*ṭhāma*), weight (*tullu*), metal content (*davvo*), and the exchange value in terms of the Khaljī currency (*mullu*),[44] of some 260 types of coins issued by various kingdoms of northern India in the twelfth, thirteenth and early fourteenth centuries. The data is given first in verses and then in tables (*jantra*).[45] For the sake of the metre, sometimes the proper names of the coins are modified in the verses; sometimes the

---

[42] Deyell 1990, p. 261.

[43] DP 136. The *iggānī* is the standard unit of currency; cf. Gupta 1969, pp. 87–89; Wright 1974, pp. 105–107.

[44] At the very outset, Pherū promises to provide these parameters for all the coins; cf. DP 3, cited in n. 18 above.

[45] These tables are preceded occasionally (e.g., after DP 77) by the prose line: *vivaraṃ jantreṇāha*, "the details are told by means of a table."

proper sequence of the denominations is changed. These are, however, correctly reproduced in the tables. Thus, the tables serve as corrective supplements to the verses.

The coins described are of five types: gold, silver, gold-silver-copper alloy (*tri-dhātu-miśrita-mudrā*), silver-copper alloy or billon (*dvi-dhātu-mudrā*) and copper. The metal content of each coin type is expressed as follows. In the case of gold and silver coins, the degree of fineness is given in the scale of 1 to 12 for gold and of 1 to 20 for silver. For coins made of alloy, the weight of each metal per 100 specimens is listed. For example, the parameters of a coin named *Paüma* (Sanskrit: *Padma*) minted at Varanasi, presumably under the reign of the Gahaḍavāla kings, are given as follows:

> The coin from Varanasi called *Paüma* is [made] of three metals. One hundred coins weigh thirty-seven *tolas,* and contain forty-one *ṭaṃkas* of eleven *vannī* eleven *java* gold; thirty-six *ṭaṃkas* of pure silver and thirty-four *ṭaṃkas* of copper.
> In each *Paüma,* there are silver, gold and copper one *māṣa* each plus seven, ten and five *javas* and zero, four and fifteen *visuvas* respectively.
> The weight of a single *Paüma* is one *ṭaṃka,* seven *javas,* sixteen *visuvaṃsas.* Know that its price is fifty-nine or sixty *jaithalas.*[46]

That is to say, each coin weighs 1 *ṭaṃka,* 7 *javas* and 16 *visuvas* and consists of 1 *māṣā,* 10 *javas* and 4 *visuvas* of gold; 1 *māṣā,* 7 *javas* of silver; and 1 *māṣā,* 5 *javas* and 15 *visuavas* of copper. The touch of the gold is 11 *vannī* 11 *java,* where *java* is one-sixteenth part of a *vannī;* this translates to 23 3/8 carats. This data is given more clearly in the table.

2.4.1 The Nomenclature of Coins

An interesting feature of the catalogue is the plethora of names of the coins. Today a coin is generally known by its denomination, but in Pherū's time, the nomenclature was formed in several ways, often after the names of ruling monarch. In the DP, the coinage is generally classified accor-

[46] DP 62–65. No specimen of this coin seems to be extant.

ding to kingdoms, and under each kingdom, the coins issued by different kings are arranged in a chronological order. Thus, for Gujarat, Pherū lists the billon coins which were issued by the respective kings in the following order.

1. *kumara/kumarapurī* (issued by Kumārapāla Caulukya, r. 1144–1173)
2. *ajayapurī* (Ajayapāla Caulukya, r. 1173–1175)
3. *bhīmapurī* (Bhīma II Caulukya, r. 1178–1241)
4. *lūṇavasā/lavaṇasapurī* (Lāvaṇyaprasāda Vāghela, r. 1242–1243)
5. *vīsalapuri* (Vīsaladeva Vāghela, r. 1244–1262)
6. *ajjanapurī / arjunapurī* (Arjunadeva Vāghela, r. 1264–1273).

Because of the metrical constraints, Pherū sometimes gives only an abbreviated form of a name in the verse, but the full form in the table. Thus, what he calls *kumara* is only a short form of the coin named *kumarapurī*, which was issued by the king Kumārapāla Cālukya who ruled from Anhilvad Patan from 1144 to 1173. But what does suffix °*purī* mean? From the Sanskrit texts and inscriptions we learn that such coins were known as *Kumāra-priya, Bhīma-priya* and so on[47] which became *Kumarapurī, Bhīmapurī*, etc., in Apabhraṃśa. Such a method of naming the coins seems to have prevailed in Gujrarat and Malwa.

In Punjab and Delhi, however, another system of nomenclature prevailed before the advent of the Muslim rule. Among the coins from Jalandhar (*jālaṃdharī mudrāḥ*) are mentioned *Jaïtacaṃdāhe, Rūpacaṃdāhe* and *Tiloyacaṃdāhe* (DP 109–110). These were presumably issued by kings named Jaitracandra, Rūpacandra and Trailokyacandra. Likewise, the coinage issued by the Tomar Rajput king Anaṅgapāla was known as *Aṇagapalāhe*, by Madanapāla as *Mayaṇapalāhe*, by Pṛthvīpāla as *Piṭhaüpalāhe* and so on (DP 111 and the table that follows). I have not been able to define the linguistic reason for this nomenclature.

Similarly coins issued by Muslim rulers are also designated after their names. Thus, *Kuvāicī* or *Kuvācīya* (DP 116) are the

---

[47] Strauch 2002, pp. 313–314, where several other occurrences are cited.

coins issued by Nāṣru-d-dīn Qubācha of Sind (r. 1203–1228) who was appointed Governor of Ūcch by Muḥammad bin Sām in 1203 and who assumed independence after the latter's death in 1206. *Samasī* (DP 118) and *Tittimīsī* (DP 120) are the coins of Shams al-Dīn Īltutmish (r. 1210–1235). Some of his coins bear also the Nāgarī legend *samasadīna* or *samasadi.*

Besides these designations based on the names of rulers, there are some which are purely descriptive. Pherū mentions gold coins bearing the figures of Sītā and Rāma. He calls these *Sīyārāma* and adds that they are of two types, *saṃyogī* (Sītā and Rāma together?) and *viyogī* (Sītā and Rāma separately?). It is not known who issued these coins before the time of Pherū. According to Parameshwari Lal Gupta, Akbar also issued a coin with the figures of Rāma and Sītā and with the Nāgarī legend *siyarāma.*[48] Pherū designates a gold coin (DP 58) and a trimetallic coin (DP 62) *Paümā* or *Padamā*; probably these bore the figure of Lakṣmī.

But there are several designations which are either nicknames or trade names for certain coins, such as *Karāriya, Khaṭṭalāga* (DP 55), *Vilāīkora* (DP 67), *Bhaṃbhaï, Egaṭipi* (DP 75) and so on. Further research is needed to interpret these names properly.

2.4.2 The Coinage of the Turkish Sulṭāns

The lion's share of the catalogue goes to coins issued by the various kings at Delhi, from the Tomar king Anaṅgapāla to Pherū's employer, Qutb al-Dīn Mubārak Shāh of the Khaljī dynasty. Before the advent of the Khaljīs, Delhi was ruled by various Sulṭāns from Mu'iz al-Dīn Muḥammad ibn Sām (r. 1193–1206) to Mu'iz al-Dīn Kaiqubād (r. 1287–1290). Of these Sulṭāns, Pherū mentions only their billon coins (DP 112–31), although they are known to have issued silver coins also.

For example, about Raḍīyya Sulṭānā (r. 1236–1240), the only female ruler of this dynasty who ruled under the name of Jalālat al-Dīn Raḍiyya, Pherū states as follows:

> Shams al-Dīn's (*samasadi*) daughter Raḍīyya (*radīyā*). Her *Radī* is twofold: [minted at] Delhi and Badaun. [These

[48] Gupta 1969, p. 119 and pl. xxvi, no. 281; see also Mitchiner 2000.

contain respectively] sixteen and a half, and twelve and three quarters *ṭaṃkas* [of silver in one hundred pieces]. [Their prices are] nineteen and thirty-one [pieces per *Ṭaṃka*].[49]

But according to Stan Goron and J. P. Goenka, there survive also a gold *ṭaṃkā* of Raḍīyya minted at Lakhnautī in Bengal and silver *ṭāṃkas* minted at Delhi, in addition to the billon *jītals* minted at Delhi and Badaun.[50] This is the only occasion when Pherū mentions the names of different mints.

Likewise, of the first rulers of the Khaljī dynasty, namely, Jalāl al-Dīn Fīrūz II Khaljī (r. 1290–1296) and his son Rukn al-Dīn Ibrahīm (r. 1296), Pherū's information is partial and mentions only the billon coins, because they were still in circulation (*vaṭṭaṃti vivahāre*; DP 132).

2.4.3 The Coinage of ᶜAlā' al-Dīn Muḥammad Khaljī

When Pherū was composing the DP in 1318, the coinage of ᶜAlā' al-Dīn and Quṭb al-Dīn was legal tender at the time of writing (*saṃpaï pavaṭṭamāṇā*) and therefore his account of this coinage is naturally very detailed and comprehensive.[51]

ᶜAlā' al-Dīn Muḥammad Khaljī (r. 1296–1316) overthrew his uncle Jalāl al-Dīn Fīrūz and ascended the throne. During his reign of two decades, a large variety of coins were issued. Pherū informs us that ᶜAlā' al-Dīn issued two varieties of *dugānī*, two varieties of *chagānī*, one variety of *igānī*, gold *Ṭaṃkās* of five denominations and weights, one silver *Ṭaṃkā* of 1 *tolā* weight, and 1 gold *dīnār*. The five kinds of gold *Taṃkas* weighed 1, 5, 10, 50 and 100 *tolās*. The 100 *tolā* coin would weigh almost 1.1 kg. Such huge pieces naturally were not used for monitory transactions but as royal gifts to foreign ambassadors or as tokens of royal favour to high nobility. This custom continued into the Mughal times.[52]

---

[49] DP 122: *samasadi suyā radīyā tassa radī dunni ḍhillīya budaüvā | saḍha sola paüṇa teraha ṭaṃkaka uṇavīsa igatīsā ||.*

[50] Goron and Goenka 2001, pp. 26–27, where all the extant coins of Raḍīyyā are illustrated and excellently catalogued.

[51] DP 134–148; cf. also Gupta 1957, pp. 35–47; Moin 1999.

[52] Cf. Gupta 1957, pp. 37–38 (Gigantic coins). See also Najm-Ul-Hasan, "Making Big Money," *Hindustan Times*, 1 May 1998, for an account of a gold

Besides these gold, silver and billon coins there survive also several varieties of copper coins issued by ᶜAlā' al-Dīn which are not mentioned by Pherū.[53] He refers to ᶜAlā' al-Dīn as *Aśvapati Mahānarendra Pātisāhi Alāvadī,* but does not inform us about his titles which were incorporated on coins, such as *sikandar al-thānī,* "the second Alexander," *yamīn al-khilāfa,* "the right hand of the Caliphate," and *nāṣir amīr al-mū'minīn,* "helper of the Commander of the Faithful."[54] Nor does he inform us about the different mints, the names of which were generally available on the coins.

2.4.4 The Coinage of Shihāb al-Dīn ᶜUmar

When ᶜAlā' al-Dīn Khaljī died in 1316 after a long reign, his powerful general Mālik Kafur installed ᶜAlā' al-Dīn's six year old son Shihāb al-Dīn ᶜUmar as the Sulṭān and proclaimed himself as the Regent. This poor child ruled just for two months, during which time the royal mint carried on its work as usual and issued coins under the ruler's name. Pherū lists gold and silver *Ṭaṃkās* of 1 *tolā* each and five types of *gānī* coins. Pherū mentions their weights, silver content and so on, but, unlike modern numismatists, he does not mention the inscriptions on the coins. The long Arabic titles of the Sulṭāns would not have fitted in his Apabhraṃśa metres in any case. Modern numismatic catalogues record these inscriptions also and inform us that on his gold coins the child king was referred to as the "Second Alexander" (*sikandar al-thānī*).[55]

2.4.5 The Coinage of Quṭb al-Dīn Mubārak Shāh

Within two months of his coronation, Shihāb al-Dīn was killed by his elder brother Quṭb al-Dīn Mubārak Shāh who escaped from prison and ascended the throne. Pherū refers to him as *Rāyabandichoḍa,* "he who released himself from the prison and

---

coin issued by the Mughal Emperor Jahāngīr. It weighed a little short of 12 kg, had a diameter of 20.3 cm (i.e., almost the width of A-4 size paper) and was supposed to be the largest gold coin in the world. In 1987 it was estimated to be worth ten million US dollars.

[53] Goron and Goenka 2001, pp. 37–39.

[54] Ibid, p. 37.

[55] Ibid, pp. 39–40.

became king" or "he who freed the prisoners on becoming the king".[56] His short rule of four years has nothing to record but his dissolute life. The only achievement was the wide range of his coinage produced by the royal mints at Delhi and in Quṭbābad (Devagiri). According to Pherū, these mints produced as many as sixty-three different types of coins: 32 varieties of gold, 20 types of silver coins, 7 kinds of *dammas* and 4 varieties of copper pieces.[57] In the first two years, the gold and silver *Ṭaṃkās* were of circular shape. These were changed to square shape in 1318, just before Pherū wrote his book. Thus, the mints issued circular and square gold *Ṭaṃkās* of different denominations up to 200 *tolas*. There were also silver coins of 20 different types, and diverse kinds of billon and copper coins. Pherū lists these meticulously with their weights and metal content. What he does not mention are Quṭb al-Dīn's grandiloquent titles, which are mentioned in the modern numismatic catalogues.

Until this time, the Sulṭāns expressed a nominal allegiance to the Caliph and mentioned his name in their coinage. Quṭb al-Dīn discarded the Caliph's name from his coins, and called himself the *khalīfa rabb al-ᶜalamīn*, "Caliph, the lord of the two Worlds," *al-imām al-a'zam*, "Most High Imām," and *sikandar al-zamān*, "the Alexander of the Age". [58]

Leaving these epithets aside, the coins themselves are said to be of a very high quality. The numismatist Nelson Wright remarks: "The coinage of Qutbuddin Mubarak stands out for its boldness of design and variety of its inscriptions. ... There is perhaps no finer coin in the whole pre-Mughal series than the broad square gold tankah of high relief struck at Qutbabad Fort."[59]

2.4.6 Accuracy of Pherū's Assays

It is to Pherū's credit that he prepared a comprehensive catalogue of Quṭb al-Dīn's coinage. An important element in

[56] DP 139: *itto bhaṇāmi saṃpaï kudubuddī rāyabaṃdichoḍassa | caürasa vaṭṭa muddā nāṇāviha tulla mullo ya ||.*

[57] DP 140: *battīsaṃ kaṇayamayā ruppamayā vīsa damma sattavihā | caüviha taṃbaya sāhā muddā savvevi tesaṭṭhī ||.*

[58] Goron and Goenka 2001, pp. 40–44.

[59] Wright 1936, pp. 107–108.

his data are the results of his assays. Today these can be compared with the modern assays to ascertain their accuracy. The first major study of the coins of the Delhi Sultanate was undertaken by H. Nelson Wright in his classic work *The Coinage and Metrology of the Sultans of Delhi*. Here he included also the results of the matellographic analyses of the coinage which were done by the assayers of the British Museum and of the Royal Mint. After the *Dravyaparīkṣā* was published, numismatists compared Pherū's statements with modern assay results published by Nelson Wright and found excellent agreement between them.

In particular, John S. Deyell compared the silver content in a series of *gānī* coins according to the analysis of the British Museum and according Pherū's assay and found that the percentage of agreement between the two assays ranges between 96.56 and 101.36 and that the percentage of variance between the two lies between 3.44 and 1.36.[60] It is indeed remarkable that there is a near-perfect agreement between Pherū's assays made in the medieval mint of Delhi and the modern analyses of the British Museum.

Of course, this degree of accuracy pertains specially to the coinage of ᶜAlā' al-Dīn and his successors Shihāb al-Dīn and Quṭb al-Dīn, the coinage which Pherū directly dealt with. With regard to the coinage of other Sulṭāns and other kingdoms, the accuracy varies, depending on the number of specimens which were available to him for examination. Some parts of the data may also have been derived by Pherū from old mint records or other trade sources and not by direct examination. Even so, preserving all these records—his own and of others—for posterity in the form of the *Dravyaparīkṣā* was indeed a remarkable achievement.

Bibliography

Agrawala, Vasudeva Sharan, 1951–1952, "Dhātūtpatti," *The Journal of the Uttar Pradesh Historical Society*, 24–25, pp. 321–335.

——— 1966, "A Unique Treatise on Medieval Indian Coins". In: *Dr. Ghulam Yazdani Commemoration Volume*, Hyderabad: Maulana Abul Kalam Azad Oriental Research Institute, pp.

[60] Deyell 1990, see the table on p. 255.

81–101. Reprinted as "Dravyaparīkṣā of Ṭhakkura Pherū" in *Indian Numismatic Chronicle,* 8, 1969, pp. 100–114.

Amarakoṣa,1997, *Nāmaliṅgānuśāsana alias Amarakoṣa of Amarasiṃha,* with the commentary *Vyākhyāsudhā* or *Rāmāśamī* of Bhānuji Dīkśita, edited with notes by Śivadatta Dādhimatha, revised by Vāsudeva Lakṣmaṇaśastrī Paṇaśīkara. (Bombay: Nirnaya Sagar Press, 1915), reprint Delhi: Chuakhamba Sanskrit Pratisthan.

Arthaśāstra, 2010, *The Kauṭilīya Arthaśāstra.* Part I: Sanskrit Text with a Glossary, ed. R. P. Gokhale, (Bombay University, 1969), 7th reprint Delhi: Motilal Banarsidass.

Blochmann, H. 1873 (tr), *The Ain i Akbari by Abul Fazl 'Allami,* vol. 1, Calcutta: Asiatic Society of Bengal. Reprint: Frankfurt: Institute for the History of Arabic-Islamic Science at the Johann Wolfgang Goethe University, 1993.

Deshpande, Vijaya Jayant, 1996, "Muṣāvijñāna or the Science of the Crucibles," *Indian Journal of History of Science,* 30.4, pp. 359–373.

Deyell, John S., 1990, *Living without Silver: The Monetary History of Early Medieval North India,* Delhi: Oxford University Press, 1990 (Oxford India Paperbacks, 1999).

Goron, Stan and Goenka, J. P., 2001, *The Coins of the Indian Sultanates: Covering the Area of Present Day India, Pakistan and Bangladesh,* New Delhi: Munshiram Manoharlal.

Gupta, Parameshwari Lal, 1957, "The Coinage of the Khilji Sultans of Delhi," *The Journal of the Numismatic Society of India,* 29, pp. 35–47.

——— 1969, *Coins,* New Delhi: National Book Trust.

Habib, Irfan, 1982, "Agrarian Economy." In: Tapan Roychaudhury & Irfan Habib (eds), *The Cambridge Economic History of India,* Volume I: *c.*1200–*c.*1700, Cambridge: Cambridge University Press, p. 50 ff.

Hoover, Herbert Clark, and Hoover, Lou Henry, 1912 (tr), Georgius Agricola, *De Re Metallica,* translated from the first Latin Edition of 1556, London: The Mining Magazine, available online at http://www.farlang.com/gemstones/agricola-metallica/page_001.

McHugh, James Andrew, 2008, *Sandalwood and Carrion: Smell in South Asian Culture and Civilization,* Ph.D. Dissertation, Harvard University.

Mehta, Makrand, 1991, *Indian Merchants and Entrepreneurs in Historical Perspective,* Delhi: Academic Foundation.

Mitchiner, Michael, 2000, *Ramatankas, Hindu Religious Tokens illustrating Themes from Ramayana,* Nasik: Indian Institute of Research in Numismatic Studies (IIRNS).

Moin, Danish, 1999, *Coins of the Delhi Sultanate,* Nasik: Indian Institute of Research in Numismatic Studies (IIRNS).

Nahata, Agar Chand, and Nahata, Bhanwar Lal (eds), 1961, *Ṭhakkura-Pherū-viracita-Ratnaparīkṣādi-sapta-grantha-saṃgraha,* Jodhpur: Rajasthan Oriental Series.

——— n.d. *Ratnaparīkṣā,* (text with Hindi trans.), Calcutta.

Nahata, Bhanwar Lal, 1976, *Ṭhakkura Pherū viracitā Dravya-parīkṣā aur Dhātūtpatti* (text with Hindi trans.), Vaishali: Research Institute of Prakrit, Jainology and Ahimsa.

Petit, Jérôme, 2008–2009, "Banārasīdās et Jean-Baptiste Tavernier: Feux croises sur l'histoire économique de l'Inde au XVIIe siècle," *Bulletin d'Études Indiennes,* 26–27, pp. 141-152.

SaKHYa, 2009 (= Sreeramula Rajeswara Sarma, Takanori Kusuba, Takao Hayashi and Michio Yano), *Gaṇitasāra-kaumudī, the Moonlight of the Essence of Mathematics, by Ṭhakkura Pherū,* edited with Introduction, Translation and Mathematical Commentary, New Delhi: Manohar.

Sarma, Sreeramula Rajeswara, 1983 "*Varṇamālikā* System of Determining the Fineness of Gold in Ancient and Medieval India". In: B. Datta et al. (eds), *Aruṇa-Bhāratī: Professor A. N. Jani Felicitation Volume,* Baroda: Professor A. N. Jani Felicitation Volume Committee, pp. 369–389.

——— 1984, *Ṭhakkura Pherū's Rayaṇaparikkhā. A Medieval Prakrit Text on Gemmology,* with an Introduction, Sanskrit *chāyā,* Translation into English and Commentary, Aligarh: Viveka Publications.

——— 1986 "Thakkura Pheru and the Popularisation of Science in India in the Fourteenth Century" in: *Sri Bhanwar Lal Nahata Abhinandana Grantha,* Calcutta: Shri Bhanwar Lal Nahata Abhinandan Samaroh Samiti, pt 4, pp. 63–72.

——— 1996, "Sanskrit Manuals for Learning Persian" in: Azarmi Dukht Safavi (ed), *Adab Shenasi,* Aligarh: Department of Persian, Aligarh Muslim University, pp. 1–12.

——— 1999, "Yantrarāja: the Astrolabe in Sanskrit," *Indian Journal of History of Science,* 34, 145–158. Reprinted in, idem,

The Archaic and the Exotic: Studies in the History of Indian Astronomical Instruments, New Delhi: Manohar, 2008, pp. 240–256.

——— 2000, "Sultān, Sūri and the Astrolabe," *Indian Journal of History of Science,* 35.2, 29–147. Reprinted in, idem, *The Archaic and the Exotic: Studies in the History of Indian Astronomical Instruments*, New Delhi: Manohar, 2008, pp. 179–198.

——— 2002, "From Yāvanī to Saṃskṛtam: Sanskrit Writings inspired by Persian Works," *Studies in the History of Indian Thought,* Kyoto, 14, pp. 71–88.

Schiffner, Carl, 1928 (tr), Georg Agricola, *Zwölf Bücher vom Berg- und Hüttenwesen ...,* in neuer Deutscher Übersetzung bearbeitet von Carl Schiffner et al, Berlin: Agricola Gesellschaft beim Deutschen Museum, V.D.I. Verlag, available online at http://www.digitalis.uni-koeln.de/Agricola/agricola_index.html.

Steingass, F., 1996, *A Comprehensive Persian-English Dictionary,* (London, 1892), reprint New Delhi: Munshiram Manoharlal.

Strauch, Ingo, 2002, *Die Lekhapaddhati-Lekhapañcāsikā: Briefe und Urkunden im Mittelalterlichen Gujarat,* Berlin: Dietrich Reimer Verlag.

Sūri, Mahendra, 1936, *Yantrarājaḥ, Mahendraguru-viracitaḥ, Malayendu-sūri-viracita-ṭīkā-sahitaḥ,* ed. Kṛṣṇaśaṃkara Keśavarāma Raikva, Mumbai: Nirnaya Sagar Press.

Thomas, Edward, 1891 *Chronicles of the Pathan Kings of Delhi,* London, reprint 1967: New Delhi: Munshiram Manoharlal.

Wilson, H. H., 1855, *A Glossary of Judicial and Revenue Terms ...,* London: Wm. H. Allen and Co.

Wright, H. Nelson, 1936, *The Coinage and Metrology of the Sultans of Delhi,* Oxford, reprint 1974: New Delhi: Munshiram Manoharlal.

Wulff, Hans E., 1996, *The Traditional Crafts of Persia: Their Development, Technology, and Influence on Eastern and Western Civilizations.* Cambridge, etc.: The M.I.T. Press.

Genealogical Discourse and Jain Sectarian Promotion. *Mantri-Karmacandra-Vaṃśāvalī-Prabandha* and the Kharataragaccha

Nalini Balbir

Abstract

As a component of a wider project on the study of the role played by Jain Śvetāmbara lay and monastic elites in society, based in particular on manuscript colophons, the present paper focuses on a large scale *praśasti*: the edited *Mantri-Karmacandra-Vaṃśāvalī-Prabandha* composed in Sanskrit by Jayasoma Pāṭhaka in 1593, and commented upon by Guṇavinaya who also wrote a versified Gujarati version of the text. Both authors are Jain monks belonging to the Kharataragaccha. Their works are praises of a Jain layman and of his lineage who, for generation, continuously sponsored this monastic order. The genealogical discourse, which spreads from the twelfth to the sixteenth century, is an essential component of the praise, as it provides an in-depth perspective to the present, represented by the leading figure of Karmacandra, who was active in the sixteenth century. It is argued in this paper that the lineage favoured action directed towards the cult-forms specific to the Kharataragaccha. Patterns of interactions between the political power on the one hand, which Karmacandra and his ancestors represented since many of them were ministers to various kings of Rajasthan, and Jain faith, on the other hand, are described, together with the modes of action developed in order to guarantee the presence of Jain ideals and actors at the state level. Far from being a fictional work, the *Vaṃśāvalī* is supported by historical documents, as the comparison with epigraphs and manuscript colophons suggests. The *Vaṃśāvalī* also appears to be a means to assert the presence of the Kharataragaccha at the court of Akbar, and to counterbalance the prevailing impression of an exclusive presence of Tapāgaccha monastic leaders given by their own literature and by the *Āīn-i-Akbarī*.

Keywords: Jainism, Medieval Jainism, Kharataragaccha, Oswals, Akbar, Jinacandrasūri, Dādāgurus, Mantri Karmacandra, Family history, Jain inscriptions, Jain manuscript colophons, Sanskrit, castes and Jain monastic orders, Genealogy, Political power and Jain faith, sixteenth century

This preliminary essay should be seen as a component of a wider project, the aim of which is to understand the role played by Jain Śvetāmbara elites in Northern and Western Indian societies. The word "elite" is a convenient designation for referring here to members of the lay communities (*śrāvaka*) or mendicants (*sādhu, sūri*) who, in various ways, have had a prominent position and come to the foreground within the group they belong to. Being part of an elite means that one has obtained the recognition of other people and is considered by them as having a specially prestigious position. Hence this term, which implies hierarchy and power, can be applied and understood only relatively—in the context of *vyavahāra*, so to say. When we deal with societies of the past, we can define various individuals, families or groups as elites only through the investigation of literary, iconographic or architectural sources. It is the minute study of this evidence and its collation that can lead us to find the recurring names and personalities of individuals and families. Gradually, we see how they emerge as figures whose role in the Jain society is more prominent than others and how it is displayed. There is no elite without display or even ostentation or, at any rate, without leaving conspicuous traces of one's activity.

For some years now, I have been working on tracing evidence about such groups or such individuals in the colophons of Jain manuscripts written on palm leaf or paper in Western India between the thirteenth and the seventeenth centuries. Besides the numerous short colophons with minimal information, there is a wide range of stylistic varieties going on to very elaborated ones which are written in Sanskrit, independently of the language of the text which they end, and often in verses. They are indeed *praśastis* and often called so in the documents. I have tried to show how these colophons, crosschecked with contemporary epigraphs whenever possible, bring to light Jain business lay families who, in close association with Jain religious teachers, act in special ways for the public promotion of their faith (Balbir 2006 and forthcoming, both in French). Thus, they enact the concept of *prabhāvanā*, 'propagation' and 'enforcement' of Jainism which is central to the doctrinal frame. In their own ways they contribute to maintaining Jainism through the centuries and guarantee its omnipresence in social environments. There are various modes to achieve such a goal. Getting any text copied is a source of merit, but there are large scale projects which imply a major financial investment (as we can suppose) and are, consequently, a way to display the group's presence. There are several instances of this process.

Commissioning the writing and illustration of *Kalpasūtra* manuscripts is one such instance (see Balbir forthcoming). The elaborate *praśastis* frequently found at the end of these manuscripts are organized in two parts: one is devoted to the spiritual genealogy of the mendicant who is the supervisor and instigator of the project, the other to the genealogy of the lay family centring around a given individual. When this is a lady, as often happens, all the male members of the family are named. The genealogy is often accompanied by the mention of notable religious deeds, such as the organization of pilgrimages or the organization of ceremonies meant to celebrate a mendicant's ascent to a higher religious status. Such details are important as they stress the continuous part played by a given group in pious activity: they distinguish themselves not only once, but by multiple acts of different types. It is this multiplicity that makes them known to others. The fact that commissioning *Kalpasūtra* manuscripts is prestigious is to be connected with the public and social role occupied by this sacred book in performance during the festival of Paryushan among Western Indian Śvetāmbara communities from at least the fourteenth century onwards.

Another prestigious and not so common an activity in the field of manuscript production is the commissioning of manuscripts of the Śvetāmbara Āgamas in their original Ardhamāgadhī language. This specification is required because we see that in the late Middle Ages it was common to have manuscripts copied, of individual Āgamas with Gujarati commentaries (*ṭabos* or *bālāvabodhas*). In comparison, copying Ardhamāgadhī exemplars appears to have been less frequent, and, therefore, all the more remarkable. Whereas the commissioning of *Kalpasūtra* manuscripts has social prestige, the commissioning of original Āgama manuscripts could illustrate the acquisition of prestige through concern for learning and culture, independently of practical interests. What we call the 'Śvetāmbara Āgamas', and seem to take as a unit, is nothing more than a myth if we turn to the manuscripts themselves. The most frequent pattern is the copying of single works, or of two three works which form a small group. Comparatively, then, other patterns again appear as distinctive and manuscript colophons underline this somewhat exceptional character. These are cases where several texts are copied one after the other. Manuscripts show that for such undertakings, which were probably rather costly although the sources do not provide any financial information, the initiative was often collective rather than individual. People associated and joined their forces, either as members of a joint family or as inhabitants of the same town. Palm leaf manuscripts from Patan provide several instances of this. What is even more outstanding are cases of extremely isolated initiatives of those who initiated the copying of the totality of the forty-five Āgamas recognized by the Śvetāmbara Mūrtipūjaks. I could trace two such instances dating back to the seventeenth century. Each manuscript is separate but all their colophons end with the same phrase: "this was text So-and-so, number so-and-so of the forty-five Āgamas" and the mention of the same family members, confirming that these were large scale projects. Unfortunately, we can now retrieve a few exemplars only, not the complete sets (Balbir 2006).

Finally, besides getting manuscripts copied, one could also collect them as bibliophiles do. This is yet another type of intellectual investment which could probably be done only by wealthy families. In the seventeenth century the colophons of several manuscripts bear the names of Sahasrakiraṇa and his two sons Vardhamāna and Śāntidāsa who were inhabitants of Ahmedabad. They bought manuscripts of Sanskrit and Prakrit texts, both Jain and non Jain, showing a wide range of interests. In short, they acted as learned collectors conscious of a literary heritage which they thought worth preserving. Śāntidāsa, the second son, is well-known as a wealthy jeweler who also invested in the construction of several temples. This family line, which distinguished itself by an activity both abundantly and innovatively, kept its important social role among Gujarati Jains all along until our times. Śāntidāsa is the distant ancestor of Kasturbhai Lalbhai, a major entrepreneur, well-known for managing various religious and research Jain institutions (Balbir 2006).

Karmacandra, the individual I will focus on now, lived in the sixteenth century and was a contemporary of Akbar. He is at the centre of a network formed by a family which was influential over many generations, rulers with whom he was in close contact because of his official position as a minister, he was a disciple of a Jain religious teacher, Jinacandrasūri, and a member of his monastic group, the Kharataragaccha. His action has been handed down to us in an ensemble of texts written in Sanskrit or Gujarati which have been collected in Jinavijaya's edition (1980). Since Karmacandra and his family are regarded as great Jains and leading representatives of the Oswals, to which they belong, some information on them is available in various secondary works published in India (Desai 1933: 571–575; Desai 1941; Bhandari 1934; Bhūtoṛiyā 1988: 99ff.; Jain 1963: 222ff.; Jain 2000: 310–312, etc.).

The focus of attention here, however, is what can be considered as the seminal primary work, the *Karmacandra-vaṃśāvalī Prabandha* (herefrom: *Vaṃśāvalī*) in Sanskrit, which has 539 stanzas and was written in 1593 (VS 1650) by Jayasoma Pāṭhaka. It is available in the excellent edition provided in Jinavijaya (1980). But no information on the manuscript evidence is provided. A look at catalogues shows that manuscripts are rather rare and localized in Rajasthan. They may have a slightly different title but all those authored by Jayasoma are one and the same work.[1] The edition lacks an index of proper names, which, therefore, has been appended to the present paper.

This work provides an original instance of interaction between laypeople and mendicants in the field of writing. Normally, the laypeople are those who praise monks. Here the pattern is reversed. This *Vaṃśāvalī* is clearly a sectarian affair in the hands of several religious teachers belonging to the Kharataragaccha who monopolized the figure of Karmacandra:

[1] See for instance the *Karmachandravaṃśotkīrtanakāvyam* mentioned in Jain 1963, p. 5. The identity of the works, beyond the differences in the title, is confirmed, for instance, by a comparison of the edition with the extracts available in Vinayasāgar and Shah 2010, p. 80 (introduction).

1. The author of the text is Jayasoma Pāṭhaka, who has to his credit several works of doctrinal and polemic interest.[2]
2. He undertook this writing, which was completed in VS 1650 (= 1593) at the instigation of his guru, Jinacandrasūri, the Kharataragaccha leader who interacted with Akbar, and is at the centre of the *Vaṃśāvalī*.
3. Although it is largely a straightforward text, the *Vamśāvalī* has been the starting point of a Sanskrit commentary, written six years later, by Guṇavinaya, a disciple of the author (printed in Jinavijaya 1980 along with the *mūla*-text).

The same Guṇavinaya also wrote a Gujarati rendering of the Sanskrit *Vaṃśāvalī* in VS 1655 (in Jinavijaya 1980: 89–101), beside other works.[3]

Thus, with three different levels of accessibility (Sanskrit verses, Sanskrit prose, and Gujarati verses) and two languages (Sanskrit plus vernacular) there was some guarantee that the message conveyed would not be ignored.[4] Given the appropriation of Karmacandra by the Kharataragaccha, it is also no surprise to read, as a final *maṅgala* to the Sanskrit work—a kind of climax to the whole undertaking—a full *paṭṭāvalī* of the Kharataragaccha in more than twenty stanzas (505–528). As usual, it starts with Mahāvīra and his direct disciple Sudharma, unfolding the line of teachers until the time when the Rājagaccha, alias Kharataragaccha, started (516) as an independent order, and ending with Jinacandrasūri the contemporary of Akbar. In other words, the supportive action of Karmacandra towards Jainism and more specifically towards the

---

[2] For more details see, for instance, Vinayasāgar and Shah 2010: 84–89 (introduction).

[3] Listed by Vinayasāgar and Shah in the introduction to the edition of the commentary on the *Damayantīkathācampū* composed by Guṇavinaya, 2010: 91–113.

[4] Jinavijaya 1980 also contains the following other documents: *Vacchāvatāṃ rī vaṃsāvalī* (1980: 102–109), *Karamacanda rī nīsāṇī* by Kavi Malharī (1980: 110), both in Rajasthani, the extract of *Jinasiṃhasūrirāsa* by Sūrajacanda dealing with Karmacandra (1980:111) and another small composition, *Mantrīśvara Karmacandra Vacchāvata suyaśa* (1980:112).

Kharataragaccha leaders is rewarded by a panegyric by authors belonging to this monastic order.

The exact expansion of this literary pattern and situation will have to be investigated further. But Karmacandra is not the only important layman to have become the focus of a *praśasti* composed and commented upon by Kharataragaccha monks. At about the same time the community leader Rūpajī had been the topic of a similar type of work written by Śrīvallabhagaṇi, a contemporary of Jinacandrasūri (see Vinayasāgar 1969). Like Karmacandra, Rūpajī belonged to an illustrious family which had rendered manifold services to Jainism: he is the son of Somajī who organized several pilgrimages at the instigation of Jinacandrasūri and started the construction of the Kharataravasahī on Mount Shatrunjaya.

In such undertakings, the monk acts as a bard for the representative of the political power and thus explicitly involves himself in worldly matters. In the *Vaṃśāvalī* another sign of the Kharataragaccha's allegiance to the Emperor, though superficial, could be seen in the way the date of composition of the work is expressed: it is given twice, first according to the Vikrama era with the help of a *bhūtasaṃkhyā* as *kha-bhūta-rasa-śaśi* (= V.S. 1650), then again at the very end, with reference to Akbar's accession to power, as dated in the thirty-eighth year of his reign "which was the cause of happiness for the whole world". This custom is known from several inscriptions of this *gaccha.*[5]

The author of the work claims accurateness for what he writes and expresses this both at the beginning and at the end. His source is what he has heard, in the way it has been heard[6] from those who know Karmacandra's family tradition. But he distinguishes between what relates to people he has not seen, that is, the distant ancestors of Karmacandra, and what he has

---

[5] See respectively stanzas 528 and 538. Compare Salomon 1998, p. 195 : "The Ilāhī era (Tārīkh-i Ilāhī) instituted by the Mughal emperor Akbar in A.D. 1556 is recorded in a Jaina inscription from Pattan (EI I, 319–324) of the *allāī* year 41 and [Vikrama] 1652 = 1596". In fact, this custom is much more widely spread than this statement would suggest. Several examples are found in KhGPLS.

[6] *yathāśrutam* (11) ; *yathāśrāvi* (535).

seen. For the former, he is neutral (*rāga-dveṣau na teṣu me*), but for the latter, he undertakes a *varṇanā*.[7] Expanded by the commentator, this means, "the exposition of qualities" in one case, and "praise" in the other.[8] Such glosses are not surprising in the Indian context where the boundary between description and celebration is very thin or hardly present.

The *Vaṃśāvalī* can be seen as a very large sized *praśasti*. It makes use of stylistic devices characterizing this literary form, such as series of relative clauses to describe the role of the person in focus:

(Saṅgrāma) śrīSerasāhisāhiḥ ... / ... *mantripade yaṃ dadhāti sma* // 236
... *yo yātrāṃ* ... *vihitavān* ... //237
yaḥ kṛtavān ... //238
yo 'nyeṣu .... //239
... *yaḥ* ... *kṛtavān* ... // 240
... *ayam* ... // 241

The contents of the *Vaṃśāvalī* expand on a period of about five centuries, beginning in the twelfth century and ending in Jahangir's time. The eponymous ancestor is Bohittha, one of the three sons of king Sāgara and his wife Mānavatī, belonging to the Devaḍāvaṃśa from the name of their native place, Devalavāṭaka (18) in Mewar. The lineage thus becomes known under the name *Bohitthahara*, said by the author to be current in his period (23). This is confirmed by epigraphic records (*bohittarāgotrīya*, °*gotra*, often abbreviated as *bo*°). The family is also commonly known as "Vacchāvat" or "Bachhawat", a vernacularised form of the name Vatsarāja who is one of its prominent members. Bohittha and Vacchāvat are two of the *gotras* attached to the Oswals.

The climax of the *Vaṃśāvalī* is the life of Karmacandra or Karmacandra Vacchāvat in the sixteenth century and his interaction with contemporary rulers and Jain monastic leaders. The focus is immediate history covering the present of the author. However, before it comes to Karmacandra him-

---

[7] *varṇayāmi* (11) ; *varṇanā* (534).

[8] *'varṇayāmi' guṇavacanair vistārayāmi*, p. 5 ; *'varṇanā' stutir mayā 'vidadhe' kṛtā*, p. 86.

self in the second half (262ff.), the text has already dealt extensively in its first half with the family *paramparā* from its very beginning, naming all its members and describing their deeds. Gaining prestige and fame are acquired through one's insertion within a group that continues over many centuries. Thus the individual dimension is only one small component. The purpose is to underline the continuity of the support offered to Jainism over the centuries by a given lineage through lavish gifts of money or gold or by "sowing the seed of their wealth in the seven fields" (*saptakṣetrī* 85) or "in a good field" (65), as is prescribed by normative texts. More broadly, the purpose is to emphasize the all-pervading generosity of the lineage because recalling the past is a way to stimulate the present: several of its members are credited with the construction of relief-centres (*satrāgāra*, *satraśālā*) in times of famine or other hardships which the population had to face. This theme is developed extensively with reference to Karmacandra himself, who could not do less than his ancestors and is so to say constrained by their action. He is *nirmama* (300), and makes no distinction of caste or family when it comes to the rescue of the needy (302). On the other hand, the pious behaviour of the lineage is a recurring theme: among the ancestors of Karmacandra are several instances of people who observed ritual fasts in public contexts (92), or who fasted unto death, like Tejapāla, son of Samadhara (63) or Nagarāja, son of Varasiṃha, who died "a sage death" in Ajmer (*paṇḍitamṛtyunā*, 227). As for Karmacandra himself, he is said to "enliven the Jina's words" (295). As can be expected, many members of the lineage acted as official community leaders known as *saṅghapati*: Śrīkarṇa's sons (49), Tejapāla (53, 63), Vīlhā (64), Kaḍuā (69). They organized large scale pilgrimages, to the main holy places of Western India such as Abu, Girnar and, primarily, Shatrunjaya, managing to get tax-exemptions (87, 238).

But even more importantly, the *Vaṃśāvalī* insists on the exclusive and traditional association of this lineage with only one section of the mendicant community, namely the Kharataragaccha. The text goes back to the thirteenth century, mentioning the association of the ancestor Śrīkarṇa with the pontiff Jineśvarasūri, who was the teacher who actually converted (*pratibodha*, 44) the lineage to Jainism. This is presented as the consequence of an auspicious omen he had when he reached Kheḍīnagara for the rainy season (40ff.) and the words said to him in a dream by the *śāsana* deity (*śāsanasūrī*, 42).[9] This dream came true. Following the teacher's preaching which they all attended, they were converted. Their adoption of right faith (*samyaktvoccāra*, 49) was concretized by the organization of a pilgrimage to Shatrunjaya and Girnar at the instigation of the monk (40ff.). This is the first instance of an enduring connection for many centuries. Epigraphic records posterior to the time of Karmacandra's life show that his sons pursued the tradition of supporting the Kharataragaccha in particular, not only Jainism as an abstraction. *Paṭṭāvali*s of the Kharataragaccha keep the memory of the special role played by certain members of this lineage in connection with the monastic careers of some of the pontiffs.[10]

Inscriptions show that all the Jina images sponsored (*kārāpita*) by members of the lineage were ritually installed (*pratiṣṭhita*) by pontiffs of this monastic order.

date (VS)	main sponsor (see the Index of proper names below for references in the *Vaṃśāvalī*)	other family members	pontiff	Jina image	source
1507	Jesala	wife Sūdī, sons Devarāja and Vacchā	Jinabhadrasūri	Śāntinātha	BJLS 915

[9] This happened in VS 1323 (according to Bhandari p. 4).

[10] See, among others, the copious extracts of the *Paṭṭāvalīvācanā*, Berlin manuscript No. 1980 (Ms. or. fol. 729) described long ago by Albrecht Weber (*Verzeichnis* II, 3, Berlin, 1892 pp. 1050ff.).

1534	Jesala	wife Sūṃdī, sons Devarāja and Vaccharāja etc.	Jinacandrasūri	Śītalanātha	BJLS 3
1566	Vacchā	wife Vīlhāde, son Ratnāka	Jinahaṃsasūri	Ajitanātha	BJLS 4
1570	Devarājamantrin, son of Jesalamantrin	wife and sons with their wives, etc.	Jinahaṃsasūri	Candraprabha	BJLS 1948
1591	Vayarasiṃha (Vairasiṃha)		Jinamāṇikyasūri	renovation of Ādinātha image with *parikara*, destroyed on arrival of Moghul chief Kammarāṃ	BJLS 2
1593	Vacchā	wife Vīlhāde, son Karmasiṃha and wife Kautagade, their son Rājā, etc.	Jinamāṇikyasūri	Neminātha	BJLS 27
1593	Karmasī (Karmasiṃha)-mantrin	wife Kautigade, son Sūrya and his wife	Jinamāṇikyasūri	Śītalanātha	BJLS 28
1593	Pithāka	his father Rājā, grandfather Karmasī, etc.	Jinamāṇikyasūri	Naminātha (main image in temple got to be made by Karmasiṃha; see below)	BJLS 1193

1593	Ḍuṃga-rasī (Ḍuṃga-rasiṃha) -mantrin	son Narabada	Jinamā-ṇikyasūri	Vimala-nātha	BJLS 41
1595	Vacchā	son Vara-siṃha, wife Vījhalade, son Harāka (Hararāja) and his wife Hīrā-de, their son Jodhā, his sons Jiṇadāsa, Bhayarava dāsa	Jinamā-ṇikyasūri	Abhinan-dana	BJLS 5

The main image is that of Naminātha which was installed in a temple dedicated to this Jina caused to be made by Karma-siṃha, a minister of Lūṇakarṇa, king of Bikaner. This is one of the few events that is dated in the *Vaṃśāvalī*:

> *kha-munīṣv-indu-varṣe* (= VS 1570) *'bhūc caityaṃ Nami-jineśituḥ* (163cd = 168cd).

Prominent members of Karmacandra's lineage showed their support to monks of the Kharataragaccha when they invested a lot of money for organizing the celebrations held on the occasion of the promotion of a monk to a higher position, especially to that of a *sūri*. They made this form of support their family speciality:

> In the beginning of the fourteenth century, Tejapāla, son of Samadhara, organized this celebration in Patan for Jinakuśalasūri, who thus succeeded his teacher Rājendracandrasūri (57).[11]

---

[11] There might have been some confusion in the name of the layman involved. According to other sources, his name was, indeed, Tejapāla, but he was the son of one Jālhaṇa and was joined in the organization of the event, in VS 1377, by his brother Rudrapāla: KhGGurvāvalī p. 69 and KhGBI p. 168,

In the middle of the same century, Kaḍuā, son of Vīlhā, did it for Jinarājasūri (80).[12]

In VS 1556 (=1499), the minister Karmasiṃha did it for Jinahaṃsasūri (168).[13]

In the sixteenth century, Karmacandra used his influence and wealth for the celebration of the title *yugapradhāna* conferred to Jinacandrasūri.[14] He also sponsored the celebration which was performed when Mānasiṃha obtained the status of an *ācārya* and became known as Jinasiṃhasūri (460-463).[15] This deed is remembered in several inscriptions and manuscript *praśastis* as well.[16]

It is even more noteworthy that the family support also went to religious forms that developed specially within the Kharataragaccha. Not only did Karmacandra and his ancestors commissioned or renovated Jain temples and Jina images, as any pious Jain would wish to do, but they took an active part in sponsoring *stūpas* and *pādukās* commemorating the past gurus of this order such as Jinadattasūri (1075–1154 CE) and Jinakuśalasūri (1280–1332). Both are among the so-called *Dādā-gurus*, who have an outstanding place because of their role as "reformers, miracle workers or creators of new Jains ... (and) are the focus of a widespread cult".[17] The *Vaṃśāvalī* states:

stūpaṃ śrīJinadattasya °Kuśalasya guror api
acīkarad guru-prītyā Phalavardhi-purī-sthitaḥ (328).

In yet another stanza (345), it is mentioned that "the pilgrimage to the *stūpa* of the guru" (Jinadatta) in Ajmer was under-

---

but there is no indication about his affiliation in the *Paṭṭāvalīvācanā* quoted in Weber, *Verzeichnis* p. 1047.

[12] This happened in VS 1432 according to KhGBI p. 215.

[13] Compare KhGBI p. 220.

[14] KhGPLS 1310 and 1311.

[15] No date is given for this event in the *Vaṃśāvalī*. But according to other sources it took place in VS 1649 (1592 CE).

[16] KhGPLS 1213. Catalogue of the manuscripts of the L. D. Institute of Indology, Ahmedabad, No. 6125 (*praśasti* of a manuscript of the *Abhidhānacintāmaṇivṛtti*).

[17] Babb 1996: 111.

taken by Karmacandra. Here *stūpa* refers to a "mortuary structure"[18] or shrine for commemoration. Karmacandra is shown as a faithful believer in the power of these gurus, personally worshipping Jinadatta and the miraculous image of Pārśva of Phalodi in Rajasthan. This is what, according to the author, got him the favour of being called by Akbar to Lahore (341ff.). Additional evidence from inscriptions shows that Karmacandra and his family commissioned several footprints of these gurus, which are the traditional form in which they are represented and worshipped, but also at least one anthropomorphic image (*mūrti*) in temples of Rajasthan and Lahore:

In VS 1644 (1587 CE), Karmacandra got *pādukās* of Jinadattasūri to be made in Phalodi, Rajasthan (KhGPLS 1192: inscription in Dādāvārī Rāṇīsar, Pokharaṇ, Phalodi).

In VS 1647 (1590 CE), Karmacandra got *pādukās* of Jinadattasūri to be made in Phalodi (KhGPLS 1200: inscription in Rāṇīsār pond, Dādāvārī, Phalodi).

In the 39th year of Akbar's reign (= 1594 CE), Karmacandra got *pādukās* of Jinakuśalasūri to be made (Kh GPLS 1201: inscription in the Jain temple, Lahore).

In VS 1651 (1594 CE) Karmacandra's sons Bhāgacanda and Lakṣmīcanda got an image (*mūrti*) of Jinakuśalasūri to be made, which was installed by Dayākamalagaṇi (KhGPLS 1204: inscription in the Śāntinātha temple, Sirohi). The names of Karmacandra's sons are also mentioned in the *Vaṃśāvalī* (331).

An inscription dated VS 1653 (1594 CE) refers to Karmacandra in connection with the installation of Jinakuśalasūri's *pādukās* (*mūlastambha prāraṃbhakartā mantri Karmacandraḥ śreyo'rthaṃ*) KhGPLS 1211: inscription in Dādāvārī, Amarasar, Jaipur).

In VS 1656 (1599 CE) Karmacandra got *pādukās* of Jinakuśalasūri made and installed in Saṅgrāmapura (KhGPLS 1223: inscription in Dādāvārī, Sanganer).

References to the past provide an in-depth perspective to the present. A similar part is played by the mention of role-models to whom certain members of Karmacandra's lineage

[18] Babb ibidem.

are compared. The concern of the minister Kaḍuā for having *ahiṃsā* observed in Gujarat is compared with the compassion of the most illustrious example of Kumārapāla in the twelfth century (82). His son, also a minister, is compared to Vikramāditya for his heroism (86). This topos is part of the discourse of praise.

But the evidence given in the *Vaṃśāvalī* is supported by external documents, such as inscriptions. Hence, it is not a praise without basis, or a fictional work. The narration follows a simple chronological order, from the early history of the lineage to Karmacandra's time. Dates, however, are totally lacking for the early period, and are not supplemented by the commentary either. Kings' and rulers' names are frequently mentioned, but for chronological information one has to turn to external sources. The *Vaṃśāvalī* is not a neutral chronicle of historical events. For events taking place in the fifteenth century onwards, dates are mentioned but only occasionally, in the form of *bhūtasaṃkhyās*, as expected for a verse text. The only available dates are:

vidhu-vāridhi-bhūtendu-pramite (1541 = 1484 CE) *vatsare*: foundation of Bikaner ascribed to Karmasiṃhamantrin at the court of King Lūṇakarṇa (160).
netra-vārdhi-bhūtendu-vatsare (1542 = 1485 CE): foundation of an alms-house by Karmasiṃha (172).
rasa-bhūteṣu-vidhu-pramita-vatsare (1556 = 1499 CE): installation of Jinahaṃsasūri (163ab and 168ab) sponsored by Karmasiṃha.
kha-munīṣv-indu-varṣe (1570 = 1513 CE): temple of Naminātha built by Karmasiṃha (163cd and 168cd).
varṣe netravasupañcadaśe (1582 = 1525 CE): extension of an alms-house by minister Varasiṃha (190).

We do not, however, have the dates of Karmacandra's life. They are known from other sources on the history of the Oswals as being VS 1586–1656 (Bhūtoṛiyā 1988: 100, *ubi alia*). Migrations, moves and the need to settle again in new places were part of the lives of the men in focus. But, led by the memory of their native place (69, 91), they are shown as periodically returning to Mewar, the region where it is located. Without explaining why, the *Vaṃśāvalī* states that one of the ancestors had to leave Gujarat for Vīramapura (91), identified by the commentary as Mahevā (= Mehuvā). The lineage is one of *kṣatriyas*, although this word is not used. The eponymous ancestor and several of his descendants had the title of *rājan*. Their successors had that of *mantrin* or *mahāmantrin*. They are said to have distinguished themselves either by participating directly in battles or by having assisted kings through their intelligence in winning wars against their rivals, which are the main historical events alluded to in the *Vaṃśāvalī*. This is a repetitive pattern. One of the favourite synonyms of *mantrin* used in the *Vaṃśāvalī* is *dhīsakhi* (306, 433, 434, 531), applied to Karmacandra.

King Sāgara fights against the chief of Mālava (20).

King Bohittha, his son, fights against enemies in Chittor (26).

King Śrīkarṇa, one of Bohittha's sons, seizes the fort of Matsyendra (= Mahor) in Mewar (29) and dies in the battle, leaving a widow with four sons (36ff.).

Tejapāla, who is Śrīkarṇa's grandson, gives horses, etc., to the king of Gurjara, gets a favour and a territory against money, becoming the ruler of Patan (53).

Kaḍuā, who is Tejapāla's grandson, serves Rāṇāka, the king of Medapāṭa (= Mewar) in Chittor, against the king of Malwa, and gets the post of prime minister (70-75).

Merā, his son, is a minister (84), but no other information is provided.

The minister Vatsarāja, four generations later, serves King Riṇamalla in Jodhpur (102). He is then sent to King Vikrama (modern name Bikā, 109, 123), whom he assists in the foundation of Bikaner, according to the *Vaṃśāvalī*.

The minister Karmasiṃha, who is Vatasarāja's son, serves King Lūṇakarṇa in Bikaner (158 ff.).

His younger brother Varasiṃha enters in the service of King Jetṛsiṃha in Bikaner (187).

Nagarāja, who is Varasiṃha's second son, is a successor to his father in the same position (205).

Saṅgrāma, one of Nagarāja's sons, is appointed as minister by King Kalyāṇamalla alias Kalyāṇasiṃha (245).

> Karmacandra, who is Saṅgrāma's son, successively serves King Rāyasiṃha of Bikaner, and Emperor Akbar in Lahore (see below).[19]

The post of minister is thus a hereditary function occupied by successive male members of the lineage. The break of four generations appearing from the account of the *Vaṃśāvalī* is not explained, but is probably a reality. It would explain why the lineage is often known as "Vacchāvāt" < Vatsarāja (see above), from the name of the individual who gave a new start, and a continuous one, to the connection between the family and the function.

Karmacandra's political career is delineated clearly. It has two phases. In the first one, he was the minister of Rāyasiṃha, the ruler of Bikaner from 1573 onwards—Rāē Singh as he is known in Tod's *Annals and Antiquities of Rajasthan.*[20] When the circumstances changed and Rāyasiṃha's power started to sway, Karmacandra left Bikaner for a transitional period in Meḍtā (336–37), before he was called by Akbar to Lahore. During the Bikaner period, Karmacandra was close to Rāyasiṃha whom he seems to have advised with common sense and cleverness in state affairs, allowing him to gain several victories and to make conquests. On the other hand, Rāyasiṃha was connected with Akbar through family links, for both he and Akbar had married two sisters, who were princesses of Jaisalmer. The ruler of Bikaner rendered multiple services to the Emperor by sending groups of valiant Rathors to every battle or war he had to fight. These are some elements which may explain why Karmacandra indirectly benefited from Akbar's attention and later became a significant advisor to him in Lahore. Hence we see how serving at a regional level could later lead to a higher position at the national level, so to say.

The *Vaṃśāvalī* does not conceal the official role of Karmacandra in state matters. It describes him as a minister full of insight, using the terminology of the *Arthaśāstra* (292) and the

---

[19] Later on, their descendants continued to have prominent political posts in Mewar until the nineteenth century : see, briefly, Somani 1982: 235.

[20] Part II, p. 1132ff.; see also Jain 1963: 226–227.

typology of cleverness known from Jain sources (*Caturbuddhinidhiḥ* 369). But it also skillfully and temperately narrates how this official role was made use of by him in favour of Jain ideals and the Jain community in a repeated process of give and take involving the minister and his superiors so that the practice of Jainism becomes, at least occasionally, a state affair.

Among the themes developed in the *Vaṃśāvalī* for matters of public action, one is a cliché which has a long life: it is the ban of *hiṃsā* during the rainy season and the period corresponding to the festival of Paryushan. This is designated by the word *amāri-ghoṣaṇā*, 'proclamation of non-killing'. Even now Jain community leaders consider it an important success to be able to get this from the political power and like to publicise the news. This process implies constraints on the professional groups (mostly low castes) who are involved in 'violent' occupations, and probably financial compensations, but this part of the story remains untold. Such authorizations are acquired through negotiations as the phrase *śaktyā yuktyā ca* (320) suggests. Thus, in exchange for his services to Rāyasiṃha, Karmacandra requires from him that oil-makers, potters and food-makers do not practice their activity during four months (281). Later, 'safety is granted to the fish' (*mīnābhayadānaṃ*, 430) of the lakes of Kashmir, and non-killing of animals proclaimed for one year in Cambay, and one day in Lahore (444ff., 404ff.). According to the text, these privileges are the result of Akbar's interaction with the Jain pontiff Jinacandrasūri. Karmacandra acted as an intermediary between the Emperor and the religious authorities. The success materialises in the form of an imperial edict (*farmān*, Skt. *phuramāna*, 398) which is sent to eleven districts (*śumba*, 404; *paḍagāna*, comm.) with the instruction to observe this for "10–15 days" (405).[21] Negotiating abilities of Karmacandra are said to have done marvels in relations with Muslims too. Through gifts of money he was able to recover more than a thousand

[21] This edict is reported to have been published in the monthly *Sarasvatī* (June 1912), but was not accessible to me. Getting such edicts proclaimed is a recurring sign of success of Jain negotiations with the political power and is a recurring theme, also in the *Vaṃśāvalī* (186, 342, 343, 370, 374, 404).

Jain images that had been seized by the Mughal Turasam Khān in Śivapurī (= Sirohi), and to give them a shelter in the Cintāmaṇi Pārśvanātha temple of Bikaner (307–308).

The way Jain concerns are introduced in state management is illustrated at the level of ritual too when Akbar is said to have asked his minister to instruct him in a Jain ritual of pacification in order to counteract the inauspicious birth of Salim's daughter. This *śāntividhi* was executed on a grand scale with public display (359–365). It is one of the high feats connected with Jinacandrasūri's biography (Babb 1996: 124).

Another form of public action is a positive undertaking for what we call today environment protection. When Karmacandra was in the service of Rāyasiṃha in Bikaner, he prohibited the cutting of all trees in the desert (321). This he got as a favour of the king. The protection of trees (*vṛkṣarakṣaṇam*, 329) is not justified by ideological reasons but by practical ones: in case of draughts, they are able to provide subsistence (through their fruit).

We find the prestigious activities centring around the scriptures, which I mentioned at the beginning of this paper, also illustrated by members of this lineage. Karmasiṃha is said to have received a *Kalpasūtra* manuscript for fourteen years (172cd), whatever this exactly means. Efforts to retrieve such a document have remained fruitless. Karmasiṃha's presence at the kingdom of Bikaner ruled by Lūṇakarṇa, however, is acknowledged in the *praśasti* of the *Ācārāṅgadīpikā* composed in VS 1573 by the Kharataragaccha leader, Jinahaṃsasūri.[22] Karmacandra is depicted as a learned man too. With his guru Jayasoma, the author of the *Vaṃśāvalī* himself, he was instructed in the text and the meaning of the eleven *Aṅgas* (316). Following this he invested a lot of money to get the Siddhānta, that is, the Śvetāmbara canon *stricto sensu* but perhaps other categories of texts as well, put to writing:

śrutajñānasya bhakty-arthaṃ śrīSiddhāntasya lekhane

---

[22] This *praśasti* is not found in the Calcutta edition (1880) of the commentary but it is quoted in full in manuscript catalogues, see W. Schubring, *Die Jaina Handschriften der Preussischen Staatsbibliothek*, Leipzig, 1944, No. 5 p. 3 or Catalogue of the manuscripts of the L. D. Institute of Indology, Ahmedabad, No. 208.

dhanaṃ dhanaṃ punar yena purā vyāpāritaṃ vidā (317).

Again, his name as a ruling minister occasionally appears in *praśasti*s of contemporary works or manuscripts. One of them is the *Damayantīcampūkāvyaṭīkā* composed by the same Guṇavinaya who wrote the *Vaṃśāvalī*.[23] Thus, Karmacandra is depicted as an example to follow both at the personal and at the public levels.

To conclude this preliminary investigation: the *Vaṃśāvalī* is an interesting piece of history writing in pre-modern India. It is the Jain contribution to and counterpart of the bardic literature well represented at the regional level in western India, especially Rajasthan. Although the *Vaṃśāvalī* makes use of literary motifs, it is not a work of fiction. It is based on reality as the comparison with inscriptions, which provides supportive evidence, tends to show. In the rhetoric at work the narration of the past appears as a significant component illuminating the narration of the present—here the interaction between a Jain official, a king of regional status, and a specific monastic community to which the family is affiliated for generations on. It underlines recurring patterns in the relations between the Jain community and political power, and in the ways the Jains manage to get practical advantages in favour of their own faith. In Karmacandra's case, there is one higher level of interaction: with an emperor, Akbar, at the national level. Primarily, the *Karmacandra-vaṃśāvalī* is a text meant for the promotion of the Kharataragaccha. We can even go so far as to say that its different versions could have been written with the view to publicise the Kharatara's role at Akbar's court in order to counterbalance the over presence of their sectarian rivals, the Tapāgaccha. For, it is known that the prevailing 'teachers of Akbar' were Hīravijayasūri, Vijayasenasūri and Bhānucandra, all of whom belonged to the Tapāgaccha. The Tapās also succeeded in getting imperial edicts against the slaughter of animals. Only their names are mentioned in the *Āīn-i-Akbarī* (Smith 1917; Vidyavijayji 1943, etc.). Jinacandrasūri, the pontiff of the Kharataragaccha, is conspicuous by his absence, as is Karmacandra. In other

[23] See Vinayasāgar and Shah 2010: 591–593 and introduction: 66–68.

words, if the Kharataragaccha did not want their role to be minimized or forgotten, their only option was to make their own publicity by themselves.

Index of Proper Names

An asterisk (*) preceding a name indicates that the person belongs to Karmacandra's lineage and can be seen in the genealogical tree, kindly prepared by Jérôme Petit.

Bibliography

Babb, Lawrence A., 1996, *Absent Lord: Ascetics and Kings in a Jain Ritual Culture*, Berkeley, etc.: University of California Press.

Balbir, Nalini, 2006, "Sur les traces de deux bibliothèques familiales au Gujarat" (XVe–XVIIe siècles). In: *Anamorphoses*. Hommage à Jacques Dumarçay. Textes réunis par Henri Chambert-Loir et Bruno Dagens. Paris : Les Indes Savantes, pp. 325–352.

——— 2010, "Is a Manuscript an Object or a Living Being ? Jain Views on the Life and Use of Sacred Texts." In: Kristina Myrvold (ed.), *The Death of Sacred Texts : Ritual Disposal and Renovation of Texts in World Religions*. Farnham: Ashgate, pp. 107–124.

——— forthcoming, "Réseaux sociaux, religieux et familiaux dans les colophons des manuscrits jaina de l'Inde occidentale". Paper delivered at the International Conference "Lecteurs et copistes dans les traditions manuscrites iraniennes, indiennes et centrasiatiques", Paris, 16–19 June 2010.

Bhandari, S. R., Bhandari, C. R., Gupta, K. A., Soni, B. A., Ratnawal, B. R., 1934, *Osvāl jāti kā itihās*, Bhanpura (Indore): Oswal History Publishing House.

Bhūtoṛiyā, Māṃgīlāl, 1988, *Itihāsa kī amara bela Osavāla (Osavāla jāti kā itihāsa)*, dvitīya khaṇḍa, Ladnun: Priyadarśī Prakāśan.

BJLS = *Bikaner Jain Lekha Saṃgraha*. A. Nahta and Bh. Nahta (eds), Calcutta: Nahta Brothers, Vīra saṃvat 2482 [= 1955] (Shri Abhaya Jaina Granthamala 15).

Cort, John E., 2004, "Jains, Caste and Hierarchy in North Gujarat." *Contributions to Indian Sociology* (n.s.) 38, 1&2, pp. 73–112.

Desai, M. D., 1933, *Jain Sāhitya no Samkṣipta Itihāsa*, Bombay.

——— 1941, "Introduction to Siddhicandra." *Bhānucandragaṇicarita*, Ahmedabad, Calcutta: Singhi Jain Series (15).

Dundas, Paul, 1999, "Jain Perceptions of Islam in the Early Modern Period." *Indo-Iranian Journal* 42, pp. 35–46.

Jain, Kailash Chand, 1963, *Jainism in Rajasthan*, Sholapur: Jīvarāja Jaina Granthamālā (No. 15).

Jain, Jyoti Prasad, 2000, *Pramukh Aitihāsik Jain Puruṣ aur Mahilāeṃ*, Delhi: Bhāratīya Jñānapīṭha.

Jayasoma, 1980, *Mantrikarmacandra Vaṃśāvalī Prabandha*, (ed. Jinavijaya Muni), Bombay: Singhi Jain Series (72).

KhGBI: *Kharataragaccha kā Bṛhad Itihāsa*, Part I, by Sāhitya Vācaspati Mahopādhyāy Vinayasāgar, Jaipur: Prakrit Bharati Academy, 2004. Second ed., 2005 (Prākṛta Bhāratī Puṣpa 161).

KhGGurvāvalī: *Kharataragacchagurvāvalī*. In: ŚrīJinapālopādhyāyādi-saṅkalita *Kharataragacchabṛhadgurvāvali*, Bombay: Singhi Jain Series (42), 1956.

KhGPLS: Mahopādhyāya Vinayasāgar, *Kharataragaccha pratiṣṭhā lekha saṃgraha* (12vīṃ śatī se lekar 20vīṃ śatī tak kharataragacchācāryoṃ dvārā pratiṣṭhita pratimā lekhoṃ kā saṃgraha), Jaipur: Prakrit Bharati Academy, 2005 (Prakrit Bharati Pushpa 182).

Mehta, Lakshman Sinh, 1983, *Vacchāvat Gotrīya Mehtā Vaṃśa*, (not consulted).

Smith, Vincent A., 1917, "The Jain Teachers of Akbar." In: *Commemorative Essays Presented to Sir Ramkrishna Gopal Bhandarkar*, Poona: Bhandar Oriental Research Institute, pp. 265–276.

Salomon, Richard, 1998, *Indian Epigraphy. A guide to the study of inscriptions in Sanskrit, Prakrit, and the other Indo-Aryan languages*, New York, Oxford: Oxford University Press.

Somani, Ram Vallabh, 1982, *Jain Inscriptions of Rajasthan*. Jaipur: Rajasthan Prakrit Bharati Sansthan (Prakrit Bharati Puspa 11).

Śrīvallabhagaṇi, 1969, *Saṅghapati Rūpajī-vaṃśa-praśastiḥ*, (ed. Mahopādhyāy Vinayasāgar), Jodhpur: Rajasthan Puratan Granthamala (107).

Tod, James, 1920, *Annals and Antiquities of Rajasthan*, London: Oxford University Press. Reprint: Delhi, Motilal Banarsidass, 1971, 1987, 3 vols.

Vaṃśāvalī: see Jayasoma.

Vidyavijayji Muni, 1943, *A Monk and a Monarch* (originally written in Gujarati). Adapted by Dolarrai R. Mankad, Ujjain.

Vinayasāgar, Mahopādhyāy and Shah, J. B., (eds) 2010, *Rasasiddha-kavīśvara-śrīTrivikramabhaṭṭa-praṇītā Damayantī-kathā -campūḥ mahopādhyāya-śrīGuṇavinaya-gaṇi-sandṛbdhayā Sārasvatī-vivṛtyā sambhūṣitā*, Ahmedabad: L. D. Institute of Indology (L. D. Series 149).

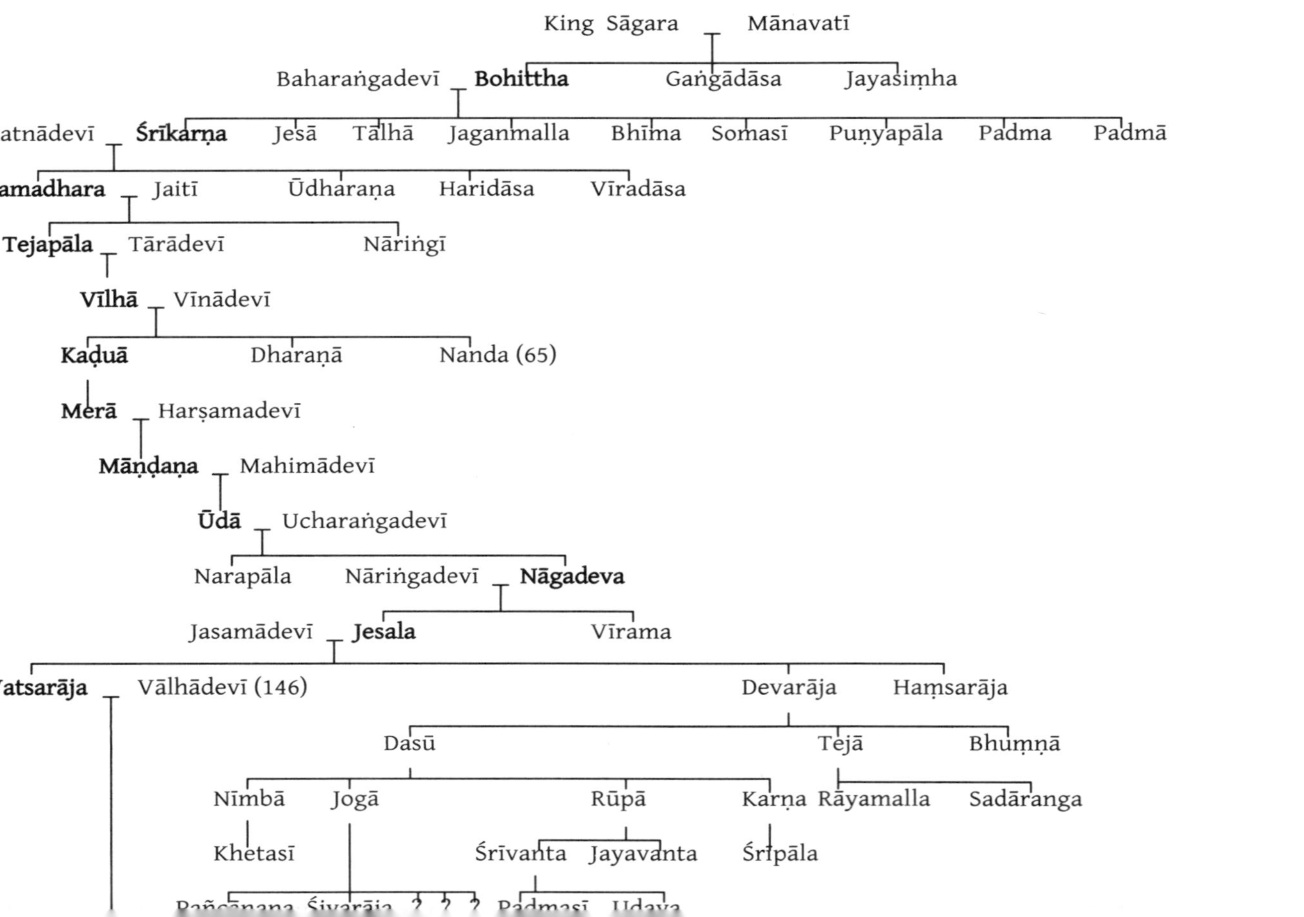

King Sāgara
Mānavatī
Baharaṅgadevī
Bohittha
Gaṅgādāsa
Jayasiṃha
Ratnādevī
Śrīkarṇa
Jesā
Tālhā
Jaganmalla
Bhīma
Somasī
Puṇyapāla
Padma
Padmā
Samadhara
Jaitī
Ūdharaṇa
Haridāsa
Vīradāsa
Tejapāla
Tārādevī
Nāriṅgī
Vīlhā
Vīnādevī
Kaḍuā
Dharaṇā
Nanda (65)
Merā
Harṣamadevī
Māṇḍaṇa
Mahimādevī
Ūdā
Ucharaṅgadevī
Narapāla
Nāriṅgadevī
Nāgadeva
Jasamādevī
Jesala
Vīrama
Vatsarāja
Vālhādevī (146)
Devarāja
Haṃsarāja
Dasū
Tejā
Bhuṃṇā
Nīmbā
Jogā
Rūpā
Karṇa
Rāyamalla
Sadāranga
Khetasī
Śrīvanta
Jayavanta
Śrīpāla

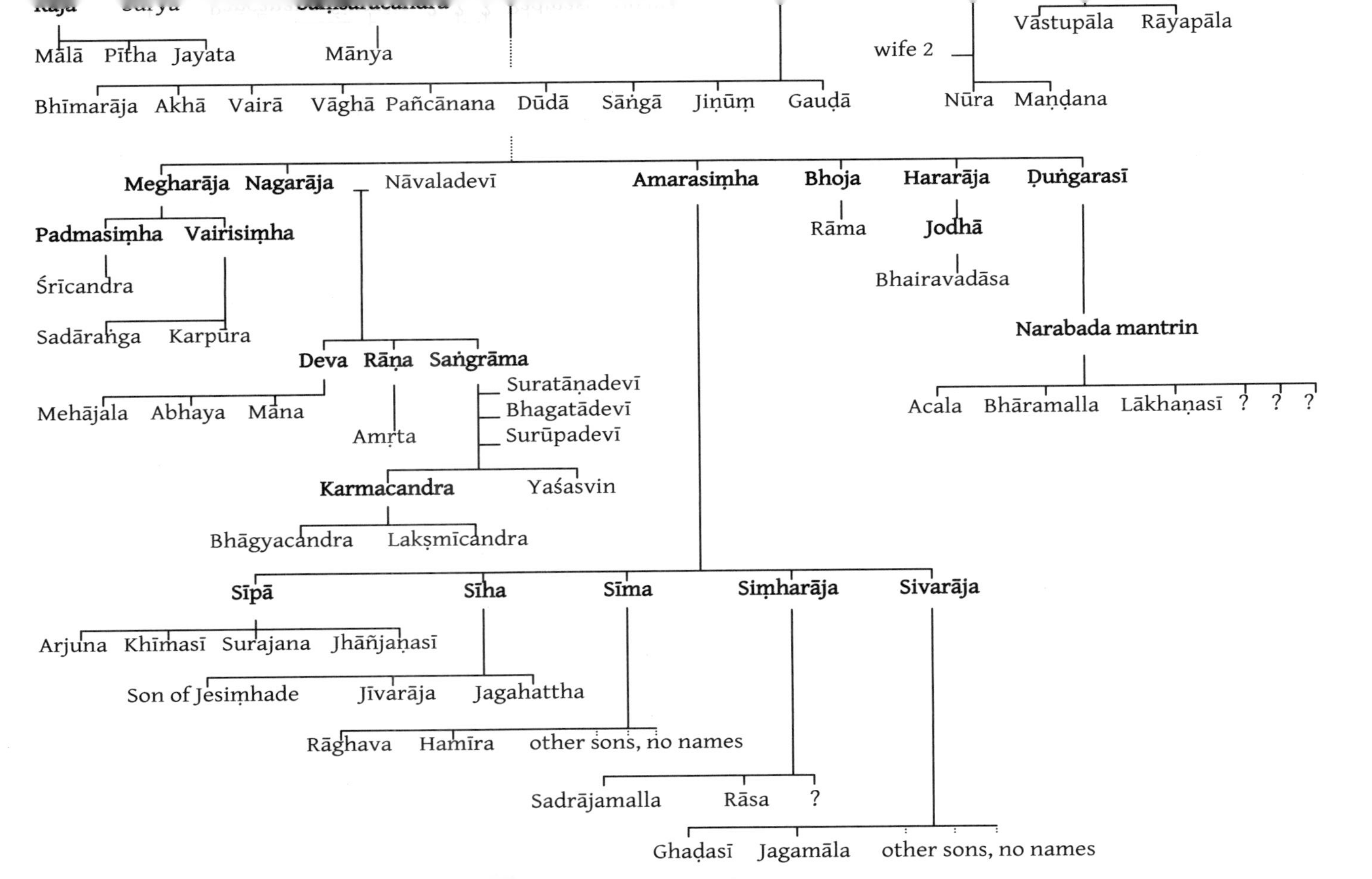

Vastupāla
Rāyapāla
Mālā
Pītha
Jayata
Mānya
wife 2
Bhīmarāja
Akhā
Vairā
Vāghā
Pañcānana
Dūdā
Sāṅgā
Jiṇūṃ
Gauḍā
Nūra
Maṇḍana
Megharāja
Nagarāja
Nāvaladevī
Amarasiṃha
Bhoja
Hararāja
Ḍuṅgarasī
Padmasiṃha
Vairisiṃha
Rāma
Jodhā
Śrīcandra
Bhairavadāsa
Sadāraṅga
Karpūra
Narabada mantrin
Deva
Rāṇa
Saṅgrāma
Suratāṇadevī
Bhagatādevī
Surūpadevī
Mehājala
Abhaya
Māna
Amṛta
Acala
Bhāramalla
Lākhaṇasī
?
?
?
Karmacandra
Yaśasvin
Bhāgyacandra
Lakṣmīcandra
Sīpā
Sīha
Sīma
Siṃharāja
Sivarāja
Arjuna
Khīmasī
Surajana
Jhāñjaṇasī
Son of Jesiṃhade
Jīvarāja
Jagahattha
Rāghava
Hamīra
other sons, no names
Sadrājamalla
Rāsa
?
Ghaḍasī
Jagamāla
other sons, no names

An Example of Buddhist-Jaina Congruence in the *Kālāmasutta**

Bhikkhu Pāsādika

Abstract

In an article by Evans in 2007 the content of the Buddha's Discourse to the Kālāmas has been doubted and relativised considerably. On the basis of a textual analysis and by drawing on relevant parallel passages the stance on the Discourse will be critically analysed. Passages pointing to the beginnings of the Jaina *syādvāda* or showing Buddhist parallels to it will be discussed especially, as an example of Buddhist and Jaina congruence.

Keywords: *Kālāmasutta*, Discourse to the Kālāmas, Jaina *syādvāda*, Buddhist parallels to *syādvāda*

According to leading indologists, certain teachings of Jainism and early Buddhism are strongly reminiscent of those of the European Enlightenment, ushering in the progress of scientific enquiry. Thus, with reference to the two soteriologies-cum-philosophies, it has been affirmed, for instance, "that as philosophies they could have been held in different ways consistently with scientific progress... The sturdy common sense of Jainism, along with its relativistic dialectic... could be parts of a growing science."[1] In the Discourse Addressed to the Kālāmas (*Kālāmasutta*), for example, the Buddha encourages contemporaries to come to know for themselves by objectively probing things. In a recent article, "Doubting the *Kālāma-Sutta*: Epistemology, Ethics, and the 'Sacred'" (Evans 2007: 91ff.), the content of the discourse has been relativised considerably. In the following I shall try to come to a conclusion, by means of textual analysis and relevant parallel passages, whether the article's relativist position is justifiable or not. I shall, in particular, discuss such passages as can—in spite of many differences between Jainism and Buddhism—be related to the beginnings of the later Jaina *syādvāda* or considered a Buddhist parallel to it.

---

* Many thanks are due to Dr Jayandra Soni for his comments on this paper and for making accessible to me B. K. Matilal's monograph on *Anekāntavāda*.

[1] See Pande 1984: 250. On the ancient Jaina thinkers' interest in problems of biology, cosmology or ontology, apart from their soteriological concern proper, see Tatia 1975.

It has been observed (Premasiri 1996: 84ff.) that the *Kālāmasutta* of the *Aṅguttaranikāya* (Morris, Warder 1961: 188-193) is considered by many scholars as enshrining the essence of the Buddha's epistemological teaching because in it he sets forth ten grounds that should not be gone by (*etha...mā...*) for ascertaining a statement's reliability. It is only on knowing things or phenomena (*dhammā*) for oneself (*yadā...attanā va jāneyyātha*), so it says in the discourse, that one should respond. The *sutta*'s ten grounds not acceptable to the Buddha as ultimate criteria are: 1) report (*anussava*), 2) tradition (*paramparā*), 3) hearsay (*itikirā*), 4) authority of holy scriptures (*piṭakasampadāna*), 5) [mere] reasoning (*takka*), 6) inference [only] (*naya*), 7) consideration of reasons [alone] (*ākāraparivitakka*), 8) taking one's stand on dogmas (*diṭṭhinijjhānakkhanti*), 9) [just] appearance of likelihood (*bhavyarūpatā*) and 10) [faith in] one's spiritual teacher (*samaṇo no garu*).[2]

In the above-mentioned article Evans very much doubts the possibility to cite the *Kālāmasutta* "as proof of the rational and empirical spirit of early Buddhist epistemology." According to him,

> the Kālāmas do not ask what is the truth, and the Buddha does not tell them how to find it. Rather the Kālāmas ask 'Who is telling the truth?' in what may have been the pursuit of sacred or quasi-magical power through the person of a teacher. The Buddha, in turn, encourages them to adopt a set of attitudes and actions, which includes choosing a teacher. The method of evaluation that the Buddha gives, which includes the famous 'know for yourselves', is found to be at least as much ethical as it is epistemological and to invoke the opinion of authority and the public. The Buddha here seems to call for a decision that is partly based on faith, and the Kālāmas respond not with independent

---

[2] For clarification of the ten grounds, most notably of *piṭakasampadāna*, see Premasiri 1996. A single parallel of the *Kālāmasutta* has been preserved in the Chinese *Madhyamāgama* (see *Taishō* I, No. 26, 438b-439c22). Unfortunately the ten grounds do not occur in the *āgama* text, whereas the four kinds of confidence (see the discussion below) (安隱, *āśvāsatva*) of the Chinese translation tally only partly—but basically—with the *assāsas* of the Pāli text.

> research, but with an act of faith in committing themselves to (and being accepted by) the Buddha [Evans 2007: 91].

Evans adds that "the sense of modernity in the Sutta should make us pause and ask whether we have been projecting our own categories of thought into it and thereby misunderstanding it." He further states that in his hermeneutical enquiry his concern is not with what the historical Buddha may have said or thought but that he is rather interested in the 'Buddha of tradition', that is "the Buddha of the Pāli *Nikāyas* as seen through the lens of the Theravāda tradition." By moving away from interpreting the *Kālāmasutta* as a "rational-empirical epistemological treatise" Evans wishes to avoid a more or less common approach that "tacitly ignores or argues away more obviously superstitious aspects" traceable in the Pāli *nikāyas.*

Evans' article of sixteen pages—against six of the original text—reads like a long commentary on the *sutta* so that, for want of space and time, only a few points he makes can be discussed here. The overall impression got from the article is that it is—if thought-provoking—highly speculative. The author draws on material from various *suttas* in different *nikāyas* in order to support his arguments for the Kālāmas' quest for a genuine teacher, and asking questions only to enable them to access "sacred or quasi-magical power". It goes without saying that the Pāli canon does include places in which great store is set by accessing 'sacred or quasi-magical power', but on grounds of textual evidence, to attribute such a motivation to the Kālāmas is but speculation. According to the discourse, due to heated debates and interschool disputes over the theses and/or doctrines (*vāda*) put forward by different ascetics and *brāhmaṇas*, the Kālāmas simply tell the Buddha that they have their doubts as to who of them is right or wrong (*ko si nāma imesaṃ bhavantānaṃ samaṇānaṃ saccaṃ āḥa ko musā ti*) and the latter, before stating his ten grounds as mentioned, confirms that the Kālāmas are in doubt. "On knowing for yourselves, Kālāmas," the Buddha continues,

> a) these things (*dhammā*) are demeritorious (*akusala*): greed (*lobha*), hatred (*dosa*) and delusion (*moha*); being

> under their sway, they lead to one's disadvantage and suffering; so they should be got rid of.
> b) These things are meritorious (*kusala*): freedom from greed (*alobha*), from hatred (*adosa*) and from delusion (*amoha*); cultivating them, they lead to one's advantage and happiness; so they should be cultivated.

Evans is certainly right to underline that the *Kālāmasutta* is at least as much ethical as it is epistemological, for the Buddha's examples of demeritorious and meritorious behaviour respectively refer to violating and complying with lay ethics. Although for his arguments Evans cites a number of *suttas*, he does not mention the discourse following the *Kālāmasutta*, namely, the 'Speech Addressed to the [Two] Sāḷhas', the *Sāḷhasutta* (Morris, Warder 1961: 193-197), being a close parallel to the former. Like the Buddha, in the *Sāḷhasutta* his disciple Nandaka several times enumerates the ten grounds not acceptable as ultimate criteria. Moreover, according to the *Sāḷhasutta*, *abhijjhā* (covetousness) is synonymous with *lobha* in the aforesaid context, *vyāpāda* (ill will) with *dosa* and *avijjā* (nescience) with *moha*; for the opposites of the above *alobha*, *adosa* and *amoha* Nandaka gives the synonyms *anabhijjhā* (selflessness), *avyāpāda* (benevolence) and *vijjā* which can be rendered both as 'true knowledge' and 'science'. After his examples of *akusala*- and *kusalacarita*, in a nutshell the Buddha presents to his audience an *ariyasāvaka's*, 'a noble disciple's/a noble one's disciple's', meditative 'divine abiding' (*brahmavihāra*), his or her cultivating loving kindness, compassion, sympathetic joy and equanimity. It is important to note that, according to the text, 'divine abiding' also includes the meditator's being *asammūḷha*, *sampajāna* and *patissata*, 'clearheaded, attentive and mindful'. In the *Sāḷhasutta* the 'divine abiding' also occurs verbatim, followed by a decisive passage not found in the *Kālāmasutta* but being crucial to our understanding—seeing through the very 'lens' of the Theravāda tradition—of the implications of *alobha*, *adosa* and *amoha* in the light of the aforementioned 'objectively probing things'. The said passage runs:

> Then he knows: There is this, there is what is wretched and there is what is exalted, and there is an escape

> beyond this sphere of perception [distorted by greed, hatred and delusion]. Thus knowing and thus realizing, his mind is released from the malign influences of... nescience... there is insight-knowledge.[3]

In the commentary to this text it is made clear that *alobha, adosa* and *amoha* not only imply gnosiology, but also presuppose scientific and yogic objectivity.[4]

Lastly, attention may be drawn to another passage in the *Kālāmasutta* which, again, has occasioned speculation: According to the *sutta*, the *ariyasāvaka,* with his mind purified by his practice, finds four kinds of confidence (*assāsa*): 1) If there are an afterlife (*paraloka*) and consequences of one's actions (*kammānaṃ phalaṃ vipāko*), he will be reborn in a heaven; 2) if not, he will, nonetheless, here and now live non-violently, peacefully, happily and free from suffering; 3) if an evildoer will have to face the dire consequences of his actions whilst he, the *ariyasāvaka*, lives non-violently and bears nobody any grudge, he will have nothing to fear; and 4) if an evildoer will not have to face any consequences of his actions, he, the *ariyasāvaka*, will be confident in that he knows himself to be 'unaffected (lit. 'pure') both ways'. [5] In Evans' words here

---

[3] See Morris, Warder 1961: 196f.: *So evaṃ pajānāti atthi idaṃ atthi hīnaṃ atthi paṇītaṃ atthi imassa saññāgatassa uttariṃ nissaraṇan ti. Tassa evam(ṃ) jānato evaṃ passato...avijjāsavā pi cittaṃ vimuccati... ñāṇaṃ hoti...*

[4] See Walleser, Kopp 1930: 307: ***So evaṃ pajānātī*** *ti so cattāro brahmavihāre bhāvetvā ṭhito ariyasāvako samāpattito vuṭṭhāya vipassanaṃ ārabhanto evaṃ pajānāti.* ***Atthi idan*** *ti atthi dukkhasaccasaṃkhātaṃ hi...* ***Hīnan*** *ti samudayasaccaṃ.* ***Paṇītan*** *ti maggasaccaṃ.* ***Imassa saññāgatassa uttariṃ nissaraṇan*** *ti imassa vipassanāsaññāsaṃkhātassa saññāgatassa uttariṃ nissaraṇaṃ nāma nibbānaṃ taṃ atthī ti iminā nirodhasaccaṃ dasseti.* ***Vimuttam iti ñāṇan*** *ti ekūnavīsatividhaṃ paccavekkhanāñāṇaṃ kathitaṃ.* This expository passage explains the canonical text as referring to the Four Noble Truths realized through insight-knowledge and to 19 kinds of 'knowledge of reviewing' (cf. *Visuddhimagga*, chapter 22, PTS ed., p. 676) on the part of the four *ariyapuggalas*. With reference to fn. 6 below it may be noted that, according to the Theravāda tradition, a 'disciple of the noble ones' can qualify as an adept in various kinds of insight-knowledge, whereas 'knowledge of reviewing' pertains to the 'noble disciples' only.

[5] See Walleser, Kopp 1930: 306: ***Ubhayen'eva suddham attānaṃ samanupassāmī*** *ti yañ ca pāpaṃ na karomi yañ ca karoto pi na karīyati...* "'Thus I know myself to be unaffected both ways'—in that I do no evil and also nothing happens to a perpetrator."

"there seems to be a contradiction... when the Buddha implies that some of his enlightened and/or meditatively advanced followers may lack epistemic certainty on rebirth and the efficacy of karma..." whereas an *ariyasāvaka* is required to be free of uncertainty about such matters.[6] Evans even goes so far as to suggest that "An act of faith, indeed, is what the Buddha's discourse here elicits, the Kālāmas' taking refuge in him at the close of the *Sutta*," instead of their 'knowing for themselves'. In reply to this it may be stressed that the Kālāmas' 'act of faith' should be seen as a reaction to the Buddha's encouraging rigorous rational enquiry and free choice on their part to find out for themselves rather than his aiming at making converts of them.[7]

Not only in respect of the above ten grounds, but also with regard to the four kinds of confidence, the intellectual milieu of the Buddha's time should be taken into consideration—characterized, *inter alia*, by lively philosophical enquiry and stiff interschool competition—but also appeasement and mutual influencing. It is a striking feature with the four *assāsa*s that they are thematically connected with the agnostic Sañjaya Belaṭṭhiputta's stance on metaphysical and moral questions. Although the *assāsa*s of the *Kālāmasutta* have a ring of positive-rational pragmatism about them, they also betray —which in the given context is somewhat exceptional in the Pāli canon—a non-committal attitude as in Sañjaya, and it is this very attitude taken near the close of the *sutta* that is meant to encourage independent inquiry and rational thought. According to the *Sāmaññaphalasutta*,[8] Sañjaya is reported as having said:

---

[6] One need not assume a contradiction here if one translates *ariyasāvaka* as 'disciple of the noble ones'.

[7] Cf. Joshi 1983: 70f.; particularly apt is the author's quoting the *Bhaddiyasutta* (*Aṅguttaranikāya* II (PTS ed.), p. 190ff.) which is largely identical with the *Kālāmasutta*, containing the ten grounds and in which the Buddha makes it clear that he does not ask anybody to accept his teaching 'as a matter of authority or out of respect for him'.

[8] See Rhys Davids, Carpenter 1890: 58f.: *'Atthi paro loko' ti iti ce taṃ pucchasi, 'atthi paro loko' ti iti ce me assa, 'atthi paro loko' ti iti te naṃ vyākareyyaṃ. Evam pi me no. Tathā ti pi me no. Aññathā ti pi me no. No ti pi me no. No no ti pi me no. ... 'N'atthi paro loko?' ti... 'Atthi sukaṭa-dukkaṭānaṃ kammānaṃ phalaṃ*

> If you ask me whether there is another world ... (or no other world) ... or whether there is any fruit, any result, of good or bad actions ... (or not any fruit, any result ...)—well, if I thought there were (or were not), I would say so. But I don't say so (1). And I don't think it is thus (or thus) (2). And I don't think it is otherwise (3). And I don't deny it (4). And I don't affirm (5) another world (or its non-existence) ... any fruit, any result, of good or bad actions (or the non-existence of such fruit or result).[9]

As in Sañjaya, in the *Kālāmasutta* the existence and non-existence of an afterlife as well as the effectiveness and non-effectiveness of the law of karma are formally questioned. Sañjaya negates the alternatives, negates his negations as well as his affirmations; the non-committal attitude reflected in the *assāsas* is that, no matter whether an afterlife exists or not, or the law of karma is effective or not, an *ariyasāvaka* remains confident. On the basis of a passage in the *Brahmajālasutta* (Rhys Davids, Carpenter 1890: 26f.), Matilal comments on Sañjaya's stance as follows:

> Out of respect for truth and out of fear of, and distaste for, falsehood (cf. *musāvāda-bhayā*) Sañjaya adopted a non-committal attitude towards questions about after-life etc. His position was that definite knowledge about such matters as after-life was impossible to obtain, and he had the boldness to confess it. Thus, I think the Pāli commentator was a bit unfair when he called him an 'eel-wriggler'.[10]

Whilst formally Sañjaya's 'agnosticism' is characterized by negations, the Jainas' concessive *syādvāda* philosophy of 'non-onesidedness' signifies reconciliatory synthesis and therefore, let me suggest, the *Kālāmasutta*'s four 'confidences' can be related to it.

---

vipāko?' ti iti ce maṃ pucchasi... 'N'atthi sukaṭa-dukkaṭānaṃ kammānaṃ phalaṃ vipāko?' ti ... No no ti pi me no ti.

[9] Adapted from Rhys Davids 1899, p. 75.

[10] See Matilal 1981: 48, 1985: 303f.

With reference to the above passage from the *Dīghanikāya* Matilal makes very apposite remarks on the origins of the Jaina philosophic doctrine of non-onesidedness, *anekāntavāda*, or its 'seven ways of non-absolutism', *syādvāda/saptabhaṅgī*. According to him (Matilal 1981: 47ff., 1985: 302ff.), one of the "forerunners of the sevenfold formula of the Jainas and of the Buddhists' tetralemma[11] is the above fivefold formula developed by Sañjaya." Matilal fully explains the meaning of *syādvāda*, cites traditional objections to it and also defends the Jaina position. He concludes his treatment of *anekāntavāda*, the "philosophy of synthesis and reconciliation" and attempt "to establish a rapprochement between seemingly disagreeing philosophical schools", with these words:

> Non-violence... was the dominant trend in the whole of śramaṇa movement in India, particularly in Buddhism and Jainism. I think the Jainas carried the principle of non-violence to the intellectual level, and thus propounded their *anekānta* doctrine... The principle embodied in the respect for the life of others was transformed by the Jaina philosophers, at the intellectual level, into respect for the views of others. This was, I think, a unique attempt to harmonize the persistent discord in the field of philosophy.[12]

---

[11] See, for instance, Katsura 2000: 201ff.

[12] See Matilal 1981: 61, 1985: 313f. On *anekānta* believed in by both the Jaina and Vaibhāṣika Buddhists see also Tatia 1960: 109ff. and Soni 2007: 477ff. As for the 'principle of non-violence at the intellectual level', cf. *Saṃyuttanikāya* V, Feer 1898: 419: *Mā bhikkhave viggāhikakathaṃ katheyyātha || Na tvam imaṃ dhammavinayam ājānāsi || aham imaṃ dhammavinayam ājānāmi || ... Sahitam me asahitan te || Āciṇṇan te viparāvattaṃ || Āropito te vādo || ... Taṃ kissa hetu || Nesā bhikkhave kathā atthasaṃhitā nādibrahmacariyikā na nibbidāya na virāgāya ... na abhiññāya na sambodhāya ... saṃvattati... ||* Bodhi 2000: 1842: "Bhikkhus, do not engage in disputatious talk, saying: 'You don't understand this Dhamma and Discipline. I understand this Dhamma and Discipline... I'm consistent, you're inconsistent. What you took so long to think out has been overturned. Your thesis has been refuted...' For what reason? Because, bhikkhus, this talk is unbeneficial, irrelevant to the fundamentals of the holy life, and does not lead to revulsion, to dispassion... to direct knowledge, to enlightenment..."

It seems reasonable to associate the Jainas' "intellectual non-violence", as proposed by Matilal, with objectivity in the sense of *sine ira et studio* and of the aforementioned *alobha, adosa, amoha.*

In conclusion, let me once more revert to the ten grounds, not considered by the Buddha acceptable as ultimate criteria. However, in a non-onesided—*syāt* as it were—sense, as Premasiri points out, the *Kālāmasutta* does not imply that the ten grounds set forth in it are absolutely irrelevant to a person in search of truth. At a preliminary stage for a truth seeker "hearing from an authoritative source", tradition, scriptures, "confidence gained as a consequence of a consideration of reasons", or a qualified teacher are admissible or even necessary as essential preconditions. "What the Buddha appears to be denying in the *Kālāma Sutta*," says Premasiri, "is that any of the grounds mentioned could be a substitute for the direct experiential understanding of the truth."[13] In this context, Joshi seems fully justified in writing that the essence of the *Kālāmasutta* is summed up in Śāntarakṣita's *Tattvasaṃgraha*, v. 3587, in which the Buddha gives the following advice:

> O monks, [only] after examining my words may [you] accept [them], not out of respect—just as the prudent [test the purity of] gold by heating, cutting and rubbing it.[14]

It is worthy of note that some of the *Kālāmasutta's* ten grounds are also mentioned in the *Devadahasutta* of the *Majjhimanikāya,*[15] in which disagreement about teachings attributed to the Nigaṇṭha Nāthaputta, that is, Mahāvīra, vis-à-vis those of the Buddha is highlighted, but from which, nonetheless, also points of agreement can be gleaned. Due to the fact that in the *Devadahadasutta* the Buddha is given as driving his point home by means of dialectic parts of which thematically are very

---

[13] See Premasiri 1996: 88.

[14] See Joshi 1983: 71. For the quoted Sanskrit verse and a canonical parallel to it see Pāsādika 2007: 398.

[15] Chalmers 1896: 218: *Saddhā ruci anussavo ākāraparivitakko diṭṭhinijjhāna(k)khanti.*

similar to his formulation of the *assāsas*,[16] as mentioned, it can be vindicated, I think, to speak of a 'Buddhist-Jaina congruence in the *Kālāmasutta*.'

Bibliography

Aṅguttaranikāya II, 1988 (second ed.). Wilts, U. K.: Pali Text Society.

Bodhi Bhikkhu (tr.), 2000, *The Connected Discourses of the Buddha. A New Translation of the Saṃyutta Nikāya*, Vol. II, Oxford: Pali Text Society in association with Wisdom Publications (Somerville MA, USA).

Chalmers, Robert (ed.), 1896, *The Majjhima-Nikāya*, Vol. II, London: Pali Text Society (PTS).

Evans, Stephen A., 2007, "Doubting the Kālāma-Sutta: Epistemology, Ethics, and the 'Sacred'". In: *Buddhist Studies Review*, Vol. 24.1, pp. 90–107.

Joshi, Lal Mani, 1983, *Discerning the Buddha. A Study of Buddhism and of the Brahmanical Hindu Attitude to It*. New Delhi: Munshiram Manoharlal.

Katsura, Shōryū, 2000, "Nāgārjuna and the Tetralemma (Catuṣkoṭi)". In: Jonathan A. Silk (ed.), *Wisdom, Compassion, and the Search for Understanding*. The Buddhist Studies Legacy of Gadjin M. Nagao. Honolulu: University of Hawai'i Press, pp. 201–220.

Matilal, Bimal Krishna, 1981, *The Central Philosophy of Jainism (Anekāntavāda)*, Ahmedabad: L. D. Institute of Indology.

——— 1985, *Logic, Language and Reality. An Introduction to Indian Philosophical Studies*. Delhi: Motilal Banarsidass.

Morris, Richard, Warder, A.K (eds), 1961, *The Aṅguttara-Nikāya*, Part I, London: Pali Text Society.

Pande, Govind Chandra, 1984, *Foundations of Indian Culture. Spiritual Vision and Symbolic Forms in Ancient India*. New Delhi: Books and Books Publishers.

Pāsādika Bhikkhu, 2007, "The Ekottarāgama Parallel to Jātaka 77." In: Konrad Klaus, Jens-Uwe Hartmann (eds), *Indica et Tibetica. Festschrift für Michael Hahn*. Wiener Studien zur

[16] E.g., *ibid.*, p. 227: *Sace, bhikkhave, sattā pubbekatahetu sukhadukkhaṃ paṭisaṃvedenti, pāsaṃso Tathāgato; no ce sattā pubbekatahetu sukhadukkhaṃ paṭisaṃvedenti, pāsaṃso Tathāgato.*

Tibetologie und Buddhismuskunde, Vienna: Arbeitskreis für tibetische und buddhistische Studien Universität Wien, Heft 66, pp. 395–403.

Premasiri, P. D., 1996, "Kālāma Sutta." In: *Encyclopaedia of Buddhism*, Vol. VI, Fascicle 1: Jarā–Kāśyapīya (pp. 84–89). Colombo: Government of Sri Lanka Publication.

Rhys Davids, T. W. (tr.), 1899, *Dialogues of the Buddha* I, London: Pali Text Society.

Rhys Davids, T. W., Carpenter, J. Estlin (eds), 1890, *The Dīgha Nikāya*, Vol. I, London: Pali Text Society.

Saṃyuttanikāya, ed. L. Veer, 1890. Wilts, U. K.: Pali Text Society.

Soni, Jayandra (2007), "*Anekāntavāda* Revisited—for *doṣas*." In: Konrad Klaus, Jens U. Hartmann (eds), *Indica et Tibetica. Festschrift für Michael Hahn*, Vienna: Arbeitskreis für tibetische und buddhistische Studien Universität Wien, pp. 477-490.

Tatia, Nathmal, 1960, "Sarvāstivāda." In: Satkari Mookerjee (ed.), *The Nava-Nālandā-Mahāvihāra Research Publication*, Vol. II, pp. 77–136.

——— 1975, *The Basic Contributions of Jainism to Indian Thought and Their Relevance in the Modern Times.* 2500th Anniversary of the Mahaparinirvana of Bhagavan Mahavira. Patiala: Guru Gobind Singh Department of Religious Studies, Punjabi University.

Visuddhimaga, 1975, Wilts, U. K.: Pali Text Society.

Walleser, Max, Kopp, Hermann (eds), 1930, *Manorathapūraṇī. Buddhaghosa's Commentary on the Aṅguttara-Nikāya*, Vol. II. London: Pali Text Society.

Composition Areas in Vidyānandin's *Satyaśāsana-parīkṣā*: the First Part of the *uttarapakṣa* in the Chapter on Vaiśeṣika

Himal Trikha

Abstract

The *Satyaśāsanaparīkṣā* (SŚP) by the Digambara author Vidyānandin is a critical investigation into the main doctrines of ten Indian schools of thought. In dealing with the Vaiśeṣika, for example, Vidyānandin uses a number of arguments, which to a large extent correspond literally to passages transmitted in other philosophical Sanskrit works of the classical and medieval period. By analysing the place where the corresponding textual material is embedded in the argumentation structure of the SŚP, various areas of composition can be established. On this basis Vidyānandin's specific achievement in the discourse can be gradually extricated. Additionally, hypotheses about the historical relation of the SŚP's arguments to other works of the philosophical literature can be formulated. This article shows the close relation between the arguments presented against inherence (*samavāya*) and text passages in the following works of Digambara authors: Samantabhadra's *Yuktyanuśāsana*, Vidyānandin's *Āptaparīkṣāṭīkā*, Prabhācandra's *Prameyakamalamārtaṇḍa* and *Nyāya-kumudacandra*.

Keywords: history of Indian philosophy, Jainism, Digambara authors, Vaiśeṣika, *samavāya*

Introduction

Research on the *Satyaśāsanaparīkṣā* (SŚP) has been scarce up to only very recent times. Gokulacandra Jain's edition—based on three manuscripts—was published in 1964 together with an English summary by Nathmal Tatia (see SŚP in the bibliography). In 2003 Jayandra Soni published an article in the context of his studies on Vidyānandin (Soni 2003). In summer 2010 Jens Borgland finished his MA thesis which provides a translation of the whole extant text, prepared with the help of Nagin Shah (Borgland 2010). My dissertation on a section of the SŚP was completed in 2009 (Trikha forthcoming a).[1]

[1] A simplified English rendering of the main focus of my German dissertation, namely the examination of Vidyānandin's confrontation with the Vaiśeṣika as a case study for the epistemic pluralism of the Jainas, will be published later this year (Trikha forthcoming b). This article provides a simplified rendering of a chapter from my dissertation, where I investigated Vidyānandin's confrontation with the Vaiśeṣika from the point of view of

This article is structured into four parts: a very short introduction into the author and his work (1. Vidyānandin's SŚP) is followed by an overview of the main line of argumentation against the Vaiśeṣika in the SŚP and of the refutation of inherence in the first part of the *uttarapakṣa* (2. Confrontation with the Vaiśeṣika). Then, methodical issues concerning textual parallels with other works of Indian philosophical Sanskrit literature will be touched upon (3. Literal correspondences with other works). Finally, the framework of the first part of the *uttarapakṣa* against the Vaiśeṣika in the context of literal correspondences with other philosophical Digambara works will be presented (4. Composition areas in the light of passages with literal correspondences to other works). Illustrations for the written presentation are partly embedded in the text and partly given at the end of the article (Figures).

1 Vidyānandin's *Satyaśāsanaparīkṣā*

The SŚP is a Sanskrit work which—in subject and method—belongs to the philosophical heritage of the Jaina tradition. The author Vidyānandin flourished in the ninth or tenth century CE. He is part of a group of Digambara authors who distinguished themselves in the Sanskrit discourse with other traditions including, for example, Samantabhadra, Akalaṅka and Prabhācandra. Nine works are assigned to Vidyānandin; his most extensive works are the *Aṣṭasahasrī* and the *Tattvārthaślokavārttika.*

The *Satyaśāsanaparīkṣā* is an 'investigation' (*parīkṣā*) into the question, whether a particular 'doctrine' (*śāsana*) is 'true' (*satya*) or not. The work has been transmitted incompletely; concise examinations of only ten (of a planned twelve) philosophical traditions are extant. The dispute with these traditions opposed to Jainism follows a concept of truth which Vidyānandin states in the introductory passage of the work:

> *idam eva hi satyaśāsanasya satyatvaṃ nāma yad dṛṣṭeṣṭāviruddhatvam. ... tac ca dṛṣṭeṣṭāviruddhatvam anekāntaśāsana eva ...*

---

composition analysis. I would like to express my sincere gratitude to Dr Jayandra Soni and Dr Birgit Huemer for their valuable comments, suggestions and corrections.

> The truth of a true doctrine, of course, does consist precisely in that that (the doctrine) is not opposed to what is perceived and to what is inferred. ... And this, (namely) being not opposed to what is perceived and to what is inferred, (obtains to) the *anekānta*-doctrine only ...[2]

Vidyānandin sketches here the line of argumentation for his work: In his detailed examinations he will try to show, that each amongst the examined doctrines is opposed to the results of two means of knowledge (*pramāṇa*), namely to *dṛṣṭa*, the result of sense perception (*pratykṣa*), and to *iṣṭa*, the result of inference (*anumāna*).

2 Confrontation with the Vaiśeṣika

Vidyānandin applies the twofold argumentation structure also to his investigation of the Vaiśeṣika. This investigation is divided in a brief *pūrvapakṣa* and a twofold *uttarapakṣa*, in which Vidyānandin attempts to show, that main tenets of the Vaiśeṣika are opposed to sense perception and inference respectively.

2.1 Main Line of Argumentation

Vidyānandin chooses the Vaiśeṣika's concept of liberation as the starting point of the discussion:

> *buddhisukhaduḥkha...saṃskārāṇāṃ navānām ātmaviśeṣaguṇānām atyantocchittāv ātmanaḥ svātmany avasthānaṃ mokṣaḥ ...*
> Liberation is the abiding of the self in itself, when the nine particular qualities of the self, namely cognition, pleasure, pain ... and disposition, are completely eliminated ..."[3]

In this concept of liberation it is intend to separate a substance (*dravya* or *guṇin*), the self, from its particular qualities (*guṇa*), cognition, pain, etc. This reflects a categorical separation that proponents of the Vaiśeṣika utilize also in other cases. This separation Vidyānandin cannot accept. He sums up his reservations as follows:

---

[2] SŚP 1,15f.

[3] SŚP (II 2) 34,4f.

> *tad etad aulūkyaśāsanam ... dṛṣṭaviruddhaṃ tadabhimatasyāvayavāvayavinor guṇaguṇinoḥ ... bhedaikāntasya tadabhedagrāhiṇā pratyakṣeṇa viruddhatvāt.*
> This doctrine (presented) here, originating from Ulūka, ... is opposed to what is perceived; for the exclusiveness of difference assumed in this (doctrine)—(namely the difference) between parts and whole, between qualities and that which is characterised by qualities ...—is opposed to sense perception, through which their difference is not grasped.[4]

The main fault of the proponents of Vaiśeṣika would therefore be that they presuppose a sharp ontological difference between entities which never occur independently in our experience: for instance, a whole (*avayavin*), like a piece of cloth, never occurs independently of its parts (*avayava*), the threads—they together form the inseparable unity of a thing (*vastu*). The Vaiśeṣika's concept of liberation, in which the unity of a substance with its qualities is to be ripped apart, is therefore—according to Vidyānandin—unfounded.

2.2 Refutation of Inherence (*samavāya*)

The proponents of the Vaiśeṣika are well aware that a thing and its constituents—the whole and its parts, etc.,—occur as a single thing and as a unity in our experience.[5] The question of how the connection (*sambandha*) between these separate entities could be thought of,[6] is answered by assuming a further entity, namely inherence (*samavāya*).[7] Inherence would be the connection through which the constituents are merged into a whole. Vidyānandin sees in the assumption of *samavāya* a displacement of the problem: if we take for granted that the connection between parts and wholes, etc., is brought about by inherence, what would then be the connection between inherence, on the one hand, and the parts and the whole on

---

[4] SŚP (II 12) 35,25f.

[5] Cf. figure 1.1., on p. 88.

[6] Cf. figure 1.2.

[7] Cf. figure 1.3.

the other?[8] This question can be put more generally by asking how inherence and an entity characterized by inherence (*samavāyin*)—be it a part or a whole—are related to each other.[9]

It is this particular problem to which Vidyānandin devotes most of his energy in the first part of his *uttarapakṣa*. He summarises the definitions of *samavāya* known in his time as follows:

> *... sa samavāyaḥ samavāyyāśrito 'nāśrito vā. yadāśritas tadā paramārthata upacārād vā.*
> This inherence ... is either based on (an entity) characterised by inherence or it is not based (on it). If it is based (on it), it does so actually or metaphorically.[10]

Vidyānandin subsumes under these two main alternatives (*vikalpa*) altogether seven sub- and subsubalternatives.[11] He scrutinises these alternatives carefully, placing argument after argument against them, in order to show that none of them holds good. He finally arrives at the conclusion that the notion of *samavāya* is a feeble construction—invented by the proponents of the Vaiśeṣika in order to conceal their untenable ontological hypothesis.

3 Literal Correspondences with Other Works

The names of the works at the bottom of figure 2 draw attention to the fact that Vidyānandin discusses ideas and theories in the examined text portion of the SŚP, which are also captured in other works in philosophical Sanskrit literature. In many cases it is not only a corresponding idea but also a similar wording of a particular theory. In order to treat these correspondences systematically it is useful to discern the different types of correspondences which, in turn, are then helpful in evaluating the composition structure of the examined text portion.

---

[8] Cf. figure 1.4.

[9] Cf. figure 1.5.

[10] SŚP (II 16f.) 36,8f.

[11] Cf. figure 2.

3.1 Quantitative Assessment of Correspondence

The relation of two corresponding text passages is classified here according to the degree of literal correspondence; the number of overlapping *akṣaras*, so to speak. The first type is an exact literal correspondence. An example is the correspondence of a passage from the SŚP with a passage from Uddyotakara's *Nyāyavārttika*:

> *anāśritaḥ samavāya iti*..[12] [=] *anāśritaḥ samavāya iti*...[13]

This is different from literal correspondence with slight variations like, for instance, the correspondence of a passage from the SŚP with a passage from Śrīdhara's *Nyāyakandalī*:

> *kurvann ātmasvarūpajño bhogāt karmaparikṣayaṃ | yugakoṭisahasrāṇi kṛtvā tena vimucyate* ||[14] [~] *kurvann ātmasvarūpajño bhogāt karmaparikṣayaṃ | yugakoṭisahasreṇa kaścid eko vimucyate* ||[15]

As a third type I record loose literal correspondences in slight paraphrase, like, for instance, between a passage from the SŚP and from Vidyānandin's *Āptaparīkṣāṭīkā*:

> *tathātmāntaḥkaraṇasaṃyogāsiddher buddhyādiguṇānutpattiḥ. tadabhāve cātmavyavasthāpakopāyāsattvād ātmatattvahāniḥ.*[16] [#] *tāvad ātmāntaḥkaraṇayoḥ saṃyogād buddhyādiguṇotpattir na bhavet. tadabhāve cātmano vyavasthāpanopāyāpāyād ātmatattvahāniḥ.*[17]

In the SŚP and in the *Āptaparīkṣāṭīkā* the same theory is expressed with a different but significant close wording. This can be differentiated from parallels according to content, which are independent from a wording like, for instance, the correspondence between passages from the SŚP and the *Nyāyavārttika*:

---

[12] SŚP (II 33^{a}) 38,7.

[13] NV 159,2; notation of correspondence: SŚP (II 33^{a}) 38,7 = NV 159,2. Literal correspondences are underlined in the exemplified way.

[14] SŚP (II 8^{b}) 35,7f.

[15] NK 285,9f.; notation: SŚP (II 8^{b}) 35,7f. ~ NK 285,9f.

[16] SŚP (II 38^{e}) 39,5f.

[17] ĀPṬ 119,8f.; notation: SŚP (II 38^{e}) 39,5f. # ĀPṬ 119,8f.

saṃsargaḥ sukhaduḥkhe ca tathārthendriyabuddhayaḥ | pratyekaṃ ṣaḍvidhāś ceti duḥkhasaṅkhyaikaviṃśatiḥ ||[18] // *ekaviṃśatiprabhedabhinnaṃ punar duḥkham: śarīraṃ ṣaḍ-indriyāṇi ṣaḍviṣayāḥ ṣaḍbuddhayaḥ sukhaṃ duḥkhaṃ ceti.*[19]

3.2 Qualitative Assessment of Correspondence

The transitions between these four types of correspondence are fluid. Determining the type may depend on the editions one uses and the manuscripts one has access to, etc. However, this quantitative assessment of the literal correspondence between two text passages forms but one criterion amongst others to judge their 'qualitative' relation: lengthy passages with a high degree of literal correspondence clearly stem from a common source. Does one of them even represent the source for the other? Is one passage therefore a quotation of the other? If so, is the quotation with an unintended or an intended alteration? a paraphrase? a mediate quotation? an independent quotation of a third work?

The following list is an overview of works which contain lengthy passages with a considerable degree of literal correspondence to the SŚP (the first three types specified above):

Epics, Purāṇas, etc.: *Mahābhārata, Devībhāgavatapurāṇa, Brahmapurāṇa, Brahmavaivartapurāṇa, Āyurvedadīpikā*
Yoga: *Tattvavaiśāradī, Yogavārttika*
Advaitavedānta: *Brahmasūtrabhāṣya, Bhāmatī*
Logico-epistemological branch of Buddhism: *Nyāyabindu, Vādanyāya, Pramāṇavārttikabhāṣya, Sāmānyadūṣaṇa*
Nyāya: *Nyāyasūtra, Nyāyavārttika, Nyāyavārttikatātparyaṭīkā, Nyāyasāra, Nyāyabhūṣaṇa, Muktāvalī, Nyāyasāratātparyadīpikā, Nyāyasārapadapañcikā*
Vaiśeṣika: *Padārthadharmasaṅgraha, Vyomavatī, Nyāyakandalī*
Śvetāmbara: *Tattvabodhavidhāyinī*
Digambara: *Āptamīmāṃsā, Yuktyanuśāsana, Nyāyakumudacandra, Prameyakamalamārtaṇḍa, Viśvatattvaprakāśa*
Other works by Vidyānandin: *Aṣṭasahasrī, Āptaparīkṣāṭīkā, Tattvārthaślokavārttikālaṅkāra, Pramāṇaparīkṣā*

---

[18] SŚP (II 10^{b}) 35,19.

[19] NV 6,3f.; notation: SŚP (II 10^{b}) 35,19 // NV 6,3f.

For our knowledge of the history of the discussed theories it would be highly desirable to determine the historical relation of the corresponding passages from these works to the SŚP. However, the succession of transmission is seldom easy to decide upon in detail for various reasons. It can be, for instance, taken for granted that not all relevant passages have been identified or that relevant works are not yet edited, have been lost, etc.

In some cases, however, the analysis of the place of argumentation—namely the place where Vidyānandin uses textual material that obviously stems from a common source—allows to draw a picture of the composition structure of the work and to present hypotheses about the historical relation of the works which transmit the literal corresponding material.

4 Composition Areas in the Light of Passages with Literal Correspondences to Other Works

Roughly eighty percent of the passages against the Vaiśeṣika from the first part of the *uttarapakṣa* in the SŚP—a text portion that covers five pages in Devanāgarī print—literally correspond to passages in other works. By contrasting these passages with their respective argumentation structure, main areas of composition emerge.

4.1 Steps and levels of argumentation

The argumentation in the first part of the *uttarapakṣa* against the Vaiśeṣika is carried out in altogether thirty main steps, on six different levels. They are represented by the numbers 12-41 in the following figure:[20]

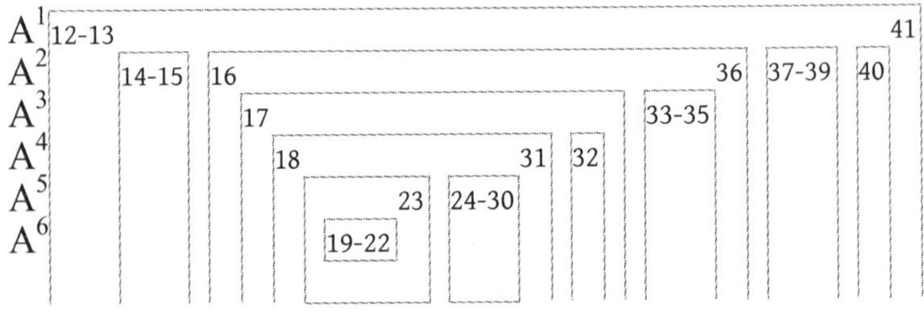

[20] SŚP (II 12-41) 35,25-39,17. Numbers 1-11 refer to the steps of argumentation in the *pūrvapakṣa*.

On the main level, A^1, Vidyānandin tries to prove that the Vaiśeṣika is opposed to sense perception, because it presupposes a sharp ontological difference between a thing and its constituents.

Inherence, the entity presupposed by proponents of the Vaiśeṣika to reconcile this difference, is notionally deconstructed on level A^2 in four big steps: general refutation of inherence [arguments 14-15], systematic deconstruction [16-36], consequences for the world view of the Vaiśeṣika [37-39] and reference to Samantabhadra as authority for the presented discussion [40].

Level A^3 pertains to the systematic deconstruction of inherence in two steps: rejection of the concept that inherence could be based (*āśrita*) on the entities characterised by inherence [17-32] and rejection of the concept that inherence is not based on them (*anāśrita*) [33-35].

On level A^4 the first alternative is rejected in two steps: rejection of the concept that inherence is actually (*paramārthataḥ*) based on the entities [18-31] and rejection of the concept that it is "based" on the entities according to metaphorical speech (*upacārāt*) [32].

On level A^5 the alternative that inherence is actually based is rejected, again in two steps: rejection of the concept that this is brought about by another connection (*sambandhāntara*) [19-23] and rejection of the notion that inherence is a connection brought about by itself (*svataḥsambandha*) [24-30].

On level A^6 four types of connection are rejected in the context of the examination of the alternative *sambandhāntara* [19-22].

The respective steps of argumentation presented here differ with regard to the question of literal correspondences with other works. Some steps do—as a whole or in part—literally correspond with passages in other works, others do not.

4.2 Passages with Literal Correspondences to Samantabhadra's *Yuktyanuśāsana*

In the group of arguments with literal correspondence to other works, those which are characterized by quotations from Samantabhadra's *Yuktyanuśāsana* stand out particularly. The numbers of the respective passages are set in bold italics and are underlined in the following figure:

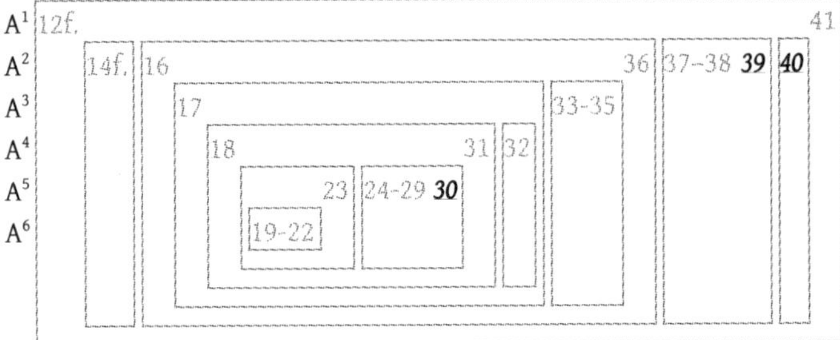

Samantabhadra is the only authority Vidyānandin mentions by name, immediately before quoting a strophe from the *Yuktyanuśāsana* in argument 40. The strophe is also referred to in an abbreviated form in arguments 30 and 39. The common characteristic of these three arguments is—from the point of view of its content analysis—that a line of argumentation is concluded with them. These arguments are further characterized—from the point of view of composition analysis—by the fact that only the reference to the strophe from the *Yuktyanuśāsana* could be identified, without any other literal correspondences. This can be seen, for instance from argument 30:[21]

> *kiṃ ca yathā samavāyaḥ svarūpāpekṣayābhedāt tadavyatiriktaghaṭanīyaghaṭakākārāpekṣayā bhedād bhedābhedātmakaḥ sidhyati tathāvayavyādyapekṣayābhedāt tadapṛthagbhūtāvayavāpekṣayā bhedāt sarvaṃ vastu bhedābhedātmakaṃ jātyantaraṃ sidhyed virodhādidūṣaṇānāṃ samavāyadṛṣṭāntenāpasāraṇād ity arhanmatasiddhis tasya tadiṣṭatvād [a]abhedabhedātmakam arthatattvaṃ tava[a] iti vacanāt. tanmatasiddhau parābhimatabhedaikāntarūpaṃ vastu khapuṣpava asad eva syāt [b]svatantrānyatarat khapuṣpam[b] iti vacanāt.*
>
> a = YA 7a b = YA 7b

4.3 Passages with Literal Correspondences to Vidyānandin's *Āptaparīkṣāṭīkā*

If we look at arguments characterized by literal correspondences with the *Āptaparīkṣāṭīkā*—another work by Vidyānan-

---

[21] SŚP (II 30) 37, 18-24. The two passages corresponding to the *Yuktyanuśāsana* are underlined and demarcated by "a" and "b".

din—a different situation can be found. These arguments are not only characterized by, but mainly consist of, textual material which is also transmitted in the *Āptaparīkṣāṭīkā* as, for example, the following passage:[22]

> [a]*syād ākūtam: samavāyasya dharmiṇo 'pratipattau hetor āśrayāsiddhatvam. pratipattau dharmigrāhakapramāṇabādhitaḥ pakṣo hetuś ca kālātyayāpadiṣṭaḥ prasajyate. samavāyo hi yataḥ pramāṇāt pratipannas*[i] *tata evāyutasiddhasambandhatvaṃ pratipannam ayutasiddhānām eva sambandhasya samavāyavyapadeśasiddher iti.*[a]
>
> [a] ~ ĀPṬ 131,1-11 ad ĀP 60ff. up to SŚP (II 36) 38,22
>
> [i] *pramāṇāpratipannas* SŚP$_{K,KH}$

The numbers of these passages corresponding to the *Āptaparīkṣāṭīkā* are set in italics and are underlined in the following figure:

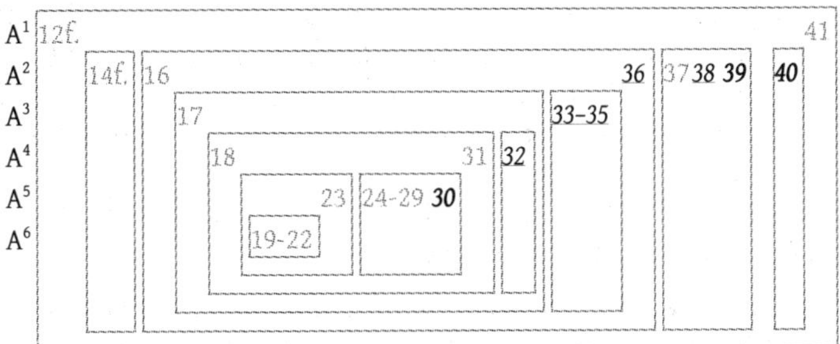

From the point of view of content analysis, it is remarkable that passages with literal correspondences to the *Āptaparīkṣāṭīkā* appear as those steps of argumentation, which pertain to 'rare' definitions of inherence. For the definition rejected in argument 32 we find an echo only in the *Vyomavatī*; the definition rejected in arguments 33 to 35 is advocated only by Uddyotakara.

4.4 Passages with Literal Correspondences to *Prameyakamalamārtaṇḍa* and *Nyāyakumudacandra*

This again differs from the last group of arguments with literal correspondences to other Digambara works, namely those that correspond to Prabhācandra's *Prameyakamalamārtaṇḍa*

[22] SŚP (II 34) 38,12-14.

and *Nyāyakumudacandra*. The numbers of the respective passages are set in normal script and are underlined in the following figure:

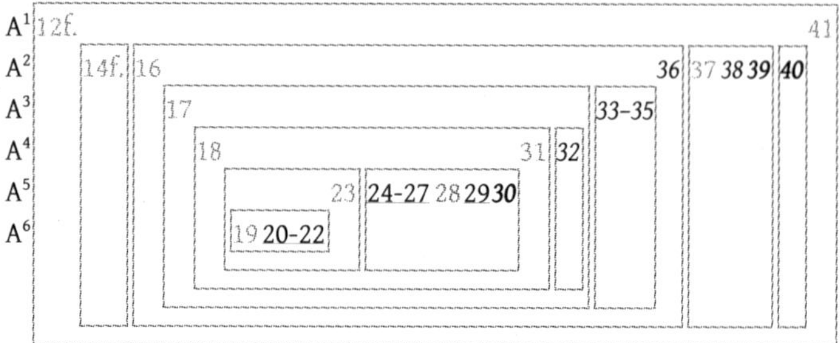

The arguments pertain to definitions of inherence which have been widely discussed. The definitions discussed on level A[6] were already rejected in the *Padārthadharmasaṅgraha* (arguments 19 to 22). The others pertain to the 'official' definition of inherence advocated in the *Padārthadharmasaṅgraha* (arguments 24 to 29). From the point of view of composition analysis, these passages are dominated by very close literal correspondences to Prabhācandra's works, but also have many parallels in other works of philosophical Sanskrit literature. See, for instance, the following passage: [23]

[β3]*nanu* [a,b]*na samavāyasya sambandhāntareṇa sambandho 'smābhir iṣṭaḥ*[i] *yenānavasthādidoṣāḥ syuḥ.*[ii] [b] [c]*api tu*[iii] *agner uṣṇatāvat*[iv] *svata evāsya sambandho yuktaḥ svata eva sambandharūpatvān na saṃyogādīnāṃ tadabhāvāt. na hy ekasya svabhāvo 'nyasyāpi. anyathā svato 'gner uṣṇatvadarśanāj jalādīnām api*[v] *tat syād*[c,a] *iti cet.*

β3 wiC up to SŚP (II 29) 37,17? a // KĀ 19,8–10; TARVV 6,27–29 ad TARV 1.1.16; ĀP 72; AS 534,14 ad ĀM 64; SVṬ 171,8 ad SV 2.27; NyViVi 416,25 ad NyVi 1.106; TRD 387,6–8 ad ṢDS 57; VTP 216,1–8 b ~ PKM 608,18f. ad PMS 4.10; NKC 297,5f. ad LT 7 [c] ~ PKM 608,21–23; NKC 297,6-8

[i] NKC om. *'smābhir iṣṭaḥ*, PKM: *yukto* instead of *'smābhir iṣṭaḥ* [ii] *yenānavasthā syāt* PKM, NKC [iii] PKM om. *api tu*, NKC *ataḥ* instead of *api tu* [iv] *uṣṇatāvat tu* PKM [v] according to *jalādīnām api tat* PKM (*jalādīnām api svata eva tat* NKC) against *jalādīnāpi tat* SŚP

[23] SŚP (II 24) 36,18-21.

4.5 Passages without Literal Correspondences to Other Works

Finally, it is worthwhile to look at the arguments for which I could not find, as yet, any literal correspondences of a high degree.[24] These arguments may in some instances touch on topics or terms, for which I found parallels to passages in other works according to content, but no literal correspondences at all—neither exactly, nor with variations, nor in paraphrase. It is possible, of course, that further research in the philosophical Sanskrit literature of the Jainas will throw a different light on these passages, however, at the present time I presume that the specific contribution of the SŚP to the discussion is represented by the arguments delineated in figure 3. The hypothesis based on the point of view of the composition analysis is supported by the point of view of content analysis: the arguments with no literal correspondences are crucial points of the argumentation, where a level or step of an argumentation is begun (arguments 12f., 16, 17, 18, 19, 37) or concluded (argument 31 and 41).

Conclusion

By the analysis of the places of argumentation, where passages with literal correspondences to other works are employed, the following picture emerges with regard to the composition structure of the first part of the *uttarapakṣa* against the Vaiśeṣika in the SŚP. Vidyānandin here continues, specifies and elaborates a line of argumentation which can be traced back to Samantabhadra's *Yuktyanuśāsana*. The arguments against inherence fall in three groups.

The first group consists of arguments, which are also transmitted literally in Prabhācandra's works and are directed against widespread definitions of inherence. It is possible that Prabhācandra took over these arguments from the SŚP; but I think it is more likely that Vidyānandin and Prabhācandra both took over these arguments from another, yet unidentified work.

The second group of arguments against inherence consists of those, which are also transmitted literally in Vidyānandin's

[24] See figure 3, numbers in bold script.

Āptaparīkṣāṭīkā. They are directed at definitions of inherence, which were rarely discussed. It is obvious, that Vidyānandin took over these arguments from one work into the other; I think it is more likely that the SŚP is the later work.

The third group of arguments against inherence consists of those, for which I have as yet not found any literal correspondences in other works at all. These arguments lay out the terminology for the framework of the discussion and I think that they were composed by Vidyānandin himself. These arguments—together with the arguments transmitted in the *Āptaparīkṣāṭikā* and the introductory and concluding arguments of the whole section—represent Vidyānandin's contribution to the discussion, not only by arrangement but also by intellectual conception.

Figures

Figure 1: Conceptualizing samavāya

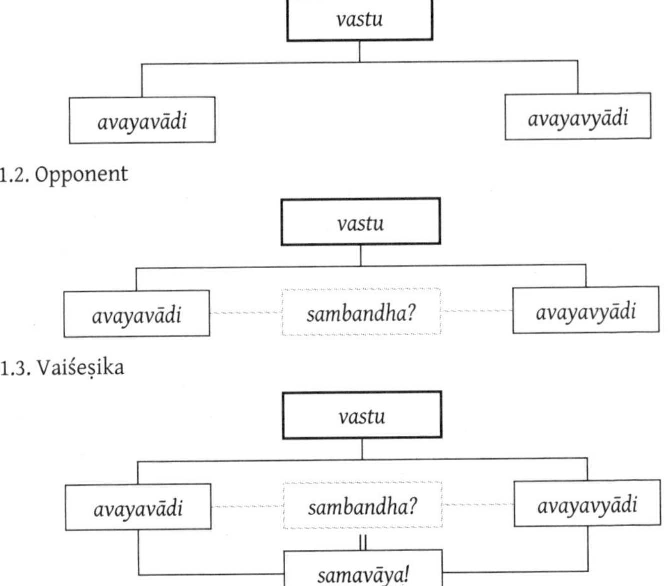

1.4. Opponent

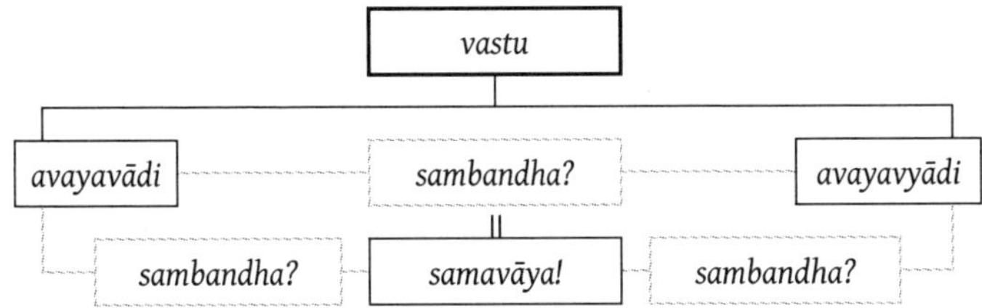

1.5. Focus of the analysis in the *Satyaśāsanaparīkṣā*

i

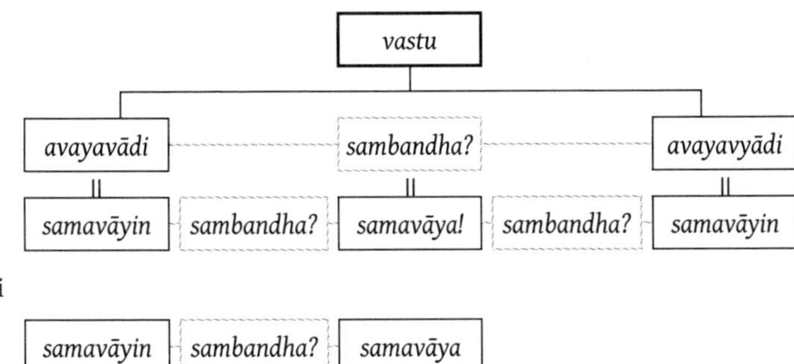

ii

samavāyin — sambandha? — samavāya

***Figure 2:** Alternatives for the relation of samavāya and samavāyin examined in the Satyaśāsanaparīkṣā*

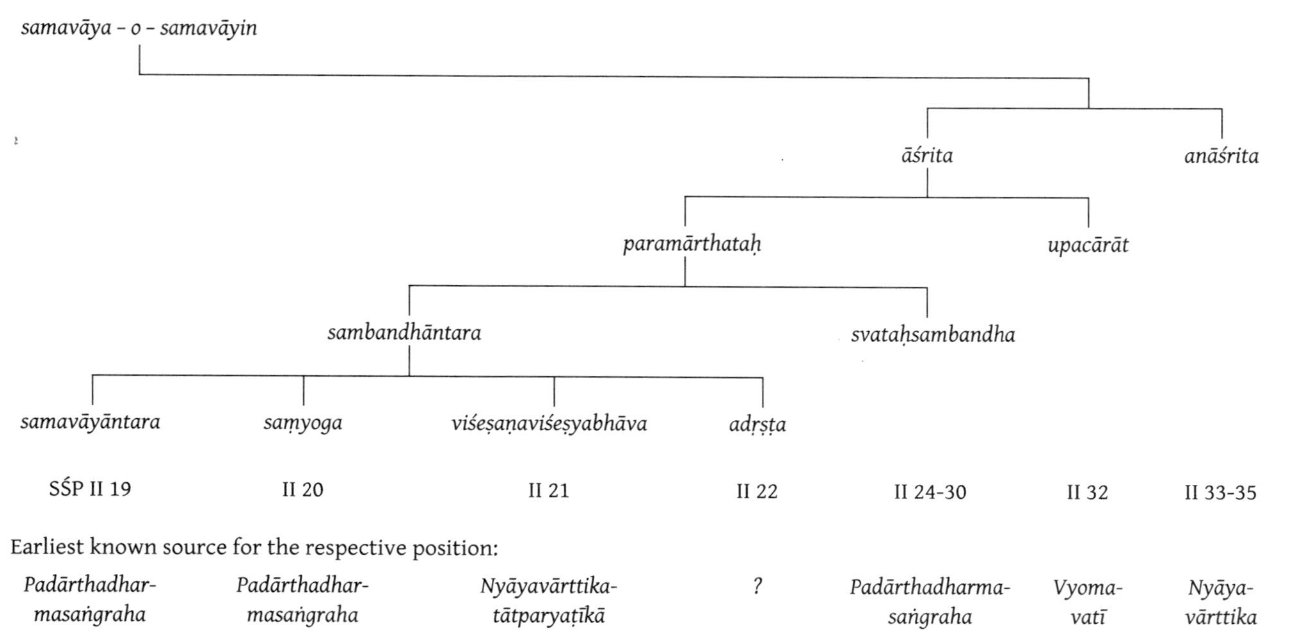

Figure 3: Areas of composition in the first part of the uttarapakṣa against the Vaiśeṣika in the Satyaśāsanaparīkṣā (SŚP II 12–41)

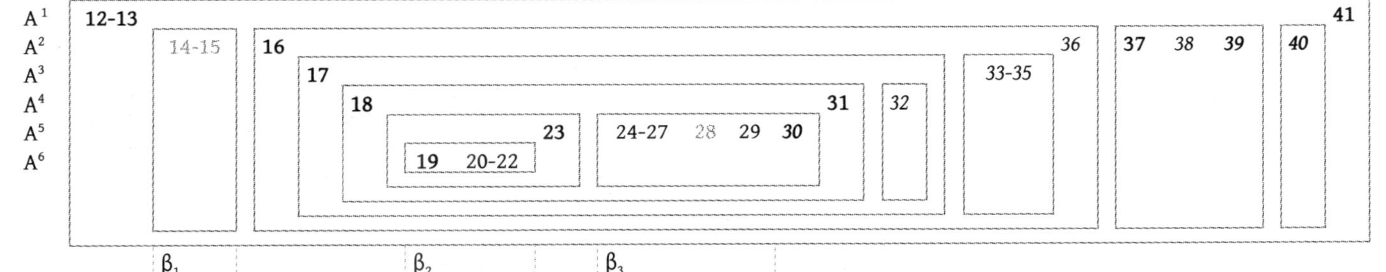

Levels of argumentation:

A¹) Attempt of the proof that the Vaiśeṣika is opposed to sense perception (12–41)

A²) General refutation of inherence (14–15), systematic deconstruction (16–36), consequences for the world view of the Vaiśeṣika (37–39), reference to Samantabhadra (40)

A³) Systematic deconstruction of inherence: rejection of the alternatives "*āśrita*" (17–32) and "*anāśrita*" (33–35),

A⁴) Examination of the alternatives for "*āśrita*": "*paramārthataḥ*" (18–31) and "*upacārāt*" (32)

A⁵) Examination of the alternatives for "*paramārthataḥ*": "*sambandhāntara*" (19–23) and "*svataḥsambandha*" (24–30)

A⁶) Examination of four alternatives for "*sambandhāntara*" (19–22)

Groups of passages according to their literal correspondence to other Digambara works

n only met with so far in the *Satyaśāsanaparīkṣā*

n Quotations from the *Yuktyanuśāsana*

n Dominated by literal correspondence to the *Āptaparīkṣāṭīkā*

n Dominated by literal correspondence to Prabhācandra's works

n Belonging to none of the above groups

$\beta_{1\text{-}3}$ Passages presumably corresponding to a yet unidentified work (see, e.g., 4.4 above)

Abbreviations and Bibliography

ĀM, *Āptamīmāṃsā* by Samantabhadra. Muni Vairāgyarativijaya (ed.), *Yaśovijayagaṇi-kṛtam Aṣṭasahasrītātparyavivaraṇam*. Poona: Śrīvijayamahodayasūrigranthamālā 15, 2004.

AS, *Aṣṭasahasrī* by Vidyānandin; see ĀM.

ĀP, *Āptaparīkṣā* by Vidyānandin Darbārīlāl Jain Koṭhiyā (ed.), *Vidyānandasvāmi-viracitā... Āptaparīkṣā svopajñāptaparīkṣālaṅkṛtiṭīkāyutā*. Sahārnapura: Vīrasevāmandir Granthamālā, 1949.

ĀPṬ, *Āptaparīkṣāṭīkā* by Vidyānandin; see ĀP.

Borgland, Jens Wilhelm, 2010, "A Translation and Investigation of Vidyānandin's *Satyaśāsanaparīkṣā*". MA Thesis, Department of Culture Studies and Oriental Languages, University of Oslo.

JMJGS, Jñānapīṭha Mūrtidevī Jaina Granthamālā: Saṃskṛta Grantha.

KĀ, *Kiraṇāvalī* by Udayana. Jitendra S. Jetly (ed.), *Praśastapādabhāṣyam with the Commentary Kiraṇāvalī of Udayanācārya*. Baroda: Gaekwad's Oriental Series 154, 1971.

LT, *Laghīyastraya*, Akalaṅka; see NKC.

MDJG, Māṇikacandra Digambara Jaina Granthamālā.

NK, *Nyāyakandalī* by Śrīdhara. Vindhyeśvarīprasāda Dvivedin (ed.), *The Bhāshya of Praśastapāda together with the Nyāyakandalī of Śrīdhara*. Benares: Vizianagaram Sanskrit Series 6, 1895.

NKC, *Nyāyakumudacandra* by Prabhācandra. Mahendra Kumar Shastri (ed.), *Nyāyakumudacandra of Prabhācandra. A commentary on Bhaṭṭākalaṅkadevas Laghīyastraya*. 2 volumes. Bombay: MDJG 38, 39, 1938–1941.

NyVi, *Nyāyaviniścaya* by Akalaṅka. Mahendrakumār Jain (ed.), *Akalaṅkadeva-praṇītasya Nyāyaviniścayasya vivaraṇabhūtaṃ Vādirājasūri-viracitaṃ Nyāyaviniścayavivaraṇam*. 2 Volumes. Kāśī: JMJGS 3, 12, 1949, 1954.

NyViVi, *Nyāyaviniścayavivaraṇa* by Vādirājasūri; see NyVi.

NV, *Nyāyavārttika* by Uddyotakara. Taranatha and Amarendramohan (eds), *Nyāyadarśanam with Vātsyāyana's Bhāṣya, Uddyotakara's Vārttika, Vācaspati Miśra's Tātparyaṭīkā and Viśvanātha's Vṛtti*. 2 Volumes. Calcutta: Calcutta Sanskrit Series 18, 29, 1936–1944. Reprint: New Delhi 1985.

PMS, *Parīkṣāmukhasūtra* by Māṇikyanandin; see PKM.

PKM, *Prameyakamalamārtaṇḍa* by Prabhācandra. Mahendra Kumar Shastri (ed.), *Prameyakamalamārttaṇḍa by Prabhācandra. A commentary on Māṇikyanandins Parīkṣāmukhasūtra.* Delhi: Sri Garib Dass Oriental Series 94, 1941, [3]1990.

ṢDS, *Ṣaḍdarśanasamuccaya* by Haribhadrasūri; see TRD.

Soni, Jayandra, 2003, "Vidyānandin's *Satyaśāsanaparīkṣā* and his Examination of the Buddhist Vijñānādvaita". In: Olle Qvarnström (ed.), *Jainism and Buddhism. Essays in Honor of Padmanabh S. Jaini,* Part II. Fremont California: Asian Humanities Press, pp. 677–688.

SŚP, *Satyaśāsanaparīkṣā* by Vidyānandin. Gokulchandra Jain (ed.), *Vidyānandi-kṛta-Satyaśāsanaparīkṣā.* Calcutta: JMJGS 30, 1964. [Numbers divided by comma refer to page and line of this edition, numbers in brackets refer to the critical text of Vidyānandin's confrontation with the Vaiśeṣika in Trikha forthcoming a.]

$SŚP_{K,KH}$, Manuscripts ka and kha used by Gokulchandra Jain in his edition of SŚP.

SŚP II, "References to the critical text of Vidyānandin's confrontation with the Vaiśeṣika". In: Trikha forthcoming a.

SV, *Siddhiviniścaya* by Akalaṅka. Mahendrakumar Jain (ed.), *Siddhiviniścayaṭīkā of Anantavīryācārya. The commentary on Siddhiviniścaya and its Vṛtti of Bhaṭṭa Akalaṅkadeva.* 2 Volumes. Kāśī: JMJGS 22–23, 1959.

SVṬ, *Siddhiviniścayatīkā*, by Anantavīrya III.; see SV.

TARV, *Tattvārtharājavārttika* by Akalaṅka. Mahendrakumār Jain (ed.), *Akalaṅkadeva-viracitaṃ Tattvārthavārtikam (Rājavārtikam) hindīsārasahitam.* 2 Volumes. Delhi: JMJGS 10, 20, 1953, [6]2001.

TARVV, *Tattvārtharājavārttikavyākhyānālaṅkāra* by Akalaṅka; see TARV.

TRD, *Tarkarahasyadīpikā* by Guṇaratnasūri. Mahendra Kumar Jain (ed.), *Haribhadrasūri-viracitaḥ Ṣaḍdarśanasamuccayaḥ ... Guṇaratnasūri-kṛtā Tarkarahasyadīpikā Somatilakasūri-kṛta-Laghuvṛttiḥ-ajñātakartṛka-Avacūrṇi-sahitā.* Vārāṇasī: JMJGS 36, 1969.

Trikha, Himal, forthcoming a, "Perspektivismus und Kritik. Polemik gegen das Vaiśeṣika in der *Satyaśāsanaparīkṣā* des Digambara Vidyānandin vor dem Hintergrund des epistemologischen Pluralismus der Jainas". Publications of the De Nobili Research Library 35. Vienna.

——— forthcoming b, "Competing world views: Perspectivism and polemics in the *Satyaśāsanaparīkṣā* and other Jaina works". In: *Proceedings of the International Conference on world view and theory in Indian Philosophy*, Barcelona 26–30 April, 2009.

wiC "without identified correspondence": passage that most likely corresponds to a yet unidentified work.

VTP *Viśvatattvaprakāśa* by Bhāvasena. V. P. Johrapurkar (ed.), Bhāvasena's *Viśvatattvaprakāśa. A Treatise on Logical Polemics.* Sholapur: Jīvarāja Jaina Granthamālā 16, 1964.

YA *Yuktyanuśāsana*, Samantabhadra. *Samantabhadra-praṇītaṃ Yuktyanuśāsanam. Vidyānanda-viracitayā ṭīkayā samanvitam Indralālaiḥ Śrīlālaiś ca sampāditaṃ saṃśodhitaṃ ca.* Bombay: MDJG 15, 1919.

Jaina Epistemology Revisited: On Erroneous Cognition

Jayandra Soni

Abstract

The aim of this revisit is to draw attention to the fact that erroneous cognition, signified by such terms as *matyajñāna*, *śrutājñāna* and *vibhaṅgajñāna* (*avadhyajñāna*), is not an insignificant aspect in Jaina epistemology. *Tattvārthasūtra* (TS) 1, 31/32, for example, says: *matiśrutāvadhayo viparyayaś ca* ("sensory knowledge, scriptural knowledge and clairvoyance 'may also' be erroneous"). This paper attempts to deal with the context in which such ideas are to be understood within the specific set of epistemological categories used in Jainism. In addition to the sūtra just quoted, recourse will be taken especially to TS 1, 9–12 (where the epistemological categories are mentioned) and to TS 2, 8–9 (especially to the two main commentaries on them) which refer to the technical term *upayoga* and its various kinds (*darśanopayoga* and *jñānopayoga*) for the context in which *matyajñāna*, etc. are used. Thus, the paper pleads for the necessity of explicitly mentioning *matyajñāna*, etc. as significant for the understanding of Jaina epistemology as a whole, especially since standard works on the theme either ignore them, or do not sufficiently emphasize their importance.

Keywords: Jaina epistemology, erroneous cognition, *Tattvārthasūtra*, *prāmāṇyavāda*, *upayoga*, theory of knowledge

The theory of cognition (*prāmāṇyavāda*) in Indian philosophy is a topic that has taken the centre-stage practically from the earliest times of philosophical activity[1] and the Jainas have not lagged behind in making their own contribution to it.[2] The words *pramā/pramiti*, *prameya*, *pramāṇa* and *pramātṛ* etymologically belong to the topic insofar as they respectively refer to cognition, the object of cognition, the means of cognition (like perception and inference), and the subject of cognition (that is, the one who cognises). In this context the question of using the word knowledge (*jñāna*) as a synonym for cognition (*pramā* or *pramiti*), as in *pratyakṣajñāna*, is an important one when

---

[1] See, for example, Dasgupta 1932: 378–388 on epistemological terms in the *Carakasaṃhitā*; also Frauwallner 1994: 66–86. See Datta 1960 for the "six ways of knowing in Vedānta".

[2] Some general studies on Jaina epistemology are, for example: Padmarajiah 1963, Dixit 1971 (p. 22, for instance, has a section with the title "Evolution of the treatment of Pramāṇa", apart from other individual sections), Shastri 1990, Bhattacharyya 1994.

speaking of *prāmāṇyavāda*. The problem has not gone by unnoticed;[3] what we are concerned with here is 'knowledge' that stands for "a cognition that is true, uncontradicted and unfalsified". It seems that it is the context which determines whether *jñāna* may be taken as a synonym for *pramā/pramiti*, without leading to any major problems in understanding the meaning of the point made when either or both terms are used. This applies to the *Tattvārthasūtra* as well.

In Indian thought, theories of error are implicit in the concern with epistemology and is based perhaps on the presupposition that human cognition/knowledge can also be fallible. In other words, taking into account the generally accepted possibility of human fallibility, Indian thinkers not only acknowledge this fact, but they also sought to explain this phenomenon. The question to which an answer was sought is: how does the occurrence of error fit into the structure of the human process of cognition? The question is significant because for the *ātmavādins*, for example, the self, or the *ātman*, intrinsically possesses knowledge (this would apply to Jaina philosophy as well insofar as, in this context, the *jīva* can be seen as the *ātman*). It is this point which has led Indian thinkers to propound several theories of error (*khyātivāda*).[4]

---

[3] Datta 1960: 19 speaking about *jñāna* and *pramā* says: "Consequently knowledge, strictly speaking, should always stand for a cognition that is true, uncontradicted and unfalsified. The ordinary division of knowledge into true knowledge and false knowledge should, therefore, be considered *as an instance of loose thinking;* the word true as applied to knowledge would then be a tautology, and the word false positively contradictory—false knowledge being only a name for falsified knowledge, which is another name for no knowledge" (my emphasis). On *cetanā, buddhi, jñāna* and *saṃvit* see, for example, Bhatt 1989: 55–57. Since experience (*anubhava*) plays an important role for the goal to be achieved in Indian philosophy, as contrasted with mere description (*lakṣaṇa*), a distinction can be drawn between 'cognition-experience' and 'knowledge-experience' when dealing with *prāmāṇyavāda*. For this in the context of Śaiva Siddhānta philosophy see Soni 1989: 100.

[4] The 'realistic' theories of error are *akhyātivāda* and *anyathākhyātivāda*. The 'idealistic' ones are *ātmakhyātivāda, asatkhyātivāda* and *anirvacanīya-khyātivāda*. For brief details see Soni 1989: 165. It seems that just as theories of error in Indian philosophy do not receive adequate treatment when dealing with epistemology in general, the same holds true for Western philosophy, to judge, for example, from the statement: "Many contemporary

When (and if) the occurrence of error is dealt with in a basic treatment of Jaina epistemology then it is either in very general terms or dismissed with very briefly.[5] The reason for this might simply be that the topic has not roused much interest in the case of Jainism. The *Tattvārthasūtra* (TS, *c.* fifth-century CE) is the fundamental and first Sanskrit work for basic Jaina philosophy by the Jaina thinker Umāsvāmin/Umāsvāti, written in the sūtra style of the other systems of Indian philosophy. The reference to erroneous knowledge in it appears briefly (in fact in only two sūtras, as we shall see below), after the basic tenets of Jaina epistemology are given in TS 1, 9–12, and after each of the *pramāṇas* referred to there are then described in sūtra format till 30/31.[6] For the context of this paper a good starting point would first be to see what the *pramāṇas* are in TS 1, 9–12:[7]

matiśrutāvadhimanaḥparyāyakevalāni jñānam (1, 9): Sensory knowledge, scriptural knowledge, clairvoyance, telepathy and omniscience [these five are means of

philosophers rate error theories poorly" (Chris Daly and David Liggins 2010: 209). The context of these error theories is certainly different because, e.g. they do *not* explain *how* an error may occur (say, on account of defective perception). When Daly and Liggins suggest that "there are exactly two fundamental sources of knowledge: perception and thought" (224–225), and if "thought" could be seen as a synonym for inference (*anumāna*) then there may be sufficient grounds for a fruitful comparative study, especially when one reads such statements as: "Given any putative source of evidence *S* for a proposition *P*, an error theory about *P* may either dispute whether *S* is a source of evidence, or it may claim that *S*'s evidential support for *P* is defeated by the counter-evidence that the error theory marshals" (225).

[5] See Shastri 1990: 463–464, for example, albeit under the chapter dealing with *ajñāna*, ignorance. The pages referred to here are under the section "The Cause of Wrong Knowledge". Padmarajiah 1963 and Soni 2000 who also deal with the basics of Jaina epistemology do not have anything significant to say about erroneous knowledge/cognition.

[6] The number after the stroke refers to the sūtra in the Śvetāmbara version of the TS.

[7] The translation is based on Jain 1992 and the Sanskrit text of it is quoted from the 1955 edition of Pūjyapāda's *Sarvārthasiddhi* (SS), regarded by the Digambaras to be the first commentary on the TS. The Śvetāmbaras say that Umāsvāti wrote an auto-commentary, the *Svopajñabhāṣya*; quotations from it are from the 1932 ed. given under Umāsvāti.

valid] knowledge.

tat pramāṇe (1, 10): These [five] are the two [*parokṣa* and *pratyakṣa*] *pramāṇas*.

ādye parokṣam (1, 11): The first two [*mati* and *śruta*] are indirect (*pramāṇas*).

pratyakṣam anyat (1, 12): The others [the three: *avadhi*, *manaḥparyāya* and *kevala*] are direct (*pramāṇas*).

As is well-known, not only is the distinction between *parokṣa* and *pratyakṣa* unique to Jainism, but also the various means of cognition/knowledge listed under them and described in TS 1, 13–30/31.[8] The explicit reference to error (*viparyaya*) is then mentioned later in two sūtras, TS 1, 31/32 and TS 32/33, which also give the reason why knowledge could be erroneous:

matiśrutāvadhayo viparyayaś ca (TS 1, 31/32), *sadasator aviśeṣād yadṛcchopalabdher unmattavat* (TS 1, 32/33).

since sensory knowledge, scriptural knowledge and clairvoyance are also [or: can also be] erroneous knowledge on account of not distinguishing between the real and the unreal, like [that of] a lunatic/drunkard, which is[/can be] accidental.

It may be noted that in terms of the classification of means of cognition/knowledge into the two types given in TS 1, 11–12, the first two, *mati* and *śruta*, are *parokṣa*, indirect means, and the third, *avadhi*, is *pratyakṣa* or the direct means. In the context of the error that can occur through them, it is insignificant whether the means in question is indirect or direct. What is important is the outcome, the (false) cognition or knowledge that results. Why precisely only these three are chosen as possibly being erroneous from the list of *pramāṇas*, does not seem to be justified, not even in the commentaries. Our task now is to analyse the statements in order to understand the Jaina point here on erroneous cognition. The best starting point would be to see what the commentaries to these sūtras say.

---

[8] See Soni 2002 for the list of the epistemological categories according to Umāsvāti and Akalaṅka.

Sarvārthasiddhi (SS) on TS 1, 31/32:

viparyayo mithyety arthaḥ | kutaḥ? samyagadhikārāt | 'ca' śabdaḥ samuccayārthaḥ | viparyayaś ca samyak ceti | kutaḥ punar eṣāṃ viparyayaḥ? mithyādarśanena sahaikārtha-samavāyāt sarajaskakaṭukālābugatadugdhavat | nanu ca tatrādhāradoṣād dugdhasya rasaviparyayo bhavati | na ca tathā matyajñānādināṃ viṣayagrahaṇe viparyayaḥ | tathā hi, samyagdṛṣṭir yathā cakṣurādibhī rūpādīn upalabhate tathā mithyādṛṣṭir api matyajñānena | yathā ca samyagdṛṣṭiḥ śrutena rūpādīn jānāti nirūpayati ca tathā mithyādṛṣṭir api śrutājñānena | yathā cāvadhijñānena samyagdṛṣṭiḥ rūpiṇo 'rthān avagacchati tathā mithyādṛṣṭir vibhaṅgajñāneneti |

Erroneous knowledge [here in the sūtra] has the meaning [what is cognised] 'incorrectly'/'wrongly'. [Objection:] How [can this be], because the topic is about [what is] right/correct.[9] [Reply:] The word 'ca' has the meaning of conjunction, [*mati*, etc., are/can be] erroneous *and* right.[10] [Objection:] Again, how are/can these be erroneous? [Reply: this happens] because of the co-inherent equivalence [in the soul of what is wrong and what is right] with false belief, like milk turns bad (*kaṭuka*) in a pumpkin gourd (*ālābu*) with impurity. [Objection:] On account of the fault there in the container, there is a change/error (*viparyaya*) in the fluid of the milk. There cannot in the same way (*tathā*) be a change when *matyajñāna*, etc., grasp an object [of cognition]. [Reply:] It is in the same way; just as one who has the right view perceives form, etc., through the eyes and so on, so too also [in the case of] the wrong view

[9] The reference is not only to TS 1, 1: *samyagdarśanajñānacāritrāṇi mokṣa-mārgaḥ* | 'Right faith, right knowledge and right conduct [together] are the path to liberation', but also to the section here dealing with *pramāṇa* (TS 1, 10: *tat pramāṇe*) which states the source of valid or correct knowledge/cognition.

[10] The meaning would be that *mati*, *śruta* and *avadhi* are indeed valid means of knowledge, as said in TS 1, 9. TS 1, 31/32 now says that these are also, in the sense of 'can also be', in error at the same time. It is interesting to note that this statement coming after so many sūtras leads to another, qualified understanding of TS 1, 9.

through *matyajñāna* (sensory non-knowledge). Just as one who has the right view knows and perceives form, etc., through *śruta* (scriptural knowledge), so too also the wrong view through *śrutājñāna* (scriptural non-knowledge). And just as the right view understands the meanings of forms, so too, the wrong view through knowledge that is a fraud/deception.

It is noteworthy that this sūtra and its commentary come towards the end of the description of basic Jaina epistemology —noteworthy because they refer back to TS 1, 9 which has to be understood with the qualifications expressed here. In keeping with the general method in Indian theories of error the very means of cognition/knowledge acknowledged as *pramāṇa*, that is, that they are valid as such, *may* also in certain cases *not* be valid means of knowledge, and hence may cognise an object in a way it is not. The point of this sūtra and its commentary then is that the *pramāṇas* in question should be seen as *having the possibility* of being in error as well, apart from the obvious possibility of being valid means. The sūtra hints at this interpretation with the use of the word "*ca*" and the sense of the verb (i.e. 'may') that has to be supplied to it is given in the commentary. That is why the interpretation is not that the means *are* in error, but that they *could be, might or may also be* so, in other words the cognition/knowledge they yield could be both valid and invalid.[11] This would further have to be understood as meaning that only upon assessing their conclusions can one say whether the result is valid or not. These means err because of *mithyādarśana* and/or *mithyādṛṣṭi*, as the commentary says. We shall return to this point in order to discuss how the error/falsity is to be decided upon.

The question could be asked whether the possibility of the fallibility of the *pramāṇas* mentioned here in TS 1, 31/32 could not have been included together with the *pramāṇas* in question when they were first listed in TS 1, 9, at least in the commentaries. This point will also be taken up below. Here, in elaborating the sūtra, the commentator explicitly mentions

---

[11] See Tatia 1994: 23. His translation of TS 1, 31/32 is: "Empirical, articulate and clairvoyant knowledge may be enlightened as well as deluded".

matyajñāna, *śrutājñāna* and *vibhaṅgajñāna* (as a synonym for *avadhyajñāna*); that is, *mati*, *śruta* and *avadhi* can also be erroneous; and hence are responsible for *ajñāna*, because their cognition could also be erroneous. Thus, we have sensory non-knowledge, scriptural non-knowledge, and the last would be non-clairvoyance. The point of the analogy of milk becoming bad in a dirty gourd is that when *ajñāna* is present, when it dirties correct cognition/knowledge, the result is error; without *ajñāna* the same means would function validly. Let us now turn to the Śvetāmbara commentary on this sūtra.

The *Svopajñabhāṣya* on TS 1, 31/32:

> *matijñānaṃ śrutajñānam avadhijñānam iti viparyayaś ca bhavaty ajñānaṃ cety arthaḥ | jñānaviparyayo 'jñānam iti | atrāha | tad eva jñānaṃ tad evājñānam iti | nanu cchāyātapavac chītoṣṇavac ca tad atyantaviruddham iti | atrocyate | — mithyādarśanaparigrahād viparītagrāhakatvam eteṣām | tasmād ajñānāni bhavanti | tad yathā | —matyajñānaṃ śrutājñānaṃ vibhaṅgajñānam iti | avadhir viparīto vibhaṅga ity ucyate |*
>
> Sensory knowledge, scriptural knowledge, clairvoyance [with regard to these three] there is [or: can be] error also, non-knowledge, this is the meaning [of the sūtra]. An error in knowledge is non-knowledge. Here an objector says: one and the same knowledge is non-knowledge! These two (knowledge and non-knowledge) are absolutely contrary, like shade and sunshine (*ātapa*), cold and heat. To this (*atra*) we reply: these (three above-mentioned means of knowledge grasp what is false on account of comprehending [the object of knowledge] through false belief,[12] that is why they are non-knowledge. That is to say [they lead to]: sensory non-knowledge, scriptural non-knowledge, non-clairvoyance. *Avadhi* (clairvoyance) that is an error is [here in the commentary] called *vibhaṅga* (fraud/deception).

---

[12] The sense also seems to be: these *pramāṇas* grasp (their respective objects) erroneously because they grasp them through false belief.

The *Svopajñabhāṣya* on TS 1, 31/32 continued:

> *atrāha—uktaṃ bhavatā samyagdarśanaparigṛhītaṃ matyādi-jñānaṃ bhavaty anyathā 'jñānam eva iti | mithyādṛṣṭayo 'pi ca bhavyāś cābhavyāś cendriyanimittān aviparītān sparśādīn upalabhante, upadiśanti ca sparśaṃ sparśa iti rasaṃ rasa iti, evaṃ śeṣān | tat katham etad iti | atrocyate | —teṣāṃ hi viparītam etad bhavati |*
>
> Here an objector says: You said, Sir, [an object of knowledge] grasped through right belief is [valid] sensory knowledge, etc., otherwise [i.e., without right belief] it is non-knowledge. Even in the case of one who has a wrong view—for both who are capable and incapable (*bhavyāś cābhavyās*) [of having valid cognition]—perceives touch, etc., without error through the senses, and indicates touch as touch, taste as taste, in the same way the rest [of the senses like hearing and smelling]. How is this so? Here we reply: there is error here with these [means of knowledge].

These two parts of the Śvetāmbara commentary on TS 1, 31/32 say in essence the same thing about the basic problem as the Digambara SS commentary on it: both begin by mentioning the problem of referring to *mati*, *śruta* and *avadhi* first as *jñāna* (in TS 1, 9) and now in TS 31/32 as *viparyaya*, as being in error also—namely, that they could be *ajñāna*—leading to a contradiction of terms with regard to the same means of cognition/knowledge. The opponent in the Śvetāmbara commentary says that this is as contradictory as shade/sunshine and cold/heat. The reason for the error in both commentaries is attributed to *matyajñāna*, *śrutājñāna* and *vibhaṅgajñāna* (*avadhyajñāna*). As we already saw, the SS commentary explains this occurrence on the analogy of milk turning bad through the impurity in the vessel in which it is stored; through *ajñāna* cognition/knowledge 'turns bad'.

At the end of the commentary on TS 1, 31/32, the *Svopajñabhāṣya* has no link to the next sūtra, TS 1, 32/33. The SS on the other hand says *atrocyate*, "here [with regard to the reason why mati, etc., could err] the *sūtrakāra* says" (quoted again from above):

matiśrutāvadhayo viparyayaś ca (TS 1, 31/32), *sadasator aviśeṣād yadṛcchopalabdher unmattavat* (TS 1, 32/33).

Sensory knowledge, scriptural knowledge, clairvoyance are [or: can be] erroneous knowledge also; on account of not distinguishing between the real and the unreal, knowledge (*upalabdhi*) is [/can be] accidental, like [that of] a lunatic/drunkard.

The SS on TS 1, 32/33:

sad vidyamānam asad avidyamānam ity arthaḥ | tayor aviśeṣeṇa yadṛcchayā upalabdher viparyayo bhavati | kadā cid rūpādi sad apy asad iti pratipadyate, asad api sad iti, kadācit sat sad eva, asad apy asad eveti mithyādarśanodayād adhyavasyati | yathā pittodayākulitabuddhir mātaraṃ bhāryeti, bhāryām api māteti manyate | yadṛcchayā yadāpi mātaraṃ mātaiveti bhāryam api bhāryaiveti ca tadāpi na tat samyagjñānam | evaṃ matyādināṃ api rūpādiṣu viparyayo veditavyaḥ | tathā hi, kaścin mithyādarśanapariṇāma ātmany avasthito rūpādyupalabdhau satyām api kāraṇaviparyāsaṃ bhedābhedaviparyāsaṃ svarūpaviparyāsaṃ ca janayati | ...[13]*| tatas tanmatyajñānaṃ śrutājñānaṃ vibhaṅgajñānaṃ ca bhavati | samyagdarśanaṃ punas tattvārthādhigame śraddhānam utpādayati | tatas tanmatijñānaṃ śrutajñānam avadhijñānaṃ ca bhavati |*

Sat is [what is] real and *asat* [what is] unreal, this is the meaning [of the words in the sūtra]. There is error with regard to both because the cognition/knowledge (*upalabdhi*) is accidental, since it is without distinction [between what is real and what is not]. Sometimes, as a consequence of wrong belief (*mithyādarśana*), it [the cognition/knowledge] regards form, etc., even if they are real, to be unreal, [and] even if they are unreal to be

---

[13] About nine lines of the ed. used here have been omitted, in which the three kinds of error (with regard to the cause/*kāraṇa*, difference and identity/*bhedābheda*, and nature/*svarūpa* of the object of cognition/knowledge) are elaborated with reference to some (*kecit*) views which are not accepted by the Jainas because they are opposed to what is known through perception and inference (*dṛṣṭeṣṭaviruddhāt*). These errors come about as a consequence of wrong belief (*mithyādarśanodayāt*).

real; sometimes it considers the real as real, even the unreal as unreal: just as the mind, bewildered/ perplexed as a consequence of [the ill-effect of] bile, regards the mother as the wife, [and sometimes] considers even the wife as the mother. Sometimes, although by chance/accident, when it regards the mother as the mother and the wife as the wife, then this too is [strictly speaking] not right knowledge. In this way, the error of sensory knowledge, etc., [namely, of *śruta* and *avadhi* as well] is to be understood with regard to [a cognition/ knowledge of] form, etc. That is to say, the transformation which takes place *(avasthita)* in a person/soul on account of wrong belief gives rise to a mistake with regard to: [1] the cause, [2] difference and identity and [3] the intrinsic nature [of an object], even when there is a cognition of form, etc. ... Thus, there is (in these) sensory non-knowledge, scriptural non-knowledge and non-clairvoyance. Right belief, on the other hand, produces conviction in the knowledge *(adhigame)* of things in reality. Thus there is in this [valid] sensory knowledge, scriptural knowledge and clairvoyance.

The key factor, then, in the Jaina theory of erroneous cognition/knowledge is wrong belief (*mithyādarśana*), which the SS contrasts with right belief (*samyagdarśana*). Wrong belief leads to a cognition of an object such that it is seen as what it is not. It does not matter whether the object, by fluke, is seen as it really is, if wrong belief is responsible for it. The obvious question is how does one know that this is the case, that wrong belief is the responsible factor? The answer becomes complex because it involves a discussion of what right belief is, a term which takes us back to TS 1, 1 for its specific Jaina significance. Before entering into this discussion, let us see what the *Svopajñabhāṣya* has to say on this very same TS 1, 32/33.

The *Svopajñabhāṣya* on TS 1, 32/33:

yathonmattaḥ karmodayād upahatendriyamatir viparīt-agrāhī bhavati | so 'śvaṃ gaur ity adhyavasyati gāṃ cāśva iti loṣṭaṃ suvarṇam iti suvarṇaṃ loṣṭa iti loṣṭaṃ ca loṣṭa iti

> *suvarṇaṃ suvarṇam iti tasyaivam aviśeṣeṇa loṣṭaṃ suvarṇaṃ suvarṇaṃ loṣṭam iti viparītam adhyavasyato niyatam ajñānam eva bhavati | tadvan mithyādarśenopahatendriyamater matiśrutāvadhayo 'py ajñānaṃ bhavanti |*
>
> Just as: a lunatic/drunkard whose sensory cognition/knowledge is seduced as a consequence of karma, grasps [an object of cognition] wrongly—he considers a horse to be a cow and the cow a horse, a lump of earth gold and gold a lump of earth, a lump of earth a lump of earth, gold gold, without distinction, the wrong consideration that a lump of earth is gold, gold a lump of earth, is certainly non-knowledge—so too, because the sense organs are seduced by wrong belief, even sensory knowledge, scriptural knowledge and clairvoyance are [or could in fact be] non-knowledge.

This commentary gives a direct hint with regard to the point just mentioned about how right belief (*samyagdarśana*) becomes wrong (*mithyādarśana*), namely, as a consequence of karma. In the context of the discussion here the reference is specifically to the *ghātiyā* karmas: "which have a directly negative effect on the qualities of the soul" and "are divided into four groups on the basis of which soul-quality they affect; thus we have perception-obscuring (*darśanāvaraṇīya*), knowledge-obscuring (*jñānāvaraṇīya*), energy-obstructing (*vīryāntarāya*), and bliss-defiling (*mohanīya*) karmas" (Jaini 1979: 115). In addition to this, that is, as a result of the negative effects of the different types of karma, the soul's quality states (*guṇasthānas*) are also affected in its journey of purification, of ridding itself of all karmas. There are fourteen quality states of the soul and by way of example only the first may be mentioned here for a better understanding not only of the complexity behind the Jaina theory of errors, but also for the context of what is intended in the commentaries quoted above: "1. Mithyādṛṣṭi: The lowest state, in which the soul suffers from "wrong views" (mithyā-darśana) because of the presence of darśana-mohanīya karmas and the anantānubandhī type of passions (kaṣāya)" (ibid., p. 272).

We postponed above two points for discussion: firstly, how the error/falsity is to be decided upon and secondly, the question whether the possibility of the fallibility of the *pramāṇas* mentioned in TS 1, 31/32 could not have been included together with the *pramāṇas* in question when they were first listed in TS 1, 9, at least in the commentaries.

The answer to the first question can be regarded as being implicit in the reference above to the Jaina theory of karma and the associated quality states of the soul. Obviously, if *mati*, *śruta* and *avadhi* lead to a knowledge that is not in keeping with the Jaina view of reality as contained in its canonical (Āgama) and pro-canonical works (like the TS itself) these means of cognition/knowledge would be erroneous. This answer, however, is not adequate because the basic problem remains: how is the basic Jaina view to be interpreted if there are differences of opinion not only among the different Jaina groups, like the Digambaras and Śvetāmbaras, but vis-à-vis non-Jaina views? Although this problem does not concern us directly here (we are dealing with the sūtras on error), it may be said that in terms of basic Jaina philosophy the TS is an authoritative work for both the Jaina traditions and that "their respective versions of this work show predictable disagreement on such controversial matters as the nudity of the mendicant and the partaking of food by the kevalin" (Jaini 1979: 82). In the examples of the two commentaries quoted above, we saw that the basic view in both is "almost identical" (to quote Jaini again from the same place when he speaks generally about the two TS versions and their commentaries). In other words, what within the Jaina perspective is regarded as false or correct is based directly on how each tradition understands or interprets the content of the cognition/knowledge concerned.

The other part of the answer to the question about error/falsity concerns its position when compared with non-Jaina views. Here the problem would be more easily solved because, on the one hand, the Jaina could 'integrate' the opponents' views within its theory of manifoldness (*anekāntavāda*) and regard them accordingly as being valid only partially and, on the other hand, highlight the specific points of differences, for example in terms of its ontology, metaphysics and epistemology.

The second question about the fallibility of the *pramāṇas*

mentioned in TS 1, 31/32 being included together with them when they were first listed in TS 1, 9 can be simply answered by saying that this is how the text has it and there can be no further discussion on the matter. However, it is certainly of academic interest because, as already mentioned, certain means of cognition/knowledge are said to be *pramāṇa*, valid means, and that some of these very means may also be invalid. We saw this objection at the very beginning of the SS commentary on TS 1, 31/32 when it asks how these *pramāṇas* could err because the topic under discussion is about what is right or correct (referring to *samyagdarśana*, etc. and to *pramāṇa* as basically being what is valid). This indicates that the commentary is indeed aware of the problem. The fact that TS 1, 31/32 leads to a qualified interpretation of TS 1, 9 (see fn. 9), to repeat, raises the question as to why this was not done in the first place. It may be suggested that the reason is to keep the two aspects separate: *mati*, *śruta* and *avadhi* belong to the list of *pramāṇas* listed in TS 1, 9–12 and that because of the commentaries to TS 2, 8–9, new aspects are introduced which not only refer to the earlier sūtras under discussion but list *matyajñāna*, *śrutājñāna* and *vibhaṅgājñāna* (*avadhyajñāna*) as three of the eight kinds of *jñānopayoga*. The answer to the question requires a brief reference to the two sūtras just mentioned.

The two sūtras just mentioned, TS 2, 8–9, are cryptically short in the usual sūtra format: *upayogo lakṣaṇam* and *sa dvividho 'ṣṭacaturbhedaḥ* (*upayoga* is the 'sign' [of the soul] and it [*upayoga*] is of two kinds [*jñānopayoga* and *darśanopayoga*, and these in turn are respectively of] eight and four kinds).[14] (We just mentioned the term *jñānopayoga* to which our three means of error, *matyajñāna*, *śrutājñāna* and *vibhaṅgajñāna*/*avadhyajñāna* are three of its eight kinds.)

The new aspect of *upayoga* and the various types of *pramāṇas* listed under it, broaden the scope of the Jaina theory of error even further. In addition to TS 1, 31/32, TS 2, 8–9 also draw our attention back to the sūtras at the beginning of the

[14] We are interested only in the eight kinds of *jñānopayoga*, which refer to many of the *pramāṇas* in TS 1, 9. The four kinds of *darśanopayoga*, however, are: *cakṣurdarśana*, *acakṣurdar°*, *avadhidar°* and *kevaladar°*.

text when the *pramāṇas* are first dealt with, and the question about their now different understanding would apply in this case again. The context of TS 2, 8–9 is the nature of the soul in which the actions or functions of *upayoga* as *jñānopayoga* and *darśanopayoga* (determinate or specific perception and indeterminate or bare perception respectively) are mentioned in the commentaries to them. This aspect calls for a study in itself as, and has been dealt with, for example, in Soni 2007.

The theory of error in Jainism seems to fulfil two functions. On the one hand, it may be seen as a theory that belongs to the general category of theories of error (*khyātivāda*), as with the 'realistic' ones (*akhyātivāda* and *anyathākhyātivāda*) and the 'idealistic' ones, *ātmakhyātivāda*, *asatkhyātivāda* and *anirvacanīyakhyātivāda* (see fn. 4). On the other hand, if one includes the aspect of *upayoga*, as indicated above because it belongs to the theme, then it would be an aspect that is specifically Jaina. The reason for this would be that the soul's actions or functions of *upayoga* as *jñānopayoga* and *darśanopayoga* hint at the *guṇasthānas*, which apply specifically to the 'Jaina path of purification'. In this context, the question of error here would be unique to a Jaina adept. In addition to the reference to the first *guṇasthāna* mentioned above, *mithyādṛṣṭi*, here the eleventh may also be quoted in conclusion in order to show that the ladder of the *guṇasthānas* entails both going up and down its rungs—a significant feature of the Jaina doctrine: "Upaśānta-moha: The state attained through the suppression of saṃjvalana passions; from here a fall to the lower states is inevitable. Progress is possible only for those who are able to eliminate the passions, a process which must begin at the eighth guṇasthāna" (Jaini 1979: 273].[15]

Bibliography

Bhatt, Govardhan P., 1989, *The Basic Ways of Knowing. An In-depth Study of Kumārila's Contribution to Indian Epistemology.*

[15] The eight, ninth and tenth *guṇasthānas* (*apūrva-karaṇa*, *anivṛtti-karaṇa* and *sūkṣma-sāmparāya*) belong together and "comprise the śreṇi (ladder), in which the aspirant may either suppress (upaśama) or eliminate (*kṣapaṇa*) the no-kaṣāyas (secondary passions) and the subtle forms of the saṃjvalana passion" (Jaini 1979: 272).

Delhi, etc.: Motilal Banarsidass.

Bhattacharyya, Hari Mohan, 1994, *Jaina Logic and Epistemology*. Calcutta, etc.: K. P. Bagchi.

Dasgupta, S., 1932, *A History of Indian Philosophy*. Volume II. Cambridge: University Press.

Daly, Chris and Liggins, David, 2010: "In defence of error theory". *Philosophical Studies* 149, pp. 209–230. DOI 10.1007/s11098-009-9346-1.

Datta, D. M., 1960, *The Six Ways of Knowing. A Critical Study of the Vedānta Theory of Knowledge*. Calcutta: University of Calcutta.

Dixit, K. K., 1971, *Jaina Ontology*. Ahmedabad: L. D. Institute of Indology (Lalbhai Dalpatbhai Series No. 31).

Frauwallner, Erich, 1994, *Erich Frauwallner's Posthumous Essays*. Tr. from the German (1984) by Jayandra Soni. New Delhi: Aditya Prakashan.

Jain, S. A., 1992: See Pūjyapāda

Jaini, Padmanabh S., 1979, *The Jaina Path of Purification*. Delhi: Motilal Banarsidass Publishers.

Padmarajiah, Y. J., 1963, *A Comparative Study of the Jaina Theories of Reality and Knowledge*. Delhi, etc.: Motilal Banarsidass.

Pūjyapāda (sixth century), 1955 ed.: *Sarvārthasiddhi* [a commentary on Umāsvāti's *Tattvārthasūtra*]. Kāśī: Bhāratīya Jñānapīṭha, edited [and translated into Hindi] by Phūlacandra Śāstrī. See also Tatia 1994.

——— 1992, *Reality. English Translation of Shri Pujyapada's Sarvarthasiddhi*. Tr. S. A. Jain, Madras: Jwalamalini Trust, second edition [reprint of the first edition published in 1960 in Calcutta: Vira Sasana Sangha]. See also Tatia 1994.

Shastri, Indra Chandra, 1990, *Jaina Epistemology*. Varanasi: P. V. Research Institute.

Soni, Jayandra, 1989, *Philosophical Anthropology in Śaiva Siddhānta. With Special Reference to Śivāgrayogin*. Delhi: Motilal Banarsidass Publishers.

——— 2000: "Basic Jaina Epistemology" in *Philosophy East and West*, vol. 50, number 3, pp. 367–377.

——— 2002: "Epistemological Categories in the *Akalaṅkagranthatraya*" in Dragomor Dimitrov et al. (eds): *Śikhisamuccayaḥ. Indian and Tibetan Studies*. Wien: Arbeitskreis für tibetische und buddhistische Studien Universität Wien (Heft

53), pp. 185–192.

——— 2007: "Upayoga, according to Kundakunda and Umāsvāti" in *Journal of Indian Philosophy*, 2007, 35, pp. 299-311.

Tatia, Nathmal, 1994: *Tattvārtha Sūtra. That Which Is. Umāsvāti/ Umāsvāmī with the combined commentaries of Umāsvāti/ Umāsvāmī, Pūjyapāda and Siddhasenagaṇi.* Translated with an introduction. San Francisco, etc.: Harper Collins Publishers.

Umāsvāti/Umāsvāmin (c. fifth century), 1932 ed., *Sabhāṣyatattvārthādhigamasūtra*, ed. Paṇḍita Manoharalāla, Bombay: Presa Sarveṣṭa Iṃdiyā. See also Tatia 1994.

Is the *Syādvāda* True Only From a Certain Point of View?

Anne Clavel

Abstract

The *syādvāda*, also called "sevenfold predication" (*saptabhaṅgī*), is usually considered to be a fundamental tenet of the Jaina doctrine of multilateralism, since it prevents a predicate from being absolutely attributed to a subject. Nevertheless, such a conception raises a tricky problem: if the adverb *syāt* has to be understood in every statement even though the word is not explicitly expressed, as Jaina philosophers seem to confirm it (e.g. Akalaṅka's *Laghīyastraya*, stanza 63), would not the Jaina tenets and especially the Tīrthaṅkaras' teachings expose themselves to the objection of having only a relative value? So, one can ask, for instance, how the sevenfold predication could apply to a statement like "omniscience is a means of knowledge", without wrecking the whole doctrine. This paper aims at dealing with this problem. Indeed, a thorough study of some philosophical texts reveals that expressions like *paramārthataḥ*, *tattvataḥ*, *ekāntena* or *añjasā* (which may mean 'absolutely') enable us to lay down that some statements hold true absolutely and then escape the sevenfold predication.

Keywords: *syādvāda*, sevenfold predication (*saptabhaṅgī*), multilateralism, empirico-practical standpoint, transcendental standpoint

1 According to common interpretation, the *syādvāda*, also called "sevenfold predication" (*saptabhaṅgī*), constitutes a cornerstone of the Jaina doctrine of multilateralism, since it prevents a predicate from being absolutely attributed to a subject.[1] According to Jainism, in order to consider a single state of affairs as exhaustively as possible, one has to submit every predicative relation between a subject (x) and a predicate (A) to a structural rule made up of seven propositions, which are not conceived of as alternative truths, but are all endowed with the same truth-value. The whole set, which expresses all the possible ways to combine two contrary predicates, A and ¬A, is built on the following pattern:

[1] Besides, this significance is evidenced by the fact that the term *syādvāda* is sometimes used in a wider sense, as a synonym of *anekāntavāda*; cf. Matilal (1981: 25), Padmarajiah (1986: 334–335), Nyāyavijayajī (2000: 328).

(S_1) in some respect (*syāt*), *x* is only (*eva*) A;
(S_2) in some respect, *x* is only ¬A;
(S_3) in some respect, *x* is A and ¬A;
(S_4) in some respect, *x* is only inexpressible;
(S_5) in some respect, *x* is A and inexpressible;
(S_6) in some respect, *x* is ¬A and inexpressible;
(S_7) in some respect, *x* is A, ¬A and inexpressible.[2]

A significant logical problem results from the rule according to which no judgement can escape the *syādvāda*.[3] Being an inheritance from the canonical texts,[4] this rule endures in the logicians' works. For instance, Akalaṅka (*c.* 720–780) utters in the *Nyāyaviniścaya*, stanza III.68ab:

---

[2] Among the many instances that are given by Jaina philosophers, Akalaṅka provides a significant illustration of the *saptabhaṅgī* in the *Tattvārthavārttika* (RVār *ad* TS IV.42, I, p. 253.4–6): (1) *syād asty eva jīvaḥ,* (2) *syān nāsty eva jīvaḥ,* (4) *syād avaktavya eva jīvaḥ,* (3) *syād asti ca nāsti ca,* (5) *syād asti cāvaktavyaś ca,* (6) *syād nāsti cāvaktavyaś ca,* (7) *syād asti ca nāsti cāvaktavyaś ca.* The order of the third and the fourth propositions is reversed, without having the least consequence on the whole structure, because despite appearances both propositions contain exactly the same predicates; they only differ insofar as S_3 and S_4 combine them differently: when two contrary predicates—here existence and non-existence—are attributed simultaneously to a subject, language is not able to express the content of these predicates in a single word; simultaneity is accurately rendered by the term "inexpressible", but this adjective totally erases the semantics of the contrary predicates. Cf., among others, Uno (2000: 48–49) and Clavel (2010: 157–158).

[3] Another important problem, that has frequently aroused modern scholars' interest, concerns the compatibility of the *saptabhaṅgī* with two logical principles, i.e. the principles of contradiction and of excluded-middle. I have tried to show elsewhere that both of them are respected by Jaina philosophers, even though the *syādvāda* precisely consists in combining contrary predicates, and asserting that contradictory propositions concerning one and the same object are equally valid: on the one hand, in spite of its apparent ambiguity, each occurrence of the word *syāt* in the *saptabhaṅgī* expresses different circumstances in the seven propositions; on the other hand, the coexistence of the seven propositions aims at offsetting the inadequacies of language, which is never able to express simultaneously the different facets characterising one and the same state of affairs at a single point of time. Cf. Clavel 2010.

[4] This inheritance from the eleventh *aṅga*, the *Viyāhapannatti* or *Bhagavatīsūtra*, has been underscored by Dundas (2002: 231).

(α) *prayogavirahe jātu padasyārthaḥ pratīyate* /
[Even] when it (i.e. the word *syāt*) is not used, the meaning of the word is always understood.[5]

The universality of this rule raises a serious difficulty. If the *saptabhaṅgī* applies to every statement, whatever its subject and its predicate may be, how could a judgement still be endowed with an absolute value? In this way, the philosophers' claim to establish accurately the nature of reality, the cognitive process and so on, would be necessarily bound to fail. Moreover, the Jaina tenets and especially the Tīrthaṅkaras' teachings would not be immune to the criticism of being relative. If a statement like "omniscience is a means of knowledge" can be subjected to the sevenfold predication, the cognitive validity of omniscience would not be guaranteed anymore, because according to the traditional pattern of the *saptabhaṅgī*, it could be said: (S_2) in some respect, omniscience is only no means of knowledge; (S_3) in some respect, omniscience is and is not a means of knowledge; (S_4) in some respect, omniscience is only inexpressible, etc. Thus, the perfection which the essential nature of omniscience is precisely based on would be contradicted.

This paper aims at reconsidering this problem, which may prove sufficient to destroy the whole doctrine, as it has been noticed by the opponents of Jainism, such as Bhāsarvajña.[6] Nevertheless, it seems that Jaina philosophers themselves provide means to solve the difficulty. In this respect, Akalaṅka's *Laghīyastraya* (LT 63), Vidyānandin's *Tattvārthaślokavārtika* (TŚV I.6.56 *ad* TS I.6) and Malliṣeṇa's *Syādvādamañjarī* (SVM 23.126–128 *ad* ADV 23) deserve particular attention, because these texts include a new formulation of the rule.

---

[5] NVi III.68ab, II, p. 352.13. The context makes it clear that the word Akalaṅka is talking about is *syāt*, as Vādirāja's commentary reveals it. NViV *ad* NVi III.68ab, II p. 352.14–16: ***jātu*** *kadācit prakaraṇādisannidhisamaye* ***padasya*** *syādityādeḥ* ***prayogasya viraho*** *'nuccāraṇaṃ tasmin sati* ***arthaḥ*** *syātkārāder abhidheyaḥ atiprasaṅgānuktakalpatvanivṛttilakṣaṇaḥ* ***pratīyate*** *prakaraṇādisahāyād eva śabdād avagamyate.* The *pratīka*-s are in bold characters and are left in Sanskrit when they are glossed by the commentator.

[6] Bhāsarvajña has voiced this argument in his *Nyāyabhūṣaṇa* (p. 560). Cf. Joshi (2000: 107).

2.1 The stanza LT 63 runs as follows:

(β) *aprayukto 'pi sarvatra syātkāro 'rthāt pratīyate |*
vidhau niṣedhe 'py anyatra kuśalaś cet prayojakaḥ ||
Even when it is not used, the word *syāt* is understood according to the meaning, everywhere, in affirmation, in negation too and elsewhere [too] if the author is skilful.[7]

When Vidyānandin (ninth or tenth century),[8] who is deeply indebted to Akalaṅka for his epistemological conceptions, draws a comparison between the two particles used in the assertions of *syādvāda*—the adverb *syāt* ("in some respect") and the restrictive particle *eva* ("only")—he employs, in the first two *pāda*-s of TŚV I.6.56, a phrasing that sounds similar to LT 63:

(γ) *so 'prayukto 'pi vā tajjñaiḥ sarvatrārthāt pratīyate |*
yathaivakāro'yogādivyavacchedaprayojanaḥ ||
Even when it (i.e. the word *syāt*) is not used, it is understood by those who are experts in these [matters] everywhere according to the meaning, exactly as the word *eva*, which aims at excluding unrelatedness, etc.[9] [is understood even when it is not used].[10]

---

[7] LT 63, p. 22.1–2.

[8] Scholars waver between two possible datings of Vidyānandin. Some of them consider that this Digambara philosopher flourished during the first half of the ninth century (775–840): Koṭhiyā's conclusions have been accepted, among others, by Mahendra Kumar Jain (Introduction to SVi, p. 49) and Soni (1999: 161). Nevertheless, more recent developments seem to favour a later dating (900–950): following Dhaky, Malvania and Soni (2007: 542) regard Vidyānandin as Māṇikyanandin's contemporary.

[9] In this context, the term *ādi-* refers to two other possible interpretations of the particle *eva*, i.e. *anyayogavyavaccheda* (exclusion of relatedness to another thing) and *atyantāyogavyavaccheda* (exclusion of absolute non-relatedness). The logical implications of each interpretation have been studied by Uno (2000: 43–46).

[10] TŚV I.6.56ab, p. 137.5.

This sentence is later quoted by Malliṣeṇa (thirteenth century)[11] who uses himself a parallel formulation of this rule in his commentary on the stanza 23 of Hemacandra's *Anyayoga-vyavacchedadvātriṃśikā*:

> (δ) *yatrāpi cāsau na prayujyate tatrāpi vyavacchedaphalaiva-kāravad buddhimadbhiḥ pratīyata eva. yad uktam:* [TŚV I.6. 56]
> Wherever it (i.e. the word *syāt*) is not used, it is really understood by wise [people], as well as the word *eva* —the result of which is an exclusion—[is understood wherever it is not used]. What has been said [in TŚV I.6.56].[12]

Despite minor differences, these four occurrences of the rule are obviously built on a common pattern. First of all, the grammatical structure always reveals an opposition between the explicit wording of some statements (the word *syāt* is not expressed) and their implicit meaning (the word *syāt* has to be understood). The concessive sense is conveyed by the particle *api*, either combined with a participle (β, γ) or associated with a subordinate clause (δ), or by the locative case alone (α: *prayogavirahe*). Then, this parallel structure between the four formulations of the rule is underlined by similar lexical choices: the presence of the same verbal form *pratīyate*, as well as the use of the prefix *pra-* set before the root YUJ in the noun *prayoga* (α), the past passive participle *prayukta* (β, γ) or the present passive indicative *prayujyate* (δ). Whatever form of the root is chosen, it is always associated with a negation, either syntactically (δ) or lexically (α: *viraha-* as final member of the compound; β, γ: privative prefix *a-*).

But insofar as the different formulations insist on the absolute universality of the rule—through an adverb (α: *jātu*; β, γ: *sarvatra*) or through the correlative system *yatra... tatra...* (δ)

---

[11] Dhruva, in his introduction to the *Syādvādamañjarī* (p. xiv), maintains that Malliṣena lived during Siddharāja Jayasiṃha's and Kumārapāla's reign, who ruled the Gujarat in the first and the second half of the twelfth century CE. However, as Malliṣeṇa says at the end of his work that it was composed in Śaka 1214 (i.e. 1292 CE), he should belong to the second half of the thirteenth century CE.

[12] SVM *ad* Hemacandra's AVD stanza 23, lines 126–130, p. 143–144.

—they all bear a contradiction. There are namely two possible interpretations:

1. either the rule really holds true absolutely; in such a case, since formulations like NVi III.68ab, LT 63, etc. escape the sevenfold predication, they constitute precisely exceptions to the rule set out.
2. either the *syādvāda* also applies to NVi III.68ab, LT 63, etc.; then, the contradiction resulting from the conjunction of the *modus* and the *dictum* deprives these assertions themselves of their rule status. It can be said: in some respect, the word *syāt* is not understood everywhere.

Whatever assumption is adopted, the consequence is the same although the reasoning is different: one assertion at least cannot be subjected to the sevenfold predication. With this preliminary conclusion we would then encounter a disagreement with the usual conception we mentioned at the very beginning.

2.2 Nevertheless, the last three formulations we have listed provide two precious clues that do not appear in NVi III.68ab. The first one results from the word *arthāt*. If it is to be understood as we do, i.e. as meaning "according to the sense" rather than "through the force of circumstances", it brings a possible restriction in the formulations (β) and (γ): *arthāt* may then imply that the word *syāt* could be sometimes omitted if the context or the import of the assertion makes it clear. The second clue is more conclusive, because it appears in the four formulations of the rule. The authors always introduce a restriction by specifying who is able to understand the word *syāt* when it is implicit. This restriction is expressed sometimes by the conditional clause "if the author is skilful" (β: *kuśalaś cet prayojakaḥ*), sometimes by the instrumental case (γ: *tajjñaiḥ* "by those who are expert in these [matters]"; δ: *buddhimadbhiḥ* "by wise [people]"). Such a restriction tempers the apparent unconditionality of the main clause. For, if the adverb *syāt* were to be added in a systematic way and without discernment, no skill or no knowledge would be required.

In his commentary on the LT entitled *Syādvādabhūṣāṇa*, Abhayacandra (thirteenth century CE?) shows us the way in specifying that the skill concerns the empirico-practical realm: "*cet*, if he is ***kuśalaḥ***, [if] he is clever in the empirico-practical realm" (*ced yadi **kuśalaḥ** syāt vyavahāre prabuddhaḥ syāt*).[13] This explanation seems to mean that the contradiction may be solved thanks to the distinction between two realms of reality, the empirico-practical one and the ultimate one. But if some propositions escape the *syādvāda*, how then can we discover which ones are concerned? Since the word *syāt* may be implicit, every proposition supposed to hold true absolutely should contain an explicit clue so as to prevent the reader from understanding the word *syāt*.

3.1 Let us now examine Akalaṅka's works, especially his *Laghīyastraya* and *Nyāyaviniścaya*, in order to find out concrete manifestations of such a skill in accordance with the rule expressed in these texts. This perspective sheds new light on terms which one usually attaches no importance to. The word *añjasā* and its derivative *āñjasam* represent indeed the most emblematic case of the clues we are looking for.

3.1.1 In order to determine the context in which these terms appear, let us firstly survey two illuminating stanzas in which they occur, namely LT 11cd–12ab (ε) and NVi III.88 (ζ). For the moment, *añjasā* and *āñjasam* are deliberately left in Sanskrit.

(ε) *avikalpadhiyā liṅgaṃ na kiñcit sampratīyate ||*
nānumānād asiddhatvāt pramāṇāntaram āñjasam |
No inferential sign is known by a non-conceptual thought, neither from inference because [inference] is not established; *āñjasam*, another means of knowledge [establishes inference].[14]

(ζ) *ādye parokṣam aparaṃ pratyakṣaṃ prāhur āñjasam |*
kevalaṃ lokabuddhyaiva mater lakṣaṇasaṅgrahaḥ ||
Āñjasam, the first two [kinds of cognition] (i.e. sensuous cognition and testimonial cognition) are called, according to tradition, 'the indirect means

[13] SVBh *ad* LT 63, p. 86.11–12.

[14] LT 11cd–12ab, p. 5.6–7.

> of knowledge' (*parokṣa*), [while] the rest is called 'perception' (*pratyakṣa*). Sensuous cognition is included in the name [of perception] only in order to be in accordance with the common idea.[15]

3.1.2 Among the meanings given in dictionaries, two main interpretations emerge, depending on whether a concrete meaning is insisted upon (namely the idea of straightness, of quickness) or a more intellectual one (the idea of accuracy, of conformity with truth).[16] But neither of them seems really suitable in the present contexts.

We hardly understand what the idea of immediacy, earlier preferred by Balcerowicz in 2003,[17] could mean in the context of LT 11cd–12ab and how it would provide a convincing interpretation in the other passages. Two years later, Balcerowicz suggested quite a different interpretation, since he used the adverbs "correctly" and "rightly" to translate the terms *añjasā* and *āñjasam*.[18] Although this second attempt is closer to

---

[15] NVi III.88, II, p. 363.23 & 33. The first half of the *anuṣṭubh*-stanza refers more or less explicitly to TS I.9–12 (p. 12–13): *matiśrutāvadhimanaḥparyāya-kevalāni jñānam || 9 || tat pramāṇe || 10 || ādye parokṣam || 11 || pratyakṣam anyat || 12 ||* (9) Cognition [is fivefold]: sensuous, testimonial, clairvoyant, telepathic and omniscient. (10) The set made up of these [five kinds divides into] two means of knowledge. (11) The first two [kinds of cognition] (i.e. *mati* and *śruta*) constitute the indirect means of knowledge. (12) The remaining [kinds] constitute perception.

[16] According to Monier-Williams's *Dictionary*, the adverb *añjasā* can mean "straight on, right, truly, justly; quickly, soon, instantly" (11a), and the adjective *āñjasa* "immediate, direct" (133c). Böhtlingk-Roth's *Dictionary* gives three different meanings for *añjasā* (vol. I, col. 80): "1. gerades Weges, stracks, geradeaus; 2. alsobald, sogleich; 3. in Wahrheit, der Wahrheit gemäss". Apte's *Dictionary* does not provide any other meanings.

[17] Balcerowicz (2003: 356) translates LT 11cd–12ab as follows: "No inferential sign can be known through non-conceptual comprehension (viz. perception) or through inference, because it is not established; [hence] another cognitive criterion (suppositional knowledge, *tarka*) is immediately [called for]."

[18] Balcerowicz (2005: 362) renders *añjasā* as "correctly" in NVi I.3 (2005: 373) and NVi III.83 (2005: 362): "Perception is correctly [taken to be] lucid [cognition]; the other [type of cognitive criterion] is testimonial cognition which is free of misapprehension, divided into [such varieties as] recognition etc. By way of summary, there are two cognitive criteria." Then he uses the adverb "rightly" to translate *āñjasam* in NVi III.88 (2005: 366): "Two first

the interpretation I am setting out, it seems to me that they do not manage to express the specificity of the Sanskrit terms, because these two adverbs cannot make clear, at which level of reality this correctness or this rightness applies.

Vādirāja's and Abhayacandra's commentaries are an invaluable help for us because, unlike Prabhācandra, they have not carefully avoided glossing the terms *añjasā* and *āñjasam*. While commenting on NVi I.3, Vādirāja glosses *añjasā* with *tattvataḥ* ("in conformity with reality").[19] Then, in order to explain the occurrence of *āñjasam* in NVi III.88, he uses a more explicit wording, namely *paramārthataḥ* ("from the transcendental point of view").[20] Abhayacandra follows the same path in his analysis of LT 11cd–12ab.[21] So, if we trust these two commentators, *añjasā* and *āñjasam* are meant to endow the judgement with an absolute value.

3.1.3 In order to check whether this interpretation is valid or not, let us consider NVi III.88 and LT 11cd–12ab more thoroughly. NVi III.88 is especially convenient and illuminating because this passage concerns a famous point of the Jaina philosophical tenets. The stanza is built on an opposition between two classifications of the means of knowledge: the former one, developed by the canonical tradition and confirmed by Umāsvāti's *Tattvārthādhigamasūtra* and the new one, usually

---

two (*sic*) [kinds of cognition, viz. sensuous cognition (*mati*) and testimonial cognition (*śruta*),] were rightly termed [by Umāsvāmin in TS 1.11] indirect cognition, whereas the remaining [kinds, viz. clairvoyance (*avadhi*), mind-reading (*manaḥ-pāryāya*) and absolute knowledge, were termed] direct cognition. However, it is only in order to be in agreement with people's opinion, that sensuous cognition is incorporated into the definition of [perception]."

[19] Cf. NViV *ad* NVi 1.3, I p. 87.1: ***añjasā*** *iti tattvata ity arthaḥ.*

[20] NViV *ad* NVi III.88, II p. 363.30–31: *tad idam ubhayam api pramāṇam* ***āñjasaṃ*** *na vyavahāramātraparikalpitam, paramārthataḥ* (...). This remark appears once Vādirāja has specified that the ancient classification was not in agreement with the mere empirico-practical realm. While commenting on NVi III.83, Vādirajā does not gloss *añjasā*.

[21] SVBh *ad* LT 11cd–12ab, p. 30.15–16: ***āñjasaṃ*** *pāramārthikaṃ na mithyā vikalpātmakam abhyupagantavyaṃ* (...). The whole passage is quoted and translated below, see also fn. 24.

adopted by Jaina logicians and, among others, Akalaṅka.[22] The word *añjasā* is used in this structure since it contrasts with the compound *lokabuddhyā* ("in order to be in accordance with the common idea").

We remember that according to the traditional division the cognition called *pratyakṣa* includes the three supra-sensory kinds of cognition: clairvoyance, telepathy and omniscience are conceived of as the only real forms of perception, because the soul knows reality directly, through its own powers, without using any other faculty, be it sensory or mental. On the other hand, the cognition produced thanks to a sensory faculty, together with testimonial cognition, is classified as mediate knowledge. In the later classification however, sensuous cognition has been moved to *pratyakṣa* so as to constitute the empirical component of perception, whereas clairvoyance, telepathy and omniscience, still belonging to *pratyakṣa*, became its transcendental part. With the word *lokabuddhyaiva*, the stanza ascribes this change concerning the way *pramāṇa*-s are classified, to a concession with regard to common practice, in other words to the empirico-practical use. But the restriction expressed by the particle *eva* lets us understand that, even though Akalaṅka has adopted the new classification of *pramāṇa*-s, he still considers that, strictly speaking, the term *pratyakṣa* is supposed to be used only with what concerns supra-sensory kinds of perception. Thus, the former codification, inheritance of the traditional teachings—as it is shown by the verb *prāhur*, which here has its strong meaning: "to hand down by tradition"—still holds true from the transcendental point of view or absolutely, that is without taking common practice into account. "Absolutely" or in French "*dans l'absolu*", is the translation I propose in order to render the whole specificity of the terms *añjasā* and *āñjasam*. Thus, the last stanza quoted above now reads:

---

[22] Cf. for instance LT 3: *pratyakṣaṃ viśadaṃ jñānaṃ mukhyasaṃvyavahārataḥ | parokṣaṃ śeṣavijñānaṃ pramāṇe iti saṅgrahaḥ ||* Perception [is] clear cognition, [it is twofold] because of [the division between the] transcendental [standpoint] and [the] empirico-practical [standpoint]; the indirect means of knowledge [comprises] the remaining cognition. These are the two means of knowledge in summary.

(ζ) The first two [kinds of cognition] (i.e. sensuous cognition and testimonial cognition) are absolutely called, according to tradition, 'the indirect means of knowledge' (*parokṣa*), [while] the rest is called 'perception' (*pratyakṣa*). Sensuous cognition is included in the name [of perception] only in order to be in accordance with the common idea.

Inasmuch as the stanzas NVi I.3 and NVi III.83 share some common features with NVi III.88 because both are devoted to the definition of the *pramāṇas*, it is not surprising that this interpretation of *añjasā* and *āñjasam* fits in very well with the context.[23]

3.1.4 The occurrence found at the beginning of the *Laghīyastraya* seems more stimulating because, unlike the others, it is not really concerned with the problem of definition. In order to put LT 11cd–12ab back in its context, all we can say is that Akalaṅka is endeavouring to establish that cognising the relation of invariable concomitance between a *probans* and a *probandum*, requires the cognitive validity of a peculiar *pramāṇa*, different from inference and from perception—here understood as sensuous perception. But all his argumentation would be meaningless if this *pramāṇa* were not absolutely valid, if it could be questioned anyway. Such is the explanation given by Abhayacandra when he examines the import of the word *āñjasam* in the context:

> Thus, with the idea that inference too does not grasp the invariable concomitance, there is **another means of knowledge** grasping this [invariable concomitance]: it is called **inductive reasoning.** It must be understood that

---

[23] NVi I.3, I, p. 57.15–16: *pratyakṣalakṣaṇaṃ prāhuḥ spaṣṭaṃ sākāram añjasā | dravyaparyāyasāmānyaviśeṣārthātmavedanam ||* According to tradition, perception is said to be absolutely defined as the cognition of itself and of an object [under its different aspects:] substance, mode, universal and particular, cognition which is clear and has a definite content. NVi III.83, II p. 359.30–31: *pratyakṣaṃ añjasā spaṣṭam anyac chrutam aviplavam | prakīrṇaṃ pratyabhijñādau pramāṇe iti saṅgrahaḥ ||* Absolutely, perception [is] clear [cognition]; the other [cognition] is testimonial [cognition] when deprived of error; [this testimonial cognition] is divided into recognition, etc.; these are the two means of knowledge in summary.

> [this inductive reasoning], which consists in concept, is **āñjasaṃ**, that is concerns the transcendental point of view and is not false, because otherwise the cognitive validity of inference [would] not [be] correct.[24]

Thus, the stanza LT 11cd–12ab acquires another import if *āñjasam* is understood as meaning "absolutely":

> (ε) No inferential sign is known by a non-conceptual thought, neither from inference because [inference] is not established; another means of knowledge [establishes inference] absolutely.

Using the word *añjasā* or *āñjasam* assures the unconditional validity of a statement, because its validity is not limited to the empirico-practical point of view.

3.2 It is likely that in Akalaṅka's works we shall find other words with a similar meaning, for instance *tattvataḥ* or *paramārthataḥ*, as the commentators' glosses show. LT 7cd comes within this use. Akalaṅka characterises the object of knowledge as follows:

> *tad dravyaparyāyātmārtho bahir antaś ca tattvataḥ ||*
> Thus, in conformity with reality (*tattvataḥ*), the object [of knowledge], which consists in substance and in modes, is external as well as internal.[25]

The word *tattvataḥ* could be considered as the sign of a tautology. Since the object of knowledge is nothing but reality, sometimes called *vastu*, sometimes *tattva*, LT 7cd may lay itself open to the criticism of circularity, because it would amount to saying: "*x* is such-and-such in conformity with *x*". However, if *tattvataḥ* specifies the level of reality or the point of view according to which the statement holds true, the whole stanza gets a new significance. Insofar as the two sets of opposite features (on the one hand *dravyaparyāyātmā* and on the other hand *bahir antaḥ*) already account for the complex nature of

---

[24] SVBh *ad* LT 11cd–12ab, p. 30.14–17: *tan nānumānam api vyāptigrāhakam iti tadgrāhakaṃ* **pramāṇāntaraṃ** *tarkākhyaṃ.* **āñjasaṃ** *pāramārthikaṃ na mithyā vikalpātmakam abhyupagantavyaṃ, anyathānumānaprāmāṇyāyogāt.* See fn. 21.

[25] LT 7cd, p. 3.23.

reality, the *saptabhaṅgī* is no more required to express multilateralism.

3.3 Thanks to words such as *añjasā* and *tattvataḥ*, a wise reader is warned not to subject systematically and without discernment every statement to the *syādvāda*. Nevertheless, one would rightly wonder if Akalaṅka constitutes an exception among Jaina philosophers. Would he be the first to feel it necessary to point out which statements escape the sevenfold predication? Before him, Jinabhadra in his *Viśeṣāvaśyakabhāṣya*[26] offers an exemplary case. The stanzas 94–95 explain how conceiving sensuous cognition as being a part of mediate cognition as well as a part of perception does not lead to a contradiction but can be accounted for, thanks to the doctrine of multilateralism.

> **(α_1)** Sensuous cognition and testimonial cognition are the indirect means of knowledge, because they are caused by [something] else than the soul, inasmuch as it is based on the memory of a relation grasped before, as inference.
> According to a unilateral thesis, **(β)** a [cognition] based on an inferential sign is [a variety of the] indirect means of knowledge while **(γ)** clairvoyance, etc. is perception; **(α_2)** the [cognition] produced by sensory faculties or by understanding is conventional perception.[27]

I shall not consider the problems of interpretation at issue in this passage that have been developed in a previous paper.[28] What matters for the present purpose, is to notice that Jinabhadra voices two different analyses of the cognition that is produced by sensory faculties or by understanding when it is

---

[26] Jinabhadra Gaṇi Kṣamāśramaṇa must have flourished during the second half of the sixth century CE: 484–588 CE according to Vidyabhusana (1971: 181), 489–593 CE according to Malvania (introduction to ViBh, volume I, p. 1).

[27] ViBh 94, I, p. 24.20–21: *honti parokkhāiṃ maisuyāiṃ jīvassa paraṇimittāo | puvvovaladdhasambandhasaraṇao vāṇumāṇaṃ va ||* ViBh 95, I, p. 24.26–27: *egantena parokkaṃ liṅgiyam ohāiyaṃ ca paccakkhaṃ | indiyamaṇobhavaṃ jaṃ taṃ saṃvavahārapaccakkhaṃ ||*.

[28] Cf. Clavel (forthcoming).

not based on an inferential sign: it is included in *parokṣa* (α_1) insofar as one considers the standpoint of the soul; but it is held as *pratyakṣa* (α_2) if the immediacy is judged according to the standpoint of sensory and quasi-sensory faculties. In contradistinction to this multilateral treatment, Jinabhadra examines the other kinds of cognition in a unilateral way, as it is attested by the instrumental case *egantena* (Skt. *ekāntena*): whatever the standpoint is, a cognition depending on a mark that is external to the cogniser, belongs to *parokṣa* (β), whereas a supra-sensory cognition belongs to *pratyakṣa* (γ). In these last two cases the characterisations of *pratyakṣa* or *parokṣa* are given absolutely, because one view solely is correct: such is the import of *egantena*. In this context, this term does not aim, as it often does, at suggesting the partiality of the statement and implying that from another standpoint we could provide another analysis, which would itself be unilateral. Concerning these two kinds of *pramāṇa*, Jinabhadra claims the necessity of a unilateral description. But, characterising a statement as unilateral does not systematically reduce its truth-value: a description can be true in spite of its unilateralism.

4 Finally, it appears that few statements of some philosophers' teachings really escape the sevenfold predication. So, every statement is concerned by the rule set forth in LT 63, unless a sign leads the reader in the opposite direction. But then, the author generally uses a word that is meant to exclude the understanding of *syāt*: in the passages we briefly surveyed, this function is fulfilled by the terms *añjasā*, *āñjasam*, *tattvataḥ* and *ekāntena*, and the list may still have to be completed. The alternative is embodied in LT 63; among the two different ways of interpretation that were voiced at the beginning of this paper in order to solve the paradox, the second hypothesis seems to be the good one: as the rule set out by LT 63 also applies to this stanza, it can be deduced that some statements do escape the *syādvāda*. For, only a statement that holds true absolutely is able to talk about the *vyavahāra* (the empirico-practical realm) in the terms of a law. As we can see, the assertions that escape the *syādvāda* share a common feature: they are meta-statements. On the other hand, when the rule explicitly expresses that the word *syāt* has to be understood everywhere, we should add: in all the statements that are uttered from the empirico-practical standpoint. Nevertheless, whatever point of view is adopted, the empirico-practical or the transcendental, both types of assertion always concern one and the same reality. One is the result of the knowledge par excellence, omniscience, whereas the other is obtained by every cognition limited by the power of *karman*. Insofar as the word *syāt* is the token of the empirico-practical point of view, the statements about the validity of omniscience are by no means affected by the sevenfold predication: omniscience is not only higher than *syādvāda*, but the sevenfold predication also draws its validity from this perfect cognition, because the *syādvāda* constitutes finally an ersatz cognition of omniscience. The partial and relative nature of the statements uttered in everyday life results from the fact that a cognition produced by a non-omniscient cogniser is by nature diffracted. So, there is no contradiction when we say that the *syādvāda* must apply to all the predications expressed from the empirico-practical point of view, and to these only.[29]

Bibliography

Abbreviations and Primary Sources

LT, *Laghīyastraya* by Akalaṅka. In: *Śrīmadbhaṭṭākalaṅkadevaviracitam Akalaṅkagranthatrayam. Svopajñavivṛtisahitam Laghīyastrayam, Nyāyaviniścayaḥ, Pramāṇasaṅgrahaś ca*. Mahendra Kumar Jain (ed.), Ahmedabad: Sarasvatā Pustak Bhaṇḍār (Singhi Jaina Granthamālā 12), 1996, second ed. (first ed. 1939), pp. 1–26.

NBhū, *Nyāyabhūṣaṇa* by Bhāsarvajña. In *Śrīmadācāryabhāsarvajñapraṇītasya Nyāyasārasya svopajñaṃ vyākhyānaṃ Nyāyabhūṣaṇam*. Svāmī Yogīndrānanda (ed.), Varanasi: Ṣaḍdarśana Prakāśana Pratiṣṭhānam (Ṣaḍdarśana Prakāśana Granthamālā 1), 1968.

NVi, *Nyāyaviniścaya* by Akalaṅka. In: *Nyāyaviniścayavivaraṇa of Śrī Vādirāja Sūri, the Sanskrit Commentary on Bhaṭ Akalaṅkadeva's Nyāyaviniścaya*. Mahendra Kumar Jain (ed.), Delhi: Bhā-

[29] This solution has already been sketched by some scholars, for instance Dundas (2002: 230–231) and Joshi who notes (2000: 98): "And thus the doctrine of *anekānta* can be applied to everything in the world."

ratīya Jñānapīṭha Prakāśana, 2 volumes, 2000, second ed. (first ed. Varanasi, 1949 and 1954).

NViV, *Nyāyaviniścayavivaraṇa* by Vādirāja. See NVi.

RVār, *Rājavārttika* by Akalaṅka. In: *Tattvārthavārttika [Rājavārttika] of Śrī Akalaṅkadeva*. Mahendra Kumar Jain (ed.), Delhi: Bhāratīya Jñānapīṭha Prakāśana (Jñānapīṭha Mūrtidevī Jaina Granthamālā 10 and 20), sixth ed. 2 volumes, 2001 (first ed. 1953 and 1957).

SVBh, *Syādvādabhūṣaṇa* by Abhayacandra. In: *Laghīyastrayādisaṃgrahaḥ: 1. Bhaṭṭākalaṅkadevakṛtaṃ Laghīyastrayam Anantakīrtiracitatātparyavṛttisahitam, 2. Bhaṭṭākalaṅkadevakṛta Svarūpasambodhanam, 3-4. Anantakīrtikṛtalaghubṛhatsarvajñasiddhī ca*. K. Bh. Nitve (ed.), Bombay: Manikacandra Digambara Jaina Granthamālā Samiti (Manikacandra Digambara Jaina Granthamālā 1), 1915, pp. 1–103.

SVi, *Siddhiviniścaya* Akalaṅka. In: *Siddhiviniścaya of Akalaṅka edited with the commentary Siddhiviniścayaṭīkā of Anantavīrya*, Mahendra Kumar Jain (ed.), Delhi: Bhāratīya Jñānapīṭha Prakāśana (Jñānapīṭha Mūrtidevī Jaina Granthamālā 22–23), 2 volumes,1959.

SVM, *Syādvādamañjarī* by Malliṣeṇa. In: *Syādvādamañjarī of Malliṣeṇa, with the Anyayoga-Vyavaccheda-Dvātriṃśikā of Hemacandra*, A. B. Dhruva (ed.), Delhi: Akshaya Prakashan (Bombay Sanskrit and Prakrit Series LXXXIII), 2005 (repr. of Poona 1933 ed.).

TS, *Tattvārthādhigamasūtra* by Umāsvāti. In: *Tattvārtha Sūtra, That Which Is*. N. Tatia (tr.), San Francisco: Harper Collins, 1994.

TŚV, *Tattvārthaślokavārtikam* by Vidyānandin. In: *Śrīmadvidyānandisvāmiviracitaṃ Tattvārthaślokavārtikam*. Manoharlāl (ed.), Ahmedabad: Sarasvati Pustak Bhandar (Saraswati Oriental Research Sanskrit Series 16), 2002.

ViBh, *Viśeṣāvaśyakabhāṣya* by Jinabhadra. In: *Ācārya Jinabhadra's Viśeṣāvaśyakabhāṣya*. In 3 volumes: vols I and II: *with auto-commentary*, edited by D. Malvania; vol. III: *with Śrīkoṭyāryavādigaṇi's vivaraṇa*, Edited by D. Malvania and B. J. Doshi, Ahmedabad: L. D. Institute of Indology (Lalbhai Dalpatbhai Series 10, 14 and 21), 1966–1968.

Secondary Sources

Balcerowicz, Piotr, 2003, "Is 'Inexplicability Otherwise' (*anyathānupapatti*) Otherwise Inexplicable?" *Journal of Indian Philosophy* 31 (2003), pp. 343–380.

——— 2005, "*Pramāṇas* and Language: a Dispute between Diṅnāga, Dharmakīrti and Akalaṅka", *Journal of Indian Philosophy* 33 (2005), pp. 343–400.

Clavel, Anne 2010, "Pourquoi sept plutôt que quatre? Étude comparée de la *saptabhaṅgī* et de la *catuṣkoṭi*". In Franco and Zin 2010, pp. 151–168.

——— forthcoming, "Sensuous Cognition—*Pratyakṣa* or *Parokṣa*? Jinabhadra's Reading of the *Nandīsūtra*". In: Peter Flügel and Olle Qvarnström (eds), *Jaina Scriptures and Philosophy*, London, Routledge.

Dundas, Paul 2002, *The Jains*. London, etc.: Routledge, second revised ed. (first ed. 1992).

Franco, Eli and Zin, Monika (eds), 2010, *From Turfan to Ajanta. Festschrift for Dieter Schlingloff on the Occasion of his Eightieth Birthday*, Lumbini: Lumbini International Research Institute, two volumes, 2010.

Joshi, L. V., 2000, "Nyāya Criticism of *Anekānta*". In Shah 2000, pp. 95–110.

Malvania, Dalsukh and Soni, Jayendra (eds), 2007, *Encyclopedia of Indian Philosophies, Volume X: Jain Philosophy* (Part I), Delhi: Motilal Banarsidass, 2007.

Matilal, Bimal K., 1981, *The Central Philosophy of Jainism (Anekānta-Vāda)*, Ahmedabad: L. D. Institute of Indology (Lalbhai Dalpatbhai Series 79), 1981.

Nyāyavijayajī, Muniśrī, 2000, *Jaina Philosophy and Religion*, Delhi: Motilal Banarsidass, 2000, repr. (first ed. 1998). N. J. Shah (transl.), *Jaina Darśana*, Ahmedabad: Jaina Sarasvati Bhavana, 1921.

Padmarajiah, Y. J., 1986, *A Comparative Study of the Jaina Theories of Reality and Knowledge*, Delhi: Motilal Banarsidass, 1986 (first ed. Bombay: Jain Sahitya Vikas Mandal, 1963).

Shah, Nagin J. (ed.), 2000, *Jaina Theory of Multiple Facets of Reality and Truth*, Delhi, Motilal Banarsidass: Bhogilal Leherchand Institute of Indology (Series 13), 2000.

Soni, Jayandra, 1999, "Aspects of Jaina Epistemology with Special Reference to Vidyānandin". In Wagle and Qvarnström 1999, pp. 138–168.

Uno, Atsushi, 2000, "A Study of *Syādvāda*". In: Shah 2000, pp. 33–59.

Vidyabhusana, S. C., 1971, *A History of Indian Logic*, Delhi: Motilal Banarsidass, 1971 (first ed. Calcutta, 1920).

Wagle, N. K. and Qvarnström, Olle, (eds), 1999, *Approaches to Jaina Studies: Philosophy, Logic, Rituals and Symbols*, Toronto: Centre for South Asian Studies (South Asia Studies Papers 11).

Jaina *Havelī* Temples in Northern India: Sources, Developments and Ritual Use

Julia A. B. Hegewald

Abstract

The Jaina community in South Asia has developed a number of temple types to house sacred objects and to provide an environment for worship and religious contemplation. This paper focuses on the *havelī* or courtyard temple type, which is particularly common in northern India and of later periods, starting from about the fifteenth century CE. Jaina *havelī* temples have been arranged around a central courtyard and are introverted structures. The open courtyard spaces were often enclosed from above, creating multi-storeyed halls used for the performance of rituals. The presence of numerous arcades surrounding the open or covered court areas favours the creation of manifold image chambers, which have also been developed on multiple superimposed levels. The complex spatial form of the Jaina *havelī* temple resembles domestic courtyard-houses and is related to Islamic courtyard mosques. This paper describes the forms and variations of Jaina *havelī* temples, examines their ritual use, suggests sources for their spatial layout and illustrates the wide-ranging effect this type has had on other Jaina temple types especially during the modern period.

Keywords: Jainism, *havelī*, courtyard temple, Islam, mosque, ritual dynamics, modern architecture

Introduction

This paper focuses on the description, analysis and interpretation of Jaina temples following the courtyard or *havelī* temple type. Temples belonging to this group have been planned around an inner courtyard space. They are found throughout the subcontinent, with a particular concentration in the north. Examples in this paper have been drawn from Rajasthan in the north-west, from Delhi, Haryana and Uttar Pradesh in the central northern region and from Bihar and West Bengal in eastern India. Most *havelī* temples date from comparatively late periods, starting from about the fifteenth century, with a peak of popularity between the sixteenth and nineteenth centuries. The paper outlines structural and stylistic developments of the temples, including issues such as the progression from open to roofed courtyard forms, and the creation of multiple shrines on horizontal and various superimposed vertical levels. Furthermore, it examines how the spatial layout of this kind of temple construction lends itself especially well to Jaina ritual requirements. The paper concludes by suggesting possible sources for the *havelī* temple paradigm and by introducing the issue of modern continuity in contemporary instances relating to this prominent type of Jaina temple architecture.

1.0 Courtyard Temples in Northern India

Havelī temples are particularly widespread in towns and cities. The old bazaar areas of places such as Delhi, Agra and Allahabad have a high density of constructions of this kind. However, temples following this form of planning can be found in smaller towns, villages and even in the countryside as well. When found outside an urban environment, courtyard temples are frequently surrounded by a second enclosure wall, although their design itself creates a walled and inwardlooking temple environment. This can be seen in the Digambara Jaina Temple at Pavapuri in Bihar, which has been set into a second larger courtyard space. The delineation of the outer court has been formed out of consecutive flights of buildings of surrounding monastic rest houses and temple offices. The Digambara Jaina Pārśvanātha Temple at Khaniyan near Jaipur, the Digambara Jaina Baṛī Mandir at Namdev Chowk in Sanganer—the latter two in Rajasthan—and the Śrī Cantāmana Pārśvanātha Temple at Ajimganj in West Bengal are located at the centre of walled gardens.[1]

1.1 Approaching Jaina Havelī Temples

On the outside, most courtyard temples are relatively unadorned. Because of their plain exterior design, the temples can be difficult to identify. They strongly resemble the local vernacular architecture, following the *havelī* house style.

[1] Nevertheless, not every *havelī* temple located outside an urban area has been surrounded by a further free-standing wall. The Candraprabhu Temple at Candravad in Uttar Pradesh is situated far away from the next village or settlement and is not enclosed by a second delineating element. However, it is noteworthy, that the temple has a free-standing *toraṇa* gateway, imitating the design of the ancient Buddhist gates at Sanchi, which indicates at least a second sacred boundary without an actual physical wall. The site of Candravad was claimed by the Jaina community after the discovery of the present principal icon, which was found to have been buried in the ground. The temple complex was being entirely renovated and rebuilt in 1999 and it will be interesting to see whether a separate enclosure wall will be added during this enlargement process.

Straightforward cases of courtyard temples either have no or very few small window openings. Generally, these have been integrated into the upper portion of their external walls.

On the whole, *havelī* temples are entered through a single gate on one side, leading into a central, usually square, courtyard. The open court is surrounded by shaded arcades, with a deeper pillared hall positioned on one side. This deeper section houses the main sacred statue (*mūla-nāyaka*). A small but typical example is the *havelī* temple next to the Bhāṇḍāsar Jaina Temple at Bikaner in Rajasthan (Plate 1).[2]

In courtyard temples, the visitor usually steps through a door or more elaborate porch into an arcade, then out into a court, which usually lies lower than the surrounding covered passages, and up into the sanctum on the opposite side of the quadrangle, furthest away from the entrance. At other sites, the local terrain or the integration into densely populated city quarters, has dictated the location of the temple entrance on the lateral side of the courtyard. The normally straight linear ritual dynamic reflected in the movement of the devotees, which has been superimposed on a centralised temple building, may have been derived from the long tradition of *maṇḍapa*-line temples. In the latter temple type, access to an image chamber (*garbha-gṛha*) is provided along an axis of halls (*maṇḍapas*) and additional building elements, leading to the most sacred of religious icons positioned at the furthest end of a line of architectural structures, creating a linear ritual approach.

1.2 Shrines and Halls in Courtyard Temples

The deeper hall, positioned on one side of the courtyard and acting as a sanctum, can replace the narrower colonnade, commonly found on the other sides. In temples of this kind, the pillared halls are wide and open spaces, which combine the properties of a *maṇḍapa* and that of a *garbha-gṛha*. Yet in most instances, the hall-like image chamber has been posi-

---

[2] Whereas this *havelī* temple is typical with regards to its layout and design, it is unusual by being smaller than the neighbouring Bhāṇḍāsar Jaina Temple and by fulfilling the role of a subsidiary shrine in a larger temple complex. It is more common for courtyard type temples to be major independent constructions.

tioned behind the arcade encircling the inner court on all four sides (Plate 2). The dividing line between 'shrine' and 'hall' has usually simply been created by pillars and not by doorways with walls, and subsequently is relatively fluid. In examples such as the Candraprabhu Temple at Candravad and the Ādinātha Temple at Allahabad, both in Uttar Pradesh, the visitor having crossed the open courtyard passes at first through the arcade, which on the shrine side represents a kind of narrow but elongated *maṇḍapa* equivalent, before reaching the central octagonal domed section. This element of the temple houses the principal religious sculpture and is higher and more spacious than the surrounding sections of the hall. The Śrī Cantāmana Pārśvanātha Temple at Ajimganj is a particularly complex case of a deep *havelī* temple. In addition to the arcade surrounding the courtyard on all four sides, it has a further open pillared hall, a *raṅga-maṇḍapa*, positioned between the arcade and the spacious sanctum.

In most *havelī* temples, the *mūla-nāyaka*, or other object of veneration, has been exhibited free-standing in the middle of the wide shrine area. The sacred icon can be displayed on a number of different supports. Most prevalent are: a multi-storeyed pyramidal base in the shape of a sacred mountain (*meru*), a stylised sculptural presentation of the mythical teaching auditorium of the Jinas (*samavasaraṇa*), an altar or an image pavilion placed between four pillars supporting the ceiling of the hall.[3] Such pavilions have regularly been provided with an altar-like protrusion in front, which is used for depositing offerings. The popular ritual of clockwise circumambulation (*pradakṣiṇā*) can in most situations be performed around the sacred statue, regardless of the kind of pedestal chosen for its presentation. Only in rare examples has the principal sacred representation been moved to the back of the *garbha-gṛha*, or been enclosed in a walled sanctum. The side walls as well as the high corbelled or domed ceiling of this

[3] The *mūla-nāyaka* of the Śrī Agravāla Digambara Jaina Temple in Delhi, for instance, is a statue of Candraprabhu, placed on a *meru* sculptural pedestal, while the central image and its many supplementary figural representations in the Supārśvanātha Temple (no. I) at Badaini in Varanasi in Uttar Pradesh, have been placed in an ornamental pavilion. A detailed discussion of the shapes and associated meanings of *meru*s and *samavasaraṇa*s can be found in Hegewald (2005; 2007a).

central element of the temple structure have frequently been painted and highly decorated. Such elaborately adorned spaces can be seen in the shrine sections of the Ādinātha and the Pārśvanātha Temples at Allahabad, and in most Jaina temples in the bazaar quarter of Old Delhi. The large majority of Jaina *havelī* temples in these two northern Indian cities have pyramidal *meru* pedestals, whilst it is more typical of such temples in Varanasi to exhibit the icons in a white marble image pavilion.

The openness and light of the spacious hall-like shrine areas are very different from the generally small, cubical and dark *garbha-gr̥has* commonly associated with Hindu temple architecture in India. In some instances, however, also Jaina courtyard temples have a cubical chamber constructed at the centre of the wide and open sanctum. Access to such walled image chambers inside the laterally open pillared halls is either through one or more doorways. It is especially prevalent to have three doors, of which one is usually located at the front and two at the sides of the chamber.[4]

Subsidiary sacred representations have regularly been integrated into the rear wall of the hall-like shrine element or into the internal circumambulation paths surrounding walled sanctums. There are figures of Candraprabhu, Neminātha and Mahāvīra placed into shallow wall niches in the temple wall delineating the *pradakṣiṇā-patha* behind the central image chamber of the Neminātha Temple (no. I) at Sauripur in Uttar Pradesh. A wall niche found in the same location in the Pārśvanātha Temple (no. I) in Varanasi, enshrines a sacred book for veneration. In most cases, the side arcades surrounding the courtyard protrude into the *garbha-gr̥ha* and form lateral wings on the sides of the pillared core shrine space. Frequently, these side portions contain further pavilions, altars or wall

[4] An example of the first kind of enclosed *garbha-gr̥ha* with one doorway only, is the Candraprabhu Temple at Candravad. The Digambara Jaina Temple at Pavapuri and the Śrī Cantāmana Pārśvanātha Temple at Ajimganj are representative of the variant having three entrances. The latter kind can also be associated with Jaina temples following other types, such as the *maṇḍapa*-line or the eastern concentric temple types and expresses a prevalent Jaina tendency to open up their shrines more than is typical of Hindu temples. Centralised eastern temples are highly centred structures with a focal sanctum surrounded by rings of corridors. See Hegewald (2009a: 142) for a more comprehensive description.

niches, displaying a large number of additional religious statues. Specific examples of such temples will be discussed later in this paper, in the section on multi-shrined *havelī* temples.

The facades of the image chambers, facing the courtyard area, are characterised by a lot of variation in their design. Some elevations mirror the open design of the pillars and arches found on the other three sides of the quadrangle. In most occurrences though, the design on the shrine side is more enclosed. In many instances, narrower doorways, provided with door panels and locks to secure the sacred items in the wide sanctum, have been inserted on this side.

1.3 Roof Structures above Havelī Temples

The deeper hall housing the main sacred objects, which ritually constitutes the most important element of the temple and which is the focal point to which to turn from the courtyard area, has usually been marked above by prominent roof structures. These advertise the presence of the *mūlanāyaka* below and differentiate clearly between the four sides of the central courtyard space.

Due to the relatively late construction date of most *havelī* temples (largely sixteenth to nineteenth centuries), the majority of shrines are topped by prominent bulbous domes (Plate 3).

In particular in the central and eastern regions of northern India, small pavilions or towers, locally known as *chatrīs*, have been added in the four corners. Surrounding the large dome in the middle, these create a fivefold configuration of roof forms (*pañca-yatana*). Although the *pañcā-yatana* layout of spatial structuring has a long indigenous tradition in South Asia, the resulting arrangement of four smaller *chatrīs* surrounding a large central bulbous dome can convey a distinctly Islamic impression.[5]

On the other hand, straightforward north Indian temple superstructures of the *śikhara* type, or roof structures, which are at least more akin to the *nāgara*-form of roof tower, have also been used as crowning elements positioned above the

---

[5] The pronounced impact which Islamic influences have had on Jaina temple architecture has been discussed by Hegewald (2007b). For illustrations of such roof designs, see Hegewald (2007b: figures 2, 11, 12).

core area of the hall. In Eastern India, the towers are usually more pyramidal in shape, as can be seen in the Pārśvanātha Temple at Allahabad in Uttar Pradesh. More unusual is the pyramidal roof form of the Munisuvrata courtyard temple at Rajgir.[6] Moreover, lines of three *śikhara* towers have been employed to indicate the ritually most significant section of *havelī* temples. Multiple roof structures typically indicate the presence of numerous icons (*mūrtis*) and other venerated objects below.[7]

1.4 Double and Multiple Arcades

The arcades lining the court, or at least segments of them, can be double in depth and consequently provide more space for ritual activities. In many instances, there are two parallel arcades, either running along the front side of the cloister where access is provided to the courtyard, or along its sides. The first case is illustrated by the layout of the Śrī Ravaṇḍel Digambara Jaina Temple in Rājā Bazaar in central New Delhi (founded in about 1600).[8] The asymmetrically disposed Śrī Digambara Jaina Nayā Temple in Old Delhi combines aspects of both arrangement patterns. A further interesting place for the study of variations in the disposition of arcades in *havelī* temples is Sanganer in Rajasthan. Whereas in the Digambara Jaina temples in the localities of Godikan and Patanyan only

---

[6] The latter temple architecturally marks what is considered to be the auspicious birthplace of Munisuvrata at Rajgir. An illustration can be found in Hegewald (2009a: Plate 620).

[7] Examples illustrating this point are the Digambara Meru Temple in Old Delhi and the Śrī Ravaṇḍel Digambara Jaina Temple in the centre of New Delhi. A noteworthy temple where a principal *śikhara* tower is flanked by two lateral domes, is the Śrī Cantāmana Pārśvanātha Temple at Ajimganj. In other instances, a *śikhara* tower has been positioned above the central as well as two corner shrines, positioned at the opposite side of the courtyard. The latter can be seen in the Neminātha Temple (no. I) at Sauripur and in the Digambara Jaina Temple at Pavapuri. While in the latter two examples the *śikharas* are not actually aligned, when approaching the temple from the outside, the human eye tends to merge the two levels and to perceive the constellation as consisting of three aligned roof elements. Issues of multiplicity in Jaina temple architecture have been described and analysed in Hegewald (2001; 2002).

[8] *Havelī* type Jaina temples are especially typical of the Chandi Chowk Bazaar area of Old Delhi, but the Śrī Ravaṇḍel Digambara Jaina temple is located in Rājā Bazaar, close to Connaught Place, in the centre of New Delhi. Not far from this structure is another Digambara Jaina temple, called the Śrī Agravāla Temple.

segments of the arcades are double in depth, the Baṛī Mandir, locally known as 'Badhi Mandir,' has arcades, which are three pillars deep, positioned on all four sides. In the latter example, the dual arcade also continues on the side of the court accommodating the sanctum. Through this complex spatial conception of double colonnades, the temple has been provided with a deeper *maṇḍapa* area in front of the subsequent shrine hall.

The arcades surrounding the open quadrangle, whether they are narrow or of deeper profundity, are used as supplementary *maṇḍapas* by devotees and priests, as spaces for communal worship and for the storage of ritual implements. Furthermore, additional religious representations have frequently been installed in the surrounding colonnades. They have either been placed in shallow niches, which have been integrated into the surface of wider pillars, into short wall sections inserted into the facade of the arcades, or into the long walls at the back of the corridors. The latter two cases can be seen in the inner courtyard of the Digambara Jaina *havelī* temple at Pavapuri.[9] Free-standing *mūrtis*, venerated in open corridors, or religious icons contained in small niches, can later be transformed into separate additional *garbha-gṛhas* through the insertion of walls. The Cantāmana Pārśvanātha Temple at Ajimganj illustrates this point (Plate 4). Yet, a duplication or widening of the arcaded architectural space, is most common and ritually most desirable and effective on the shrine side of the court.

2.0 Havelī Temples with Roofed Courtyards

All the temples discussed so far have an open quadrangle area, which is the most characteristic element of *havelī* temples. However, there is a pronounced tendency to cover the courtyards from above as an open court represents certain problems for the security and exclusivity of the structures. Various degrees of roof covering were available to Jaina temple builders.

---

[9] In the the Digambara Jaina *havelī* temple at Pavapuri, a representation of the deceased saint and teacher Śrī Śānti Sāgar Jī Mahārāj has been accommodated inside a niche inserted between the central pillars on the east side of the court, whilst a standing figure of Mahāvīra has been installed in the covered passage on the opposite side of the yard.

2.1 Permeable Roof Coverings

The simplest kind of covering, which still preserves much of the traditional open courtyard atmosphere, is strong metal netting or a lattice consisting of thin iron bars which has been used to cover the courtyard space from above. The metal meshing still admits light and air to the courts below but converts them into sealed cages. Birds and monkeys, who might be attracted by food offerings and shiny metal objects, are kept out through this method. Similarly, human intruders, intending to remove statues and other precious objects, are prevented from entering the temple compounds from above.[10] Such makeshift coverings, consisting simply of thin metal bars creating a protective grid above the entire open courtyard area, are popular in Sanganer, Ajimganj, Delhi and Allahabad.[11] In addition to a thin metal grid, the Ādinātha Temple at Allahabad has a barrel-vaulted metal frame, suspended above the quadrangle. The frame has been covered with plastic sheeting and creates an improvised roof almost entirely obscuring the large dome positioned above the sanctum of the temple.

2.2 Enclosing Formerly Open Courtyards

The temple at Allahabad with its provisional sun and rain shelter constitutes a simplified version of a much more pervasive form of *havelī* temple, in which the courts have been

---

[10] Image theft is common in India and during my fieldwork I encountered many Jaina temples, which had been robbed of all their precious statues. Particularly targeted are sculptures in metal, which often are solely removed for their material value. Entirely disregarding the spiritual or historic worth of such icons, the figures are molten down and reduced to their primary substance: bronze, brass or gold. This then provides the basic material for new items such as jewellery or for the religious sculptures of other religious groups. The Ādinātha Temple at Dhanupura outside Arrah, for instance, had all its movable statues stolen. In August 1999 those of the neighbouring Bālā Biśrāma Jaina Temple too were all lost in a well-organised temple burglary.

[11] Metal grids covering courtyard spaces are not only found in the region of north and eastern India and they are not exclusively associated with *havelī* type temples. There are other types of temple structures contained in walled courtyards, which have been sealed off from above by protective metal screens. Instances of *maṇḍapa*-line temples in connection with such protective grids from the region are the Ādinātha and the Sumatinātha Temple complexes, both at Ayodhya in Uttar Pradesh. In the latter example, the courtyard area is so spacious and the area to be covered so large, that additional pillars had to be raised inside to support the metal grid from below.

permanently enclosed with solid roof structures. In some cases these have clearly been fitted at a later stage, in others they appear to have been part of the original design scheme of the temples. Although the essential feature of the *havelī* temple, the open courtyard space has been covered in these instances, the previously open design, or at least their architectural antecedents, can still clearly be seen in the architecture. The former courtyard areas usually still lie deeper than the surrounding building elements, and have not been filled with pillars, supporting the roof structure. In order to admit light to these inward looking and enclosed temples, which do not normally have windows inserted into the outer wall of the arcades, roofed *havelī* temples have been provided with a further storey of arches or windows. This has been raised above the arcade on the ground floor and is known as a clerestorey. The inserted band of windows, located below the roof covering the court, admits light sideways to the internal former courtyard spaces (Plate 5). The raised storey of windows also accounts for the very spacious interior of these temples, which without the additional height of the upper storeys, would feel slightly oppressive. In a way such clerestoreys resemble double-storeyed *maṇḍapas*.[12]

A fascinating example, which shows the first stage in the conversion process of a formerly open yard area into a roofed structure, is the Śrī Digambara Jaina Nayā Temple in Old Delhi. In this instance, a raised storey consisting of large windows has been raised above the arcades surrounding the court (Plate 6). The second level consists only of a thin screen of arches adding height to the construction and admitting air. In this case, the temple conversion has not been completed and instead of the concluding solid roof above, the courtyard in its upward extended state remains open and has simply been covered with a metal grid. In the Śrī Digambara Jaina Baṛā Mandir Jī, located in the same locale of Old Delhi, a similar screen of windows has been constructed at a later stage above the arcades surrounding the open quadrangle. In this instance, however, the roof has been completed in the intended way.

[12] Double-storeyed *maṇḍapas* are popular amongst *maṇḍapa*-line temples as well. In this context, however, they take on a different form and are then referred to as *meghanāda-maṇḍapas* (Hegewald 2009a: 236–238).

Despite the band of windows above, the inside of this temple is much darker than in the previous example. Conversions from open to enclosed *havelī* temple arrangements were undertaken throughout the region of northern India. A further occurrence, where the upper storey of windows topped by a flat roof is again later than the original temple construction, is the Ajitanātha Temple at Batesar in Uttar Pradesh.

2.3 Temples with Roofed Courtyards

Unlike the last three cases, which are representative of temples in which the covered courtyard space constitutes a later embellishment, there are even more instances where the upper storey admitting light to the enclosed court as well as the covering roof-structures, were planned from the outset and are part of the original temple design. A good example from Uttar Pradesh is the Neminātha Temple (no. I) at Sauripur, although this kind of temple is especially widespread in Bihar. Representative illustrations from the eastern region are the Pañcāyatī Temple at Arrah[13] and the Vāsupūjyajī Temple at Bhagalpur, both in Bihar.

The Śrī Agravāla Digambara Jaina Temple in New Delhi, started in about 1500, is an unusual roofed *havelī* temple. In this temple, the clerestorey accommodates a raised arcade, which can be reached by worshippers via two staircases. Double-storeyed arcades are only present on three but not on the shrine side of the central covered area. On this face, a tall domed internal space reaches over both floor levels. Light is mainly admitted through a thin band of windows, raised above the second layer of arches below the flat roof of this section of the temple. This has only been supplemented by a few small openings at the rear of the upper arcade. As a result, the interior of this *havelī* temple is relatively dark in comparison to other Jaina constructions of this kind.[14] A similar assembly,

[13] The Pañcāyatī Temple, located on Mahajan Toli No. 2 Gali in Arrah, is a double temple and also its twin, the Nandīśvara-dvīpa Temple, has a clerestorey. In the latter, the raised storey of windows is octagonal in shape. The same is the case in the Nandīśvara-dvīpa Temple in the Digambara Jaina Baṛā Mandir at Hastinapur in Haryana, which has double bands of windows, one positioned above the other.

[14] The covered courtyard of this temple is relatively unusual, as it is in the shape of an elongated rectangle, and not square as usual.

though slightly less clear, as the temple has undergone many restorations and additions, is the Śrī Digambara Jaina Choṭā Mandir in the Chandni Chowk area of Old Delhi. Nevertheless, it is more common of this type of temple to be airy and flooded with light, and for builders to have experimented with increasing sizes and numbers of windows to admit more rather than less light to the temple interiors.

In this context, there is a clear tendency in connection with temples of this group to expand the light shafts of the raised cubical spaces lined by windows, further upwards. This has generally been achieved by extending the wall and window section above the arcade on the ground floor. The straight walls of these raised elements are then easily visible from outside and are reminiscent of temple and domestic house constructions in the Tibetan cultural area of the Himalayas.[15] This can be seen in the Supārśvanātha Temple (no. I), at Badaini, overlooking the Ganges river at Varanasi. This temple is unusual in having coloured panes of glass inserted into the raised storey of windows. The interior walls of the temple have been painted in an intense yellow colour and the glass panes, coloured in various shades of yellow, purple, orange, green, pink and blue, affect the light and atmosphere inside the temple.

In many instances, the additional vertical wall space, which has frequently been gained between the colonnades below and the ring of windows above, has been used to accommodate bands of paintings. The Pārśvanātha Temple (no. I) at Bhelupura in Varanasi, has a narrow strip of pictures below, as well as separate painted panels inserted between individual window frames above. Such paintings usually depict mythological life stories of the Tīrthaṅkaras, cosmological concepts, sacred

[15] Tall clerestoreys are a traditional construction method common in places such as Ladakh, Nepal, Tibet and other regions of the Tibetan cultural area with extreme weather conditions. Domestic houses of the Takali group of traders in the lower Mustang area of Nepal, for example, follow this planning principle. Because of harsh winds and sand storms, the houses have practically no windows integrated into their external walls. Instead, they are lit through a central light shaft, which has been raised above the core section of the house—traditionally probably a courtyard—and which receives light through a raised storey of windows, in the same manner as the roofed Jaina *havelī* temples discussed in this paper.

Jaina sites and pilgrimage maps (*tīrtha-paṭas*).[16] In the Śreyāṃsanātha Temple at Sarnath in Uttar Pradesh, which commemorates the birthplace of the eleventh Jina, the picture panels representing the life of Mahāvīra are almost as high as the windows above and one wonders whether two levels of windows might originally have been planned. An example where two actual bands of windows have been superimposed in the cubical space above the enclosed court is the Pārśvanātha Temple (no. V), which is found in the locality known as Maidagini in Varanasi (Plate 7). Despite the tall upper section with double windows, there still is room for bands of religious verses to surround the courtyard below the window segment. The interior of this temple, which is painted in crisp white, is flooded with light and conveys the feeling of an open yard, filled with sun light.

The advantages of a covered courtyard design are that the inside of the temple is protected against sun, rain, dust and to a certain extent noise. Temples developed in this way can be firmly locked and are as a result easier to protect against the adverse climate, pollution and against unwelcome trespassers.[17] From a ritual point of view, there might also have been a desire to create a sheltered *maṇḍapa*-like space at the front of the large and wide areas accommodating the image chambers, which normally have to fulfil a dual function. The enclosed courtyards allow devotees to conduct various kinds of veneration ceremonies (*pūjā*), which on the whole are not performed inside the main *garbha-gṛha*, in a spacious but sheltered section of the temple.

2.4 Arcades and Halls in Roofed Havelī Temples

In the same way as has been discussed in connection with open courtyard temples there is a certain variation in terms of the depth of the building elements on the shrine side of the

---

[16] For further details on Jaina cosmological art and architecture, and on pilgrimage maps, the Jaina *tīrtha-paṭas*, see Hegewald (2000; 2009b).

[17] Many benefits are associated with covered temple forms, which in the way described here, can still be lit by natural light. Therefore, the underlying principles of an enclosed temple space with bands of windows in the upper temple section have also been applied to other Jaina temple types, such as hall type temples. Similarly, there are modern *maṇḍapa*-line temples where light has been admitted to the *maṇḍapas* through narrow strips of windows positioned above.

covered court. It is generally more typical of roofed *havelī* temples to have only a deep hall and not a further arcade positioned on the most sacred side of the quadrangle. However, there are cases where in addition to this, the common arcade, which at the same time encircles the courtyard on the other three sides, runs along and deepens the face of the court on which the sanctum is to be found. At times only the impression of extra space has been suggested by moving the walled *garbha-gṛha* or image pedestal from the centre of the hall towards the back wall. This creates more room inside and imitates a *maṇḍapa* area in front of the cult statue. Prominent examples of this variation are the Śreyāṃsanātha Temple at Sarnath and the Pañcāyatī Temple at Arrah. The latter temple was constructed in 1824 CE by Śrī Jinendra Varṇī Jī and renovated extensively in 1922. The disadvantage of such spatial compositions is that the sacred icons on their pedestals cannot be circumambulated any longer. A noteworthy illustration of an enclosed *havelī* temple where another *maṇḍapa* has been added between the covered court and the image chamber is the Neminātha Temple (no. I) at Sauripur.

3.0 Multiple Shrines in Courtyard Temple Arrangements

Issues of multiplicity, associated with other types of Jaina temple constructions, play a significant role in *havelī* temples too. However, as the shape and planning logic of this temple type is distinct, ideas of duplication and addition have been expressed in different but clearly related ways. In *maṇḍapa*-line temples, supplements have mainly been made along one straight line, leading towards the principal image chamber, or branching off a central hall in the shape of a three-petalled cloverleaf.[18] Contrasting with this, *havelī* temples are more contained inward looking structures, which have been oriented around an inner courtyard space. This concentric planning scheme demands, or at least favours, more lengthwise or ring-shaped accumulations of sanctums, corridors and further elements, while clearly expressing the same underlying idea of repetition and multiplication.

[18] An exception is the *caturmukha* temple layout, where porches and at times *maṇḍapas* have been added on the four sides of a central *garbha-gṛha*. For a detailed discussion of issues of duplication and multiplication on horizontal and vertical planes, see Hegewald (2001; 2002).

3.1 Tripartite Temple Configurations

The basic layout of the spacious *garbha-gṛhas* of *havelī* type temples is tripartite, as it generally consists of a central open space, corresponding to the width of the courtyard, flanked by two narrower sections, representing the ends of the single or double arcades surrounding the yards. In most cases, the partition between the three elements is kept relatively open and is only indicated by rows of pillars, allowing people to look and wander freely into the side portions. The *mūla-nāyaka* is to be found in the central space, which usually is a higher double-storeyed area. In many instances, the side chambers contain subsidiary religious icons, either simply accommodated in wall niches or in separate image pavilions. In the Supārśvanātha Temple (no. I) at Badaini in Varanasi, an extra pavilion has been erected in the aisle on the right of the principal pavilion, creating a separate sanctum in the northern corner of the temple. A further example is the Śrī Digambara Jaina Nayā Temple, in which a large representation made of stone and decorated with numerous Jina figures, known as a *sahasra-kūṭa*, is housed in an additional chamber to the south. In the latter illustration, this has been delineated by short portions of walls. Whether through pillars or walls, both cases create clear double-shrined Jaina temples of the *havelī* type.

In the Śrī Agravāla Digambara Jaina Temple in New Delhi, the two side chapels flanking the focal *garbha-gṛha*, have again only been separated from the core devotional area by rows of pillars. In this instance, both side chapels house subsidiary religious statues. In other temples, the triple-shrined layout is slightly less open. This can be achieved by constructing a walled sanctum in the middle of the central space of the hall as well as contained image chambers in the side sections. Instances of the latter arrangement are the Vāsupūjyajī Temple at Bhagalpur and the Ajitanātha Temple at Batesar. In these two, it is still possible to perform *pradakṣiṇā* around the *garbha-gṛha* in the middle, and the ambulation path in the latter temple has been decorated with beautiful floral, roughly mid-eighteenth century, wall paintings. In the Pañcāyatī Temple at Arrah though, all three shrines have been moved to the rear wall of the temple and can only be accessed from the front. This creates a joint *maṇḍapa*-like area positioned at the front of the three aligned sanctums. It is common at Allahabad to amplify the separation between the three individual elements even further by having proper walls dividing the three main sacred zones, access to which is then only provided from the front through the arcade surrounding the courtyard. The sacred space inside the Pārśvanātha Temple in the same town has been partitioned in the same way. In this case, one of the lateral rooms does not contain figural images but houses a religious library with religious manuscripts and printed books. Manuscripts are regularly venerated in Jaina temples as sacred objects. In the Baṛī Mandir at Sanganer, two small self-contained cells have been constructed in the corners at the back of the shrine hall. These provide space for additional religious items in a more enclosed environment. A more unusual example of a triple-shrined temple, based on the courtyard style planning principles, is the Śrī Digambara Jaina Choṭā Mandir in Old Delhi. In this case, there is one central *garbha-gṛha*, which contains three image pavilions housing a large number of icons, and a side chapel to the south, whilst the chamber typically accommodating the third image chamber to the north contains a staircase, providing access to the roof. In this temple, a third shrine is located on the side of the quadrangle, to the south of this small but complex building.

3.2 Multiple Sanctums in Havelī Temples

There are various means in which more than three *garbha-gṛhas* can be created in Jaina courtyard temples. At its core, the Pañcāyatī Temple complex in Arrah is a triple-shrined *havelī* temple. This section, however, has been connected with a separate but interconnected temple building, housing a cosmological representation. Together, they create a fourfold temple construction. In the Śrī Digambara Jaina Baṛā Mandir Jī in Delhi, the central sanctum is occupied by the *mūla-nāyaka* of Ādinātha, raised on a tall multi-layered *meru* support. Four additional image chambers diverge from the rear of the wide shrine space, converting the construction into a five-shrined temple layout.[19] Also at Sanganer, the construction of subsidiary small temple niches is prevalent and various structures have what look like rows of minor supplementary shrines (*deva-kulikā*), or at least small delineated cells, positioned along the back of the wide pillared *garbha-gṛha* areas. Whereas the Digambara Jaina Temple at Godikan accommodates an image pavilion in the centre as well as a line of additional shrines along the rear, the temple in the locality of Pataniyan at the same site only has a principal pavilion and no further sanctums. This appears to indicate that even in temples with subsidiary image chambers along the back of the hall, the sculptural representations placed at the centre are considered to be the predominant icons of the temples.

A temple structure, which is quadruple at its centre, is the Pārśvanātha Temple (no. I) at Bhelupura in Varanasi. In this temple there is a double arcade on the south side of the courtyard. Consequently, four aligned *garbha-gṛha*s have been created to the west of the roofed temple court.[20] Because short wall sections protruding from the rear of the temple have been inserted between the four sanctums, these are clearly perceived as separate entities. Nevertheless, one can walk freely sideways from one chamber into another. In this temple even further shrine elements have been accommodated. There are two more chapels, which have been integrated into the corners of the arcade at the opposite side of the covered courtyard space. A seventh cell has been created in the large veranda providing access to the temple building, where a group of three standing Digambara *sādhus* are venerated in a pavilion. Large verandas such as this are not typical of *havelī* type temples. They are, however, remarkably common of temples based on the so-called eastern concentric temple type, which is prevalent of the east of India. The latter temple form

---

[19] Of the additional shrines at the back of the temple, one each is dedicated to Ādinātha and Śāntinātha, and two to Pārśvanātha.

[20] The image chamber to the south houses a statue of Padmāvatī, seated on a pedestal created from the coils of a snake whose multiple heads protect the goddess from behind. The other three cells contain image pavilions with multiple figural representations, all having Pārśvanātha as their main icon. Whereas the pavilion containing the *mūla-nāyaka* can be circumambulated, the flanking two shrines have image pavilions, which have been moved back to the outer wall of the temple and can only be accessed from the front.

seems in many instances to have had a direct influence on courtyard temples, creating fascinating hybrid forms of construction.

Many *havelī* temples have additional sanctums positioned on the opposite side of the often multi-shrined sacred area. These image chambers, usually flanking the entrance to the temple, have been described in connection with the latter temple example at Varanasi. Subsidiary chambers at the front of temple buildings can also be seen in the Śrī Ravaṇḍel Digambara Jaina Temple in New Delhi, where they house the festival chariots (*rathas*) of the temple,[21] and in the Neminātha Temple (no. I) at Sauripur, where they are larger and more elongated in shape than is generally the case. The latter temple has a total of five *garbha-gr̥has* as well as additional statues placed along the back of the *pradakṣiṇā-patha* surrounding the foremost image chamber.

Organised in a less conventional manner are the supplementary cells of the Digambara Meru Temple in Old Delhi. The main sacred chamber of this courtyard temple contains a large and very elaborate representation of Nandīśvara-dvīpa, the eighth island-continent of the Jaina cosmos. A corridor runs around the central shrine on all four sides and enables the worshipper to circumambulate the cosmological structure housed within the cubical sanctum. It is unusual that a door, located behind the focal *garbha-gr̥ha*, provides access to a further space from which two side chapels, one dedicated to Pārśvanātha and the other to Ādinātha, branch off. Consequently, this temple displays an axial alignment of shrines more than is routinely the case in a *havelī* temple. This, however, is counteracted by the addition of an extra image chamber, dedicated to Śāntinātha, which has been integrated into the side arcade on the south, and a religious library, which takes up the entire arcade on the west. A relatively rare temple with two open courtyards, which have been positioned side by side, is the Pārśvanātha Temple at Allahabad. A noteworthy *havelī* temple with an open and an enclosed court is the Vāsupūjya Bhagavāna Temple, located at the foot of Cūla-

---

[21] Whereas the festival chariot located in the storage room on the west is shaped like a miniature temple with a *śikhara* roof form, the *ratha* kept in the eastern chamber has been modelled in the shape of an elephant.

giri at Khaniyan near Jaipur. The roofed quadrangle area is double-storeyed and in this instance has been provided with a raised gallery.

3.3 Double Courtyard Temples

The discussion above has shown that triple and multi-shrined temple constellations are characteristic of Jaina *havelī* type temple constructions. In a way, the arrangement of a central courtyard surrounded by pillared arcades with a main *garbhagṛha* on one side lends itself particularly well to the creation of unlimited numbers of cells. These can be added at any time in the development of a temple, without actually having to construct a new structure next to a previously existing temple building. Already constructed arcades can simply be converted into additional sacred spaces by inserting walls or by merely placing an image pavilion in a temple section delineated by rows of pillars. Accordingly, multi-shrined temple constellations on a horizontal level are even more common in connection with *havelī* temples than they are with the *maṇḍapa*-line type.

Courtyard temples have often been constructed close to one another, as may be seen in the three Jaina temples located in the same narrow alleyway off Zero Street in Allahabad. Nevertheless, it is not typical to have additional free-standing small temples positioned inside the open courts of *havelī* complexes. Nonetheless, further religious icons are regularly housed in shallow niches integrated into the pillars or short wall segments associated with the arcades, or within the deep corridors surrounding the quadrangles themselves.

Despite this tendency towards manifold multiplications inside the temple structures themselves, there are double courtyard temples too. A straightforward example, where two *havelī* temples lying parallel to one another have been merged to create a double courtyard temple, is the Digambara Jaina Mandir Ṭoliyān in Sanganer. The eastern temple half is intriguing as it has three *śikhara*s positioned in one line above the multiple sculptures housed in small cells running along the rear of the spacious pillared shrine. A second twin temple at Adai Pedi is unusual by combining a *havelī* temple with a section, which follows the layout of a *maṇḍapa*-line temple. In addition to illustrating the horizontal duplication of *garbhagṛhas*, the temple further demonstrates the vertical supposition of image chambers. Below the courtyard temple sector of this double temple building is a subterranean sanctum constructed in the ground. The plain chamber houses three main Jina statues and has side niches accommodating minor religious representations.[22]

3.4 Superimposed Shrines in Havelī Temples

The last temple case has illustrated that additional *garbhagṛhas*, or more versatile spaces, can be superimposed on various vertical levels in courtyard constructions too. Subterranean image chambers are less popular with *havelī* type temples, but they do exist and are often more complex than those associated with other temple types. It is significant that although most lower sanctums in Jaina temples are found only one storey below ground level, the courtyard temple dedicated to Ajitanātha at Batesar has been provided with two underground areas, which both consist of two superimposed lower floor levels. The majority of these underground apartments are used as cool and comfortable spaces to accommodate travelling *munis*.[23] However, also image chambers have been integrated into the subterranean storeys at Batesar. Whilst the lower wall portions of these underground shrines have later been white-washed and are now unadorned, the upper sections and ceilings of these cavernous sacred places display wall paintings of outstanding quality, dating from about the mid-eighteenth century.

As with Jaina temples following different types of layout, it is common of *havelī* temples to be raised on high terraces or even to have been constructed above the ground floor level of

---

[22] There are further examples where *havelī* temples have been constructed very close to one another, although they have not been merged or interconnected to create a single unity. See, for instance, the two parallel-lying courtyard temples at the foot of Cūlagiri at Khaniyan near Jaipur.

[23] Subterranean rooms for the accommodation of Digambara ascetics can be seen at other sites too. The lower floor levels of the Sonagiri village temple in Madhya Pradesh are still used to house wandering ascetics. But also in connection with different temple types, rooms for monks and nuns as well as for lay pilgrims have been integrated into spaces positioned below temple buildings. In the Candraprabhu Temple (no. II) at Candrapuri, belonging to the *maṇḍapa* -line temple type, *dharmaśālā* rooms have been integrated into the terrace on which the temple has been raised.

a building. These lower levels have regularly been occupied by temple offices or are used as spaces for a variety of community activities, such as the accommodation of pilgrims or storage. Consequently, the yards are not always—as one would normally expect—located on the natural ground and many have been raised one level above the ground. The sensation created when climbing through a dark narrow staircase and then stepping out into a spacious open courtyard flooded with light and fresh air on the first floor of such Jaina temples, is similar to the astonishment felt upon reaching the Amar Vilas garden with its central water basin surrounded by trees, located on the fourth level of the City Palace at Udaipur.[24] This kind of double-storeyed arrangement is especially prevalent amongst *havelī* temples in the bazaar quarter of Old Delhi where the Śrī Digambra Jaina Nayā Temple and the Śrī Digambara Jaina Baṛā Mandir, one having an open and the other a roofed courtyard, are helpful examples. Double-storeyed *havelī* temples are equally typical of many towns in Uttar Pradesh, where the Śāntinātha Temple in Faizabad and the Cintāmaṇī Pārśvanātha Temple at Roshan Mohalla in Agra follow this construction principle. Even though they are particularly common in urban areas, the Neminātha Temple (no. I) at Sauripur, located in a garden in the countryside, indicates that there are no rules without exceptions and illustrates the creative variety enriching South Asian architecture in general.

The previous cases have demonstrated the predominant usage of one storey for additional practical functions, such as storage and offices, in combination with an upper level constituting a sacred area. The Digambara Meru Temple, a *havelī* temple in Old Delhi, is striking in that it clearly has two superimposed sanctums. Despite the fact that the shrine on the ground floor is not presently employed for worship, it has not been used for any other purpose. This might be due to the fact that it is still regarded as a sanctified space. Located exactly above the *garbha-gṛha* on the ground level, is the main

[24] The City Palace at Udaipur has been constructed around a steep natural rock and the raised garden is situated on the summit of this entirely enclosed and covered internal hill. See the architectural drawings by Tillotson (1987: 106). The quadrangles of the Jaina temples in Delhi, however, are located above artificially created architectural structures.

first floor Nandīśvara-dvīpa chapel. This expresses very well the enormous flexibility associated with Jaina temple constructions. Whilst supplementary image chambers can be added on further floor levels, other cells may temporarily fall into disuse. However, these can easily be re-established at a later stage, should more room be needed to accommodate sculptures or more abstract representations. This indicates a further familiar feature associated with multi-storeyed Jaina temples more generally, namely that statues on levels other than the ground floor are regularly treated with more reverence and frequently represent the key icons of a temple. Besides, the Digambara Jaina Temple at Pavapuri, which in its present form dates mainly from a reconstruction campaign in 1915, has a large number of *garbha-gṛhas* on a raised level. There is one image chamber on the ground floor, one exactly above it and three separate sanctums located above the arcade along the front of the courtyard. The latter are positioned opposite the two superimposed central shrines.[25]

Similarly, the Vāsupūjyajī Temple at Bhagalpur has a subsidiary chamber on the first floor level. Yet in this instance, the raised *garbha-gṛha* is not situated exactly above the principal sacred figure beneath, but has been raised above one of the two lateral cells on the ground floor. The upper shrine houses a *samavasaraṇa* representation incorporating a fourfold statue (*caturmukha*) of Vāsupūjyajī. Because of ongoing building work in the temple in 1999 and 2000, enlarging the temple structure, further image chambers might have been added in the meantime. Later supplements of sanctums are remarkably common in connection with Jaina temples and are often anticipated long in advance but only implemented at a later stage, when sufficient funds have been raised. In the Śrī Digambara Jaina Choṭā Mandir in Old Delhi access from the outset has been provided to the roof level. According to the priests and local worshippers at the temple, it has been planned to construct a roof temple in the future. This seems to have been the case in the Ajitanātha Temple at Batesar too,

[25] All five chambers in this temple contain icons of Mahāvīra. The particular connection of this Jina with Pavapuri is explained by the fact that Mahāvīra is believed to have reached enlightenment, preached his first sermon and died there.

where a door provides access to a small shrine integrated into the *śikhara* tower on the roof of the temple.

4.0 Sources and Continuities

Havelī temples are clearly related to and appear to reflect earlier forms of building from a domestic and non-Jaina religious context. Interestingly, however, they have also influenced subsequent architectural developments, predominantly in a Jaina religious context.

4.1 Domestic Houses and Mosques

In their basic spatial layout, courtyard temples are closely related to domestic houses constructed in the *havelī* style. Traditional north Indian houses have been arranged around a central courtyard and consequently follow a very similar design and ground plan pattern.[26] Most courtyard-house temples in the north of India are situated in urban areas, where they blend well into residential neighbourhoods. Many of these inner-city Jaina religious establishments are only identifiable through name boards or the display of religious symbols, such as swastikas or the hourglass-shaped representation of the Jaina cosmos, usually found close to the entrance gates. Other *havelī* temples have prominent gateway structures and elaborate protruding *jharokā* windows, indicating more directly the heightened status and the religious significance of the structure, as is the case in the Digambara Jaina Meru Temple in the Chandni Chowk region of Delhi.

Furthermore, *havelī* temples are reminiscent of South Asian mosques, which follow an open courtyard design surrounded by cloisters with a deep-pillared prayer hall (*līwān*) positioned to the west.[27] This is not surprising, as the prototype of the mosque as a type is supposed to have been the Prophet's own

---

[26] For details on traditional houses in the *havelī* style, see, for example, Tillotson (1994) and Pramar (1989).

[27] It is noteworthy that the shrines of Jaina temples and of Islamic mosques are both found on the west side of the open courtyard areas. The underlying logic, however, is different. In Jaina temples, image chambers are positioned on the west side in order to enable the main statue of the Jina housed inside the sanctum to face east, the auspicious direction of the rising sun. Muslims place their prayer halls in South Asia on the west side of mosque courtyards in order for worshippers to face the western *qiblā* pointing towards Mecca during prayer.

house in Medina, which is believed to have surrounded an open courtyard space.[28] Other design features, such as the frequent use of cusped arches, prominent domes, corner *chatrī* crenulations, glazed tiles, inscription bands and a lack of figural imagery contribute equally to a distinctly Islamic undertone in many Jaina *havelī* temples.[29]

On the other hand, the enclosed and inward-looking Jaina courtyard temples clearly express a typical Jaina approach to sacred architecture. This issue too, must have provided a strong impetus for the construction of temples based on this spatial layout and provided an important reason for the popularity of this temple type with the Jaina community in India. *Havelī* temples, which usually have no outer windows, are entirely shielded off from ordinary life. Light is only admitted to the temple structures from above, either through an internal open court or the protruding clerestoreys. The secluded quadrangles with their surrounding pillared arcades and the common use of white marble (or white washed facades), convey an atmosphere of purity, serenity and detachment from the ordinary world, which is representative of Jaina religious ideology and earlier temple building traditions of this faith. So far, art-historical writings have associated these characteristic features exclusively with temple compounds created by lines of interlinked *deva-kulikā* chains found most frequently in the north-western region of the subcontinent.[30] The discussion in this paper, however, has illustrated that the same issues are just as well-expressed in these later Jaina temple constructions, which so far have received little scholarly attention.[31]

---

[28] For a detailed discussion of the connection between courtyard-houses, mosques and gardens, see Bianca (1991).

[29] The issue of Islamic influences on Jaina temple architecture more generally has been discussed in Hegewald (2007b).

[30] Secluded courtyard designs have so far almost exclusively been associated with the Solaṅkī dynasty and their prominent style of building of the tenth to thirteenth centuries.

[31] A rare exception of an article, focussing on the political and social implications of *havelī* temples in Old Delhi and Jaipur, has been published by Asher (2003).

4.2 Modern Continuity and Influence on Other Temple Types

Havelī type temples are particularly common during the period lasting from the fifteenth to the nineteenth centuries, but there are also modern structures relating to this type. These are not always straightforward *havelī* temples. Many present a fusion of this and another temple type and generally are more eclectic. The Śāntinātha Digambra Temple at Shanti Vir Nagar, which was constructed in the twentieth century, has an elongated courtyard with arcades lining its two long side walls. At the end of the open court is a tall hall, accommodating a standing statue of the sixteenth Jaina Tīrthaṅkara, Śāntinātha. In this modern example, the icon has not been positioned at the centre of the large shrine area but is resting against the back wall. This location prevents the circumambulation of the monumental sculpture, an issue which has been so important in earlier constructions of this kind. This contemporary temple is equally remarkable for having three *śikhara* roof towers aligned above the elongated *garbha-gṛha.* Contrasting with earlier temples in which the presence of multiple roof components used to point towards the presence of numerous venerated figures below, this is not the case in the present construction. The sanctum is still entered through three arches but only the middle space has been occupied by a single large standing statue. Perhaps, further sculptures will be added in the future. In the present form, however, the underlying logic for such manifold roof towers has somewhat been lost and the feature of three aligned *śikharas* is used more as a decorative motif or a design element, removed from its original context and meaning. This is not unusual in the development of building forms and can also be observed with other architectural motives.[32] A very similar Jaina temple edifice was under construction at Bijolia in 1995.

Due to the widespread nature and the obvious popularity of the *havelī* temple type, which is well-adapted to practical and

---

[32] Small pavilions or *chatrīs*, which initially were designed to house figural depictions or other sacred representations, for instance, were later in their development frequently considerably reduced in size. The later forms do not usually contain statues. They are often used as roof elements for a variety of architectural constructions in a number of different architectural milieu, religious, domestic, palace, defence or in a water context.

Jaina ritual needs, temples of this kind had a major impact on other Jaina temple types throughout the region. In this context, there are temples designed on the *maṇḍapa*-line principle, which have courtyards added in front. These create hybrid constructions, which combine aspects from both temple types. Especially interesting are combinations, where features of *havelī* and centralised eastern temple types have been fused. At first this might seem like a contradiction in itself. Courtyard temples are entirely enclosed and inward looking, whereas centralised eastern temples are on their exterior open, extroverted constructions with multiple openings on all four sides. Furthermore, eastern temples have a compact centre in the form of a focal *garbha-gṛha*, surrounded by concentric layers of arcades, whilst courtyard temples have been arranged around a hollow yard. Nevertheless, combinations between these two popular types are relatively common in northern and eastern India. Amongst the clearest illustrations of this kind of hybrid is the Śreyāṃsanātha Temple at Sarnath. The central element of the temple follows the *havelī* temple layout with a roofed court surrounded by a single arcade and a wide open shrine area to the west. On the outside, however, an open pillared arcade has been added which encircles the temple on all four sides, creating a second circumambulation path surrounding the entire temple. Even more unusual for courtyard temples than the surrounding open corridor, is the fact that there are five entrances, providing access to the interior of the temple, have been integrated into each of the sides only omitting the shrine side, that is, the rear of the temple. This clearly breaks up the introverted nature of the *havelī* temple core. Straightforward courtyard temples are usually entered through one or a maximum of two doorways. Although the openings in the Śreyāṃsanātha Temple have been provided with doors, which remain shut on most days, it expresses a clear combination of two distinct approaches to temple planning, one inward looking and one extroverted. An example where a veranda has only been added at the front of a temple, but where again five doors open the sides of the closed exterior of a *havelī* type temple, is the Pārśvanātha Temple (no. V) at Maidagini in Varanasi. In its present form, the temple dates mainly from the 1930s. In the same town, in the locality known as Bhelupura, a similar constellation can be observed in the Pārśvanātha Temple (no. I). The latter temple has a large veranda with three doorways and a further six doors integrated into the outer sides of its central courtyard temple section.

Conclusion

The material presented in this paper has illustrated that Jaina courtyard temples from about the fifteenth to nineteenth centuries are highly complex structures. *Havelī* temples in northern India display a development from small and simple temple buildings to complex multi-storeyed and roofed constructions. The spatial layout of the temples makes reference to indigenous domestic house traditions in the *havelī* style, but appears to be related to Islamic forms of construction as well, which formed a popular source of inspiration during the peak of popularity of this building type. Due to the widespread nature and the obvious popularity of this type, which is well-adapted to practical and Jaina ritual needs, temples of this kind had a major impact on other Jaina temple types and on modern constructions throughout the region.

Plate 1: View into the open courtyard of the *havelī* temple in the compound of the Bhāṇḍāsar Jaina Temple at Bikaner, Rajasthan.

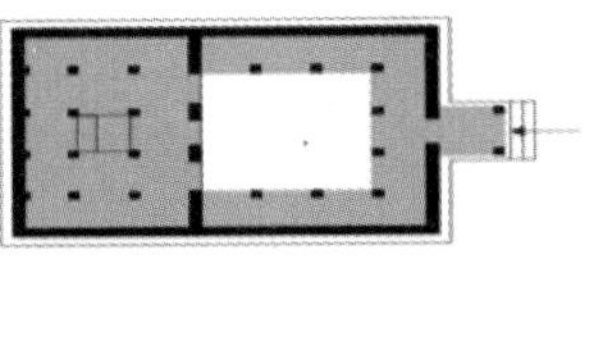

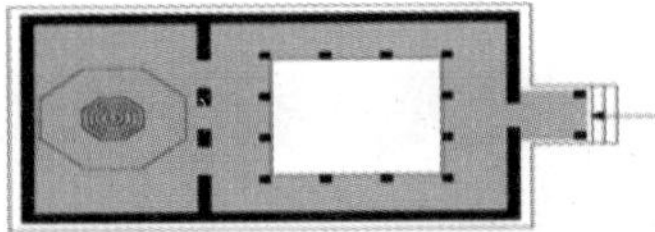

Plate 2: Jaina courtyard temples with an interrupted and continuous arcade surrounding the open quadrangle.

Plate 3: A prominent dome marks the side of the shrine in a Digambara *havelī* temple in Sanganer, Rajasthan.

Plate 4: In the Cantāmana Pārśvanātha Temple at Ajimganj, West Bengal, a subsidiary sanctum has been integrated into the colonnade.

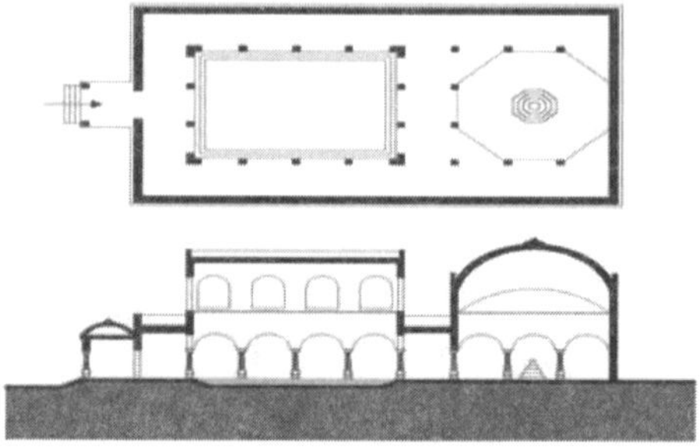

Plate 5: Plan and section of a covered courtyard temple design with a raised storey of windows below the roof.

Plate 6: The Śrī Digambara Jaina Nayā Temple in Old Delhi illustrates an incomplete conversion process from an open to a roofed *havelī* temple form.

Plate 7: Two bands of windows have been superimposed inside the clerestorey of the Pārśvanātha Temple in Maidagini in Varanasi, Uttar Pradesh.

Bibliography

Asher, Catherine B., 2003, "Hidden Gold: Jain Temples of Delhi and Jaipur and their Urban Context." In: *Jainism and Early Buddhism: Essays in Honor of Padmanabh S. Jaini*, 2 volumes. Fremont, California: Asian Humanities Press, part II, pp. 359–377.

Bianca, Stefano, 1991, *Hofhaus und Paradiesgarten: Architektur und Lebensform in der islamischen Welt.* München: Verlag C. H. Beck.

Hegewald, Julia A.B., 2000, "Oceans, Islands and Sacred Mountains: Representations of Cosmic Geography in Jaina Art and Architecture." *COSMOS: The Journal of the Traditional Cosmology Society.* No. 16, pp. 3–42.

——— 2001, "Multi-shrined Complexes: The Ordering of Space. Jaina Temple Architecture in North-Western India." *South Asian Studies.* Vol. 17, pp. 77–96.

——— 2002, "Aspects of Jaina Temple Architecture in Rajasthan and Gujarat." *South Asia Research.* Vol. 22, no. 2, pp. 107–122.

——— 2005, "Representations of the Jina's Birth and Enlightenment in Jaina Art, Architecture and Ritual". In: U. Franke-Vogt & J. Weisshaar (eds), *South Asian Archaeology 2003.* Aachen: Forschung zur Archäologie Außereuropäischer Kulturen Vol. 1 (DAI), pp. 491–499.

——— 2007a, "Meru, Samavasaraṇa and Siṁhāsana: The recurrence of three-tiered structures in Jaina cosmology, mythology and ritual." In: Gourishwar Bhattacharya, Gerd Mevissen Mallar Mitra & Sutapa Sinha (eds), *Kalhār (White Water-Lily) .Studies in Art, Iconography, Architecture and Archaeology of India and Bangladesh (Professor Enamul Haque Felicitation Volume).* Delhi: Kaveri Books, pp. 132-146 and plates: 17.1-20.

——— 2007b, "Domes, Tombs and Minarets: Islamic Influences on Jaina Architecture." In: Adam Hardy (ed.), *The Temple in South Asia.* Volume 2 of the proceedings of the 18th conference of the European Association of South Asian Archaeologists, London 2005. British Association for South Asian Studies and the British Academy, London, pp. 179-190.

——— 2009a, *Jaina Temple Architecture in India: The Development of a Distinct Language in Space and Ritual.* Monographien zur indischen Archäologie, Kunst und Philologie, Band 19, Berlin: Herausgeber Stiftung Ernst Waldschmidt, G+H-Verlag.

——— 2009b "Jala Mandirs, Tīrtha Paṭas and Cosmic Islands: Creating, Replicating and Representing Landscape in Jaina Art and Architecture." In: Gerd J. R. Mevissen & Arundhati Banerji (eds), *Prajñādhara: Essays on Asian Art History, Epigraphy and Culture in Honour of Gouriswar Bhattacharya.* New Delhi: Kaveri Books, pp. 422-437 and plates 43.1-43.20.

Pramar, V. S., 1989, *Haveli: Wooden Houses and Mansions of Gujarat.* Ahmedabad: Mapin Publishing.

Tillotson, Giles H. R., 1987, *The Rajput Palaces: The Development of an Architectural Style, 1450 - 1750.* New Haven and London: Yale University Press.

Tillotson, Sarah, 1994, *Indian Mansions: A Social History of the Haveli.* Cambridge: The Oleander Press.

Acknowledgement

I thank the Deutsche Forschungsgemeinschaft (DFG) for generously funding my research on Jaina temple architecture in India through their Emmy Noether Programme since 2002.

Interpreting New Literary Forms in Jain Medieval Literature: the *Vibudhānanda* Play in Śīlāṅka's Novel *Cauppaṇṇamahāpurisacariya*

Christine Chojnacki and Basile Leclère

Abstract

This paper concentrates on the play *Vibudhānanda*, which is integrated into Śīlāṅka's ninth-century novel, the *Caupaṇṇamahā-purisacariya*. The novel itself narrates the lives of the fifty-four Jain great men (viz. the twenty-four Tīrthaṅkaras, the twelve Cakravartins, the nine Vāsudevas and the nine Bālarāmas). It is first and foremost known as one of the oldest specimens of the Jain universal history. The *Vibudhānanda* play entails the story of Mahābala, the first Tīrthaṅkara Ṛṣabha in a previous life. In order to induce his master to become a Jain monk, Mahābala's minister Vimalamati stages in front of him a play ending in the death of the hero and the heroine. Disgusted with mundane life, Mahābala takes religious initiation. Thus, the *Vibudhānanda* has a decisive influence on the spiritual progress of the soul of Ṛṣabha, and is well integrated in the story as a whole. Nevertheless, it remains structurally distinct from the rest of the novel, as it consists mainly in dialogues between the characters, with few stage directions, thereby contrasting it with the surrounding narration. The play in the novel raises several interesting questions which will be dealt with here, for example: What kind of interaction between dramas and narratives in Jain literature does it denote? Can we deduce evidence from the *Vibudhānanda* play that a novel like the *Caupaṇṇamahāpurisacariya* was intended for oral recitation, and that the storyteller could introduce in it the performance of a short play, either helped by a troop of actors, or by assuming himself the different roles?

Keywords: Medieval Jain literature, *Caupaṇṇamahāpurisacariya*, *Vibudhānanda*, Jain universal history, Indian drama and narrative

Introduction

In early Jainism, all kinds of entertainments were condemned, insofar as they can provoke in the soul of a human being the rise of passions in their most destructive forms and thus prevent the person from following the path of the dharma which leads towards liberation. The discredit brought upon popular forms of entertainment is clearly expressed, for instance in the following instructions given in the *Āyāraṃga-*

sutta, one of the oldest Jain canonical texts dealing primarily with the conduct of the monks:[1]

> A monk should not resolve to go to places where story-tellers or acrobats perform, or where continuously story-telling, dramatic plays, singing, music, performances on the *vīṇā*, beating of time, playing on the *tūrya*, clever playing on the *paṭaha* is going on.[2]

Such an interdiction formulated by this authoritative text may have imposed a long-lasting scorn for entertainments extending, as far as we know, until the sixth century. Thus, even when Haribhadra approved of the recourse to music, singing as well as theatre in his doctrinal treatise, the *Pañcāśaka*[3], he did it reluctantly by expressly limiting them to a religious usage and permitting them only in the context of religious processions (*yātrā*):

> In this case music and singing are suitable, if they are charming with the speeches of suitable people, if they have for subject the Jinas' qualities, if they provoke the awakening to true religion and if they are deprived of mockeries.[4] Even shows like dramatic performances are suitable in this case and consist in religious dramas.[5]

Yet this authorisation, which softens the canonical injunction, shows how gradually, and probably on the model of the

---

[1] The *Āyāraṃgasutta* dates approximately from the 2nd c. BC: cf. Jacobi 1884, pp. xxxix–ilvii; Kapadia 2000 ([1]1941), pp. 105, 143; Dundas 2002, p. 23.

[2] *se bhikkū vā 2 jāva suṇeti taṃ jahā akkhāiya-ṭṭhāṇāṇi vā māṇummāṇiya-ṭṭhāṇāṇi vā mahayāhaya-naṭṭa-gīta-vāiya-taṃti-tala-tāla-turiya-paḍuppa-vāiya-ṭṭhāṇāṇi vā aṇṇatarāiṃ vā taha-ppagārāiṃ saddāiṃ ṇo abhisaṃdhārejjā gamaṇāe |* (*Āyāraṃgasutta*, II.11.14, transl. Jacobi 1884, p. 184; cf. Lévi 1963, p. 324).

[3] According to many scholars, the author of this treatise on doctrine, Haribhadra Virahāṅka, is to be distinguished from Uddyotana's master, who lived in the 8th c. (Williams 1963, pp. 4–7; Dundas 2002, p. 133).

[4] *uciyam iha gīyavāiyam uciyāṇa vayāiehiṃ jaṃ rammaṃ | jiṇa-guṇa-visayaṃ sad-dhamma-buddhi-jaṇagaṃ aṇuvahāsaṃ ||* (Haribhadra, *Pañcāśaka*, IX. 9)

[5] *pecchaṇagāvi ṇaḍādī dhammiya-ṇāḍaya-juo ihaṃ uciyā |* (Haribhadra, *Pañcāśaka*, IX. 11). The Prakrit word *ṇaḍa*, which according to the editor has *naṭa* as Sanskrit equivalent, does not mean in this context "actor", as usual, but rather "dramatic performance".

Buddhists,[6] the Jain monks became acquainted with the idea of using pleasant devices to attract people towards their dharma. Indeed, three Jain novels written in the following centuries are testimony to this evolution, since their authors, namely Dharmasenagaṇi, Haribhadra and Uddyotana resorted to the *kāvya* style and themes in order to raise the interest of their audience for religious matters. Yet such a way of writing appears to have remained highly controversial even in these times, since each of the three monks felt the need to justify it in a prefatory manifesto[7].

Among the three monks, Uddyotana (eighth century) was certainly the most audacious author in the form as well as in

---

[6] Though subject to similar canonical interdicts, the Buddhists did indulge in composing *kāvyas* and plays in order to enlighten people as early as the first to second centuries AD (Lévi 1963, p. 319). Their intention to encourage their audience on the path of Buddhism is clearly shown by the final verses of Aśvaghosa's *Saundarānanda* as well as by the lexical and structural devices consciously used by this Buddhist monk (cf. Salomon 2009, pp. 179–196; Covill 2009). Now, the acquaintance of Jain monks with the works of their Buddhist predecessors has been demonstrated. For instance, the plot of Aśvaghoṣa's *Rāṣṭrapālanāṭaka* has been taken up in a Jain legend which is evoked in the *Piṇḍanijjuti* and developed much later (*c.* 12th c.: Kapadia 2000 ([1]1941), p. 180) in Malayagiri's commentary (Bhayani 1995–1996, pp. 51–54; Bansat-Boudon 2007, pp. 40–41). Besides, the Buddhist philosopher Dharmakīrti (7th c.) alludes to this play in the *Vādyanyāya* (Steiner 1997, pp. 102–107; Bansat-Boudon 2007, pp. 46–48). Now, since the Jains knew this treatise, they must have also known the play it alluded to.

[7] Such prologues are to be found in Dharmasenagaṇi's *Vasudevahindimajjhimakhaṇḍa* (7th c.) and Haribhadra's *Samarāicchakahā* (8th c.); for an analysis, cf. Chojnacki 2008, pp. 31–42. There is also an introduction called *kahāpīḍha* in Śīlāṅka's *Cauppaṇṇamahāpurisacariya* (9th c.), and, though he wrote his *Upamitibhavaprapañcakathā* in Sanskrit, Siddharṣi was influenced in this respect by the tradition of Prakrit novels (cf. Warder 1988, §3124, 4127; Chojnacki 2008, p. 32). Apart form their prefatory manifesto, novels contain internal pieces of evidence about the still lasting discredit on entertainments: indeed, several stories show how negative the addiction to any pastime can be. Thus, in Uddyotana's *Kuvalayamālā*, the sight of a beautifully painted portrait provokes the absentmindedness of prince Kāmagajendra, who can think about nothing else but his union with the princess. In another story, prince Vajragupta, after entering an underground palace inhabited by courtesans, is seduced by them with all kinds of dances and songs, so that he even forgets for a while his duty and his kingdom.

the content of his *Kuvalayamālā*.[8] As regards the content, he did not hesitate either to develop at length the manifestations of love or to introduce various kinds of entertainments in order to win back to Jainism an audience seduced by the virtuosity of Hindu poetic compositions such as Bāṇa's *Kādambarī*. As regards the form, Uddyotana created for his novel a plot even more complex than the intricate story for which Bāṇa's work is famous. Moreover, the author of the *Kuvalayamālā* also took full advantage of the literary potentialities of Prakrit. Lastly, he was one of the earliest authors to write his novel in a mixed form of prose and verse and to give us a specimen of the *campū* genre.[9] If his audacity surely irritated the representatives of more orthodox trends of Jainism, he was nonetheless undoubtedly admired for his literary skills and his work inspired Jain authors at least until the twelfth century. Śīlāṅka, who was one of Uddyotana's close successors in the ninth century, did not only take over the form of a *campū* to write the *Cauppaṇṇamahāpurisacariya*, the *History of the Fifty Four Great Men*, in a refined Prakrit,[10] the but he also included many of Uddyotana's themes and stylistic manners.

---

[8] Even if he includes *kāvya* themes, Haribhadra does not go so far as to recognise this influence and still declares that his novel called *Samarāicca-kahā* is a *dharmakathā*, aiming at religion only. On the contrary, Dharmasena-gaṇi says in the *Vasudevahindimajjhimakhaṇḍa* that he will use *kāvya* themes and to this end he takes up a well-known metaphor already used by his Buddhist predecessor Aśvaghoṣa, that the use of love matters in his novel is comparable to the use of sugar to help a sick patient to take his medicine (cf. *Vasudevahiṇḍimajjhimakhaṃḍa* 2.2–8: *kahāo kāmiyāo logo egaṃteṇaṃ kāma-kahāsu rajjati soggai-paha-desiyaṃ puṇa dhammaṃ souṃ pi ṇecchai ya jara-pitta-vasa-kaṃḍuiya-muho iva gula-sakkara-khaṃḍa-macchaṃḍiyāīsu viparīta-pariṇā-mo / dhamm'attha-kāma-kaliyāṇi ya suhāṇi dhamm'attha-kāmāṇa ya mūlaṃ dhammo tammi ya maṃda(dā)taro jaṇo taṃ jaha ṇāma koi vejjo āuraṃ amaosaha-pāṇa-parammuhaṃ osaḍham iti uvvita(?taṃ)-maṇo'bhilasiya-pāṇa-vavaeseṇa osa-haṃ ce[va] pajjeti kāma-kahā-ratta-hitayassa jaṇassa siṃgāra-kahā-vavaeseṇa dhammaṃ ceva parikahemi.*

[9] As defined by Daṇḍin I.31 *gadyapadyamayī*: cf. Chojnacki 2008, pp. 155–174.

[10] "Śīlāṅka's work also contains some of the stylistic features mentioned by Uddyotana in his description of a mixed novel. [...] There is nothing cramped about Śīlāṅka's style, which is spacious and full and thus readable" (Warder 1988, §3126, 3129). For instance, in the first verses of the story of Ṛṣabha's previous lives, wherein is described the city of Aparājitā, there is a

Furthermore, he seems to have been gifted with an equal originality, as he went so far as to be the first novelist to include in his work the whole text of a play which he entitled the *Vibudhānanda* (*Joy for the Learned*). Thus, Śīlāṅka also appears to be the earliest Jain dramatist known to us, since the other extant Jain plays were composed in the twelfth century, at the earliest.[11] Consequently. an enquiry into the theme as well as the genre of his drama may help us to consider whether his contribution as a Jain author to Indian theatre was an original one. Besides, the pioneering insertion of the *Vibudhānanda* in the *Cauppaṇṇamahāpurisacariya* raises an aesthetic problem since the simultaneous presence of two genres could represent a threat to the coherence of the work as a whole. The analysis of these questions will further lead us to tackle two broader issues: the first is why would a Jain author want to make use of theatre and the second is what does such a novel including a play tell us about the reception of these long narrative texts in the medieval times?

Interaction between Dramas and Narratives

At first sight, the *Vibudhānanda* is endowed with all the features that distinguish Indian theatre from narrative genres. Firstly, Śīlāṅka's play consists mainly in dialogues which are introduced by the bare name of the characters and interspersed with a few other stage directions.[12] Secondly, as every

---

śṛṅkhalayamaka, a poetical ornament frequent in Prakrit novels (cf. Chojnacki 2008, pp. 112–113).

[11] The Jains might have composed *dharmikanāṭaka* at least from the 6th c. onwards, as suggested by the *Pañcāśaka*. In all likelihood, these dramas dealt mainly with the same topics as the songs mentioned by Haribhadra in the same chapter of his treatise, that is to say the edifying lives of the Jinas and of the people converted to Jain faith by them (cf. above nn. 4 and 5).

[12] These stage directions indicate most of the time how the actors must move on stage or utter their parts. The most characteristic ones refer to dramatic conventions (*nāṭyadharmī*), such as walking around the stage in order to indicate that the action has shifted from one place to another, or speaking aside (cf. Bansat-Boudon 1992, pp. 138–145, 160). For instance, the chamberlain speaks to himself (*ātmagatam* CMPC 18. 30) before addressing aloud to the jester, and Bandhumatī addresses Candralekhā aside (*apavārya* CMPC 24. 23). Elsewhere "all the characters walk about the stage" (*sarve 'pi*

play does, the *Vibudhānanda* has a mixture of passages in prose and verse, and thirdly, while the author of a novel chooses between Sanskrit or Prakrit, here again, Śīlāṅka follows the pattern of Indian theatre and assigns different languages to the characters according to their sex and condition: as is well-known, men of high rank, such as the stage-manager in the prologue, the chamberlain, the prince and the king in the play, speak Sanskrit; and the jester and all the women, such as the actress in the prologue, the princess, the queen, the maids in the play, speak Prakrit.[13]

However, in spite of these distinctive features, the play is not so different from the surrounding novel, because of the new stylistic devices Śīlāṅka deftly integrated in his *Caupaṇṇa-mahāpurisacariya*. Firstly, following Uddyotana's model and adopting the form of the *campū*, Śīlāṅka alternates between prose and verse not only in the *Vibudhānanda*, but also in the whole text of the *Cauppaṇṇamahāpurisacariya*. He did not stop there, but took care to use in his play verses which would not clash with the verses of the rest of the novel in which the *āryā* metre predominates, as is usually found in the case of Jain narrative literature. Interestingly enough, 21 of a total of 40 verses of the *Vibudhānanda* are in the *āryā* metre (7 in Prakrit[14] and 14 in Sanskrit[15]); the other most important metre being the *śārdūlavikrīdita* with 11 occurrences (roughly a quarter).[16] Thus, the *āryā* metre is by far the most dominant metre, representing about half the number of the versified sections of the work. If such a proportion is really unusual in theatre,[17] it

---

parikrāmyanti CMPC 22. 22), when the chamberlain leads the prince to the upper floor of the painting hall.

[13] As regards the inner structure of the play, cf. below and Warder 1988, §3149.

[14] VĀ I. 15, 16, 19, 21, 22, 23, 25.

[15] VĀ I. 4, 5, 6, 7, 9, 10, 11, 17, 20, 24, 30, 37, 39, 40.

[16] VĀ I. 1, 8, 13, 18, 27, 28, 32, 33, 34, 35, 36. Other metres employed by Śīlāṅka in his play: 3 *anuṣṭubh* (VĀ I. 3, 29, 31), 2 *vasantatilaka* (VĀ I. 12, 14), 2 *sragdharā* (VĀ I. 2, 38) and 1 *upājati* (VĀ I. 26).

[17] In Bhavabhūti's *Uttararāmacarita*, for instance, the dominant metre is the *anuṣṭubh*, with 90 occurrences on a total of 246 verses, while only 2 in *āryā* can be found. Incidentally, we may remark that in later Jain plays, like

may be said that it contributes in harmonising the play with the surrounding novel.[18]

If we consider now the second characteristic element of theatre, which is that it mainly consists of dialogues, we cannot, of course, say that it sharply contrasts with the rest of the novel. First of all, the nature of dialogues has changed in a novel written in the *kāvya* style. As a matter of fact, whereas the dialogues do not exist independently in old Jain novels such as the *Vasudevahiṇḍi*, they become an important characteristic in Jain novels written from the seventh century onwards. Indeed, Jain novelists had by that time borrowed from their Hindu models the *kāvya* style wherein the space given not only to descriptions but also to dialogues increases at the expense of the narration, even when the text is in prose. Consequently, the dialogues in the novels in the *kāvya* style are no longer that much distinctive of theatre. The *Kādambarī*, which was a model for Jain authors, for instance, is made up of 40% descriptions, 37% dialogues and only 22% narration. Dialogues also constitute an important element of two Jain works which are regarded as having been inspired by Bāṇa's work and written in the *kāvya* style: the *Līlāvaī* comprises 40% narration and 41% dialogues, whereas the *Kuvalayamālā* has 30% narrative passages and 32 % dialogues.

If we turn now to the *Cauppaṇṇamahāpurisacariya*, we can see that in the first chapter, into which the *Vibudhānanda* is integrated, the percentage of dialogues (53%) even exceeds that of narrative passages (40%). Moreover, Śīlāṅka has deftly integrated his play in this chapter so that the structural discrepancies do not stand out. As a matter of fact, there is no striking difference between the end of the *Vibudhānanda* and the subsequent narration: immediately after the dialogue between King Rājaśekhara and Queen Citralekhā follows the dialogue between the spectators of the play, King Mahābala and minister Vimalamati. In both passages, one character edifies the other by means of many verses on true reality of

---

Yaśaḥpāla's *Moharājaparājaya*, the *āryā* predominates like in Śīlāṅka's *Vibudhānanda* (cf. Leclère 2007, pp. 140–143).

[18] Cf. Chojnacki 2008, p. 166.

the world.[19] Conversely, the author introduces some narrative elements into his play. It especially occurs, when characters report in direct speech the words of other people: the introductory sentence, most often reduced to a verb at the passive participle and an agent at the instrumental followed by the conjunction *yathā/jahā*, is stereotyped, and one reported speech may be immediately followed by another in a way typical of the style of short stories.[20]

Lastly, the peculiar characteristic of Indian theatre concerning the different languages ascribed to different types of characters is clearly opposed to the usage of languages in narrative literature, which can usually be either in Sanskrit or in Prakrit, but rarely a mixture of both. However, Śīlāṅka has managed to partly soften the linguistic differences between the play and the rest of the novel. Indeed, the author of the *Caupaṇṇamahāpurisacaria* has restricted the linguistic variety in the *Vibudhānanda*. As a matter of fact, besides Sanskrit, there are only two kinds of Prakrit which are required for the characters appearing on stage according to their sex or their social status. In the treatises, women must speak Śaurasenī in the prose parts, and sing verses in Māhārāṣṭrī. The fool is supposed to speak a specific Prakrit called Prācyā, which is very close to Śaurasenī.[21] Consequently, since the bulk of the

---

[19] *tao rāiṇā garuya-saṃvegāvaṇṇa-hiyaeṇaṃ maṃtiṇo vimalamaissa muhaṃ paloiyaṃ / tao laddhāvasarena bhaṇiyaṃ maṃtiṇā - mahārāya ṇisuyaṃ jam aṇeṇa saṃsāra-sarūvaṃ ṇiveiyaṃ / rāiṇā bhaṇiyaṃ - kiṃ sueṇaṃ paccakkhaṃ ceva diṭṭhaṃ aṇuhavijjai ca / tao tam āyaṇṇiūṇa bhaṇiyaṃ maṃtiṇā - deva suṇasu* (CMPC 28. 1–3). Then the minister utters twelve verses in order to achieve the enlightenment of the king (CMPC 28. 4–18).

[20] While coming onto the stage, the chamberlain Mādhava reports successively the words of King Rājaśekhara, the maid Candralekhā and the astrologer Siddhādeśa, in a fashion which reminds of the narrative style : the verb of speech appears each time at the beginning of the sentence, and the speech is always introduced by *yathā* (*ādiṣṭo 'haṃ rājñā rājaśekhareṇa yathā* [...] *kathitaṃ ca me bandhumatī-sakhyā candralekhayā yathā* [...] *niveditaṃ ce me rājakulān nirgacchataḥ labdha-pratyayena siddhādeśa-nāmnā sāṃvatsarikeṇa yathā* CMPC 18. 13, 15, 16–17). In a similar way, the fool Vicitra reports first the order of his friend the prince, then a rumour he has heard (*pesio mhi jaṇaya-saṃdesuttejaviya-khattiya-vīrieṇaṃ piya-vayaṃsaeṇaṃ jahā* [...] *suyaṃ ca mae jahā* CMPC 18. 24–25).

[21] Lévi 1963, pp. 130–131; Bansat-Boudon 1992, p. 164.

novel is written in Māhārāṣṭrī, the usage of Prakrits as expected in theatre induces only one linguistic difference. Yet, even the difference between the Śaurasenī of the play and the Mahārāṣṭrī of the rest of the novel is not clearly marked. Indeed, characteristics of this dialect can indeed be traced in the speeches of the characters concerned: for instance, several imperative forms replacing the voiceless intervocalic *-t-* of the third person singular by the voiced *-d-* (as in *āṇavedu*),[22] the first person singular of the future ending in *-issam* (for instance *pekkhissam*, *gacchissam* in the maid's parts),[23] the first person plural of the present in *-mha* (as in *sunamha*).[24] However, they are comparatively few in number, and in many other instances they appear to have been replaced by the features of Māhārāṣṭrī: intervocalic dentals are dropped (for example the actress in the prologue uses *nacciyavvam* for the gerundive instead of the more regular *naccidavvam*; the jester employs the classical Prakrit form *pesio* instead of *pesido*, *suya* in the place of *suda* and *manoraha* in the place of *manoradha*; the maid resorts to the vocative *caurie* instead of *cadurie* and to the usual Prakrit form *aihi* and not the specific Śaurasenī *adidhi*. Thus, even the few typical features of the Śaurasenī dialect are not constantly used, so that the Prakrit of the play is not very different from the Māhārāṣṭrī of the novel.[25]

If Śīlāṅka has succeeded in integrating the *Vibudhānanda* in the *Caupaṇṇamahāpurisacariya* without any stylistic incongruity, however the presence of a play inside a novel raises another issue concerning the diffusion of the work as a whole. Indeed, according to a common distinction between literary works made by Sanskrit theoreticians, a novel and a play have two different types of performance: a novel is to be heard (*śrāvya*), whereas a play is to be seen (*dṛśya*). Besides, "to be heard" and "to be seen" have also been interpreted in different ways either by the Sanskrit theoreticians or by modern scholars. Thus "to be heard" has been understood at times as "to be recited in front of an audience", at times as "to be

[22] CMPC 17. 16. Cf. Pischel 1999, §351.

[23] CMPC 19. 10, 25. Cf. Pischel 1999, §521.

[24] CMPC 21. 27. Cf. Pischel 1999, §470.

[25] Cf. Bruhn 1961, p. 29.

read". For instance, basing his judgment on the length of Śīlāṅka's *Caupaṇṇamahāpurisacariya* and also on the fact that there are no "chapters for recitation" in this work, Warder concludes that this novel is intended "for private reading".[26] On the other hand, if "played" has been most of the time understood as "enacted by actors", it seems to have been sometimes interpreted as "recited expressively with a restricted enacting".[27] If we take these different interpretations into account, we are left with several options of performance for Śīlāṅka's work. The option that the play and the novel were performed each in the way that was prevalent for their respective genres, is unlikely given the evident unity of composition of the *Caupaṇṇamahāpurisacariya*, and a common mode of presentation must be postulated. Another way of eluding the problem induced by the generic heterogeneity of the work would be to surmise that it was intended for private reading only, but if it were so, why would Śīlāṅka have hinted at the enactment of the play in the prologue, and given stage directions,[28] instead of giving a mere narrative account of

---

[26] Warder 1988, §3126.

[27] In Dāmodaragupta's *Kuṭṭanīmata*, "dramatic performance is said to be of two kinds, *amiśra* or pure consisting of recitation (*pathyā*) alone, and *miśra* or mixed which combines recitation, music both vocal and instrumental, and dance with one of them preponderating over the rest" (Shastri 1975, p. 226). Similarly, in the *Abhinavabhāratī* Abhinavagupta evokes two conceptions of dramatic performance: indeed, though he thinks himself that theatre cannot be properly staged if deprived of music and dance, he nonetheless echoes the opinion of some theoreticians according to which a play can have success even when it is merely recited (ABh ad NŚ XXVIII. 7, tr. Bansat-Boudon 1992, p. 64 n. 63).

[28] Even though the stage-manager recites in the prologue a stanza stating that "this work full of good meanings, even said aloud (*gaditā*) just once, clings to the mind of people, whatever bad it could be" (*lagati jana-manasi sakṛd api gaditaiṣā kṛtir asaty api sadarthā* | VĀ I. 4a), he also says many times that it has to be played (*nāṭayitavyam* CMPC 17. 8, 19), and the actress similarly employs the same verb *nāṭ* (*nacca*, *ṇacciyavvaṃ* CMPC 17. 21–22). Besides, the verb *prayuj*, "to perform", appears in the parts of the stage-manager, when he says he will be rewarded for the pain of performing the play among a very wise assembly (*mamāpi viṣeṣa-vedinyāṃ parṣādi prayuñjā-nasya saphalaḥ pariśramo bhaviṣyati* CMPC 17. 8–9). The verb *nāṭ* and its derivatives also appear in stage directions, as early as the beginning of the play, where it is said that "the chamberlain enters playing anxiety" (*tataḥ praviśati*

representation like the famous one to be found in Damodāragupta's *Kuṭṭanīmata*?[29] Thus it seems that, on the contrary, the presence of an entire play inside the narration suggests that the whole novel was intended not only for recitation in front of an audience,[30] but for an expressive kind of performance and it could even be surmised that the story-teller probably borrowed several techniques from the actor's art of playing. The latter hypothesis is sustained by many pieces of evidence to which we will turn now.

In India, there are numerous examples attesting an association between narratives and visual arts. On one hand, there is a tradition of sculptures and paintings which are based on narratives. Some of them are presented with a complex mode of synoptic narration in which multiple episodes from a story are depicted within a single frame and the temporal sequence of events is not communicated, so it is very likely that the devotees needed the guidance of a mentor in helping them decipher representations (such as the *Jātaka* tale of a crab and a Brahmin on the Bharhut Stupa).[31] On the other hand, there is a popular tradition of narration with the support of puppets or of painted cloth, which has been maintained until recently in India.

For instance, the Garoda tradition of narrating sacred legends with the aides of *tipanu* or scroll paintings was

---

cintāṃ nāṭayan kañcukī | CMPC 18. 8: other occurrences: *nāṭyena* CMPC 19. 20; *mūrchāṃ nāṭayati* CMPC 23. 7; *parasparānurāgaṃ nāṭayataḥ* CMPC 24. 14). Even the surrounding narrative implies that the play is intended to be performed. Asked by his minister if he has heard the explanation of the cycle of existences, Mahābala replies that he has not only heard the explanation of the cycle of existences, but that he has also seen it with his own eyes (cf. below n. 47). Moreover, the argument invoked by Warder is all the weaker, since the novelists had at their disposal other means of structuring the text than dividing it in chapters, such as inserting descriptions between the episodes (Chojnacki 2008, p. 122).

[29] Cf. Lévi 1963, pp. 389–391; Shastri 1975, pp. 23–24.

[30] Indeed, there were also narrative forms which were recited without dramatisation such as in the tradition of the Pauranik (storyteller) who narrated Sanskrit tales in his own home or that of a patron (cf. Bender 1995, p. 183).

[31] Cf. Dehejia 1998, pp. 25–27.

> once widely popular in Gujarat. Itinerant Garoda story-tellers moved from village to village carrying illuminated paper scrolls. They gathered audiences around them and related stories in prose and verse, which were local versions of sacred stories from the epics and the *Purāṇas.*[32]

Within such a tradition, it would seem plausible that a narration could be dramatised and be enhanced by visual techniques. Now the first author who clearly links narration with visual arts as well as with music and dance is Uddyotana in the eighth century. As a matter of fact, in his *Kuvalayamālā*, he does not, as his predecessors do, only evoke entertainments, but he gives us vivid examples. For instance, in one of his stories, the author imagines that a monk uses Bhānu's passion for painting to lead him to enlightenment and thus he presents him a cloth illustrating the destinies of a soul (185.23–190.19) and, in a corner, the life of Bhānu himself (190.23–194.4). Uddyotana even hints at a specific procedure of presentation of such painted scrolls, when the narrator draws the attention of the audience from one part to the other by pointing to them successively:

> with the top of his stick, the Jain monk shows the sufferings in the cycle of transmigration

or when the master is showing it to Bhānu and says:

> what I have drawn here in a differentiated scene is the story of two human beings in one of their existences.

Besides, throughout the story, he uses demonstratives with which he recalls to attention the prince Bhānu:

---

[32] Cf. Jaini 1998, p. 74. Such are also the Telangana scrolls which illustrate the origin of a particular caste or the heroic deeds of one of its legendary heroes. The performers were hereditary professionals who used to be invited to villages by members of particular caste groups. They moved from one village to the next, except during the rainy season. The performances took place in the evening and continued at least for a week. [...] The narration was in the Telugu language, part in poem, part in prose. The main narrator was accompanied by four or five male members of his family; one of them joined him in singing at intervals, while the others played musical instruments (cf. Mittal 1998, pp. 58–59).

> Here there is a young man with this young woman. I have represented him with a lotus-like face saying something. I have represented the young woman more particularly here: out of shyness, she bends her head down and she writes something on the earth with her toe; her lover says something to her and she smiles (187.7–8). There, you can see a man who is weeping, his eyes closed under a flood of tears (187.23).

This example of a painted cloth, which reminds us of the paintings used by Buddhist monks in order to enlighten people,[33] suggests that the author felt the need to help the members of his audience to visualise the content of his narration, in order to better attract their attention and strike their imagination. Thus, if the story to be narrated was too long to be depicted on a cloth, one may surmise that the narrator could resort to techniques of bodily acting in order to enliven his recitation. Besides, right in the beginning of his novel, Uddyotana also directly inserts a spectacular genre called *carcarī* which is a song accompanied by music and dance, in order to justify his choice of a mixed novel which, according to the four modalities of *kathā*, "attracts" (*ākṣepiṇī*) the members of the audience before "rejecting" them (*vikṣepiṇī*), "provoking agitation" (*saṃvegajananī*) and finally "provoking disgust" for mundane life (*nirvedajananī*).

The content of this passage is as follows. Mahāvīra awoke five hundred thieves to the Jain dharma by reciting the four stanzas of his *carcarī*. With the first one, he attracted them by describing the apparent beauty of women; with the second stanza, he disgusted them by revealing the actual ugliness of the body; with the third he provoked a great agitation inside them, and with the fourth and last one, he helped them to adopt the path of Jainism leading towards liberation. The fact that this *carcarī* was intended as a song is proven not only by the precise name of the genre ascribed to it but also by its structure: within a frame in prose, verses are inserted, which are not the classical *āryā*, but specific verses called *galitaka*.

---

[33] Cf. Pinault 2000.

Besides, there is a refrain coming after each stanza, which is technically called *dhruvaka*:

> Be awoken, why do you not wake up? Do not let anything lead you astray. You must do what is to be done. At any moment, death approaches the person who is destined to die.

Thus, it seems quite probable that musical modes, different from the reading of a novel, were adopted so that it impresses more vividly the minds of the audience. Such an interpretation would have the support of Buddhist examples attested in Central Asia, in which, besides other indications alluding to a dramatised narration, as shown by Pinault, there seem to be some musical notations as to how sing the sequences.[34]

Furthermore, since Uddyotana's Kuvalayamālā is remarkably composed, such passages, which imply the intervention of visual art and musical modes, would also suggest that the dramatisation was not limited to these peculiar episodes, but extended to the novel as a whole. Indeed, other characteristics of Uddyotana's and Śīlāṅka's works are testimonies of a dramatisation of the narration. Indeed, as it was the case with Aśvaghoṣa, who was prone to write dramatic stories such as the *Sūtrālāṅkāra* with a structure akin to plays,[35] Uddyotana composed such lively stories that one may wonder whether they were narrative versions of existing plays. As a matter of fact, in the Kuvalayamālā, the stories which present the previous lives of five souls and illustrate respectively one major destructive passion (viz. anger, vanity, deceit, greed or infatuation) and its disastrous effects before the conversion, betray a dramatic structure as well as features borrowed from the theatre. Firstly, the five souls are localized in the assembly of the monk Dharmanandana, as if they were on stage. For

---

[34] Cf. Pinault 2000, pp. 149–153.

[35] As recalled by Bansat-Boudon (2007, p. 55), S. Lévi had noticed the underlying theatricality of a text such as Aśvaghosa's *Sūtrālankāra*: a prostitute tries to put the assembly off a monk whose success is a threat for her occupation. It takes a mere look of the teacher to reduce the seducing women to their white bones and their intestines. The assembly is disgusted with the mundane pleasures and at the same time, the womanly skeleton is remorseful and asks to be given the Buddhist dharma.

Caṇḍasoma, the soul suffering from anger, the monk says: "it is this man sitting on your left and on my right".[36] Besides, the five characters are described in a way reminding us of dramatic theory. The same Caṇḍasoma is presented "with red eyes like *guñjā*-berries and three waving wrinkles on his forehead; [...] his eyebrows are frowned, and his lips are quivering with rage".[37] Now, this typical portrait fits in with Bharata's teaching on the way of enacting manifestations of anger on stage.[38] One can also find in passing, other allusions to an actor playing a role. The deceitful Māyāditya is said to have a nature as moving and changing as the braids that the actors bind on their head like a turban.[39] Moreover, the very structure of these stories follows a pattern that is akin to the pattern of edifying plays: after the presentation of the main character, there is the manifestation of his passion and its consequence, followed by the remorse and, finally, the conversion. The resemblance with plays is all the more accentuated in these stories, since they present a linguistic variety, which otherwise is typical of theatre. As a matter of fact, it is in those episodes that Uddyotana chooses to resort to different kinds of dialects or pseudo-dialects to characterise social groups.[40] Furthermore, Jain novelists appear to have modelled their texts with features borrowed from the Indian theatre which enabled them to dramatise the narration. Not only did they introduce more dialogues, as in the case with Śīlāṅka's *Caupaṇṇamahāpurisacariya*, but they also created the

---

[36] *jo eso tujjha vāme dāhiṇa-pāsammi saṃṭhio mujjha |* (KM 45.12a).

[37] *bhamar'aṃjaṇa-gava-lābho guṃjā-phala-ratta-ṇayaṇa-juo || ti-vali-taraṃga-ṇiḍālo bhīsaṇa-bhiuḍī-kayaṃta-sāriccho | bhumayāvali-bhaṃgillo rosa-phuraṃ-tāharoṭṭha-juo ||* (KM 45. 12b–13).

[38] Bharata teaches that "the acting [of the furious] must be staged with consequents such as having red eyes, sweating, frowning, displaying self-confidence, biting one's lips, having trembling cheeks, rubbing together the end of the fingers" (*rakta-nayana-sveda-bhrū-kuṭī-karaṇāvaṣṭambha-dantauṣṭha-pīdaṇa-gaṇḍa-sphuraṇa-hastāgra-niṣpeṣādibhir anubhāvair abhinayaḥ prayoktavyaḥ*, NŚ VI. 77+ GOS, vol. I, p. 321).

[39] *bhaṇiyaṃ ca ṇaḍa-paḍisīsaya-jaḍā-kaḍappa-taraṃga-bhaṃgura-cala-sahāveṇa imiṇā māyāiccheṇaṃ* (KM 59. 15–16; cf. Chojnacki 2008, p. 208 n. 704).

[40] Like the villagers of Ragaḍā or the rejected people of Mathurā (cf. Chojnacki 2008, pp. 146, 209–210).

form of the *campū*, mixing prose and verse, thus appropriating the very form of Indian theatre for the *kathā*.

The introduction of this form of narration was a unique one, breaking the monotony which would have occurred in such long novels. Usually, as in theatre, assertions, questions or connectors introduce the passages in verse in a way that reminds us of the Tocharian narrative fragments in mixed prose examined by Pinault.[41] The verbs used in the introductory sentences indicate the modalities of the declamation to be adopted. As a matter of fact, the bard who announces the sunrise or the sunset declaims his verses.[42] The gods who come for the birth of a Tīrthaṅkara sing his praise[43] and the young woman who is abducted by a depraved Vidyādhara cries for help. Even when there are no introductory verbs, the fact that there are questions such as *keriso* "of which kind?", or a variant of it when there is a movement added to the description, such as *kaha* "how?", or a sentence *kā vāvarā vattium payattā* "which activities began to happen?", which break the narration and create an expectation, suggests that the verses were detached from the prose and that the intended effect was a change in the modalities of recitation. For instance, the author gives a sentence in prose saying that "there is no jewel which can be compared with the jewel represented by a Jain teacher" (14.13–14). Then, after a simple connector, such as *avi ya* "and also, moreover", he develops that idea in several verses which have a specific structure and rhythm, different from the prose, with many comparisons which are always in favour of the master. To take another example, when Śīlāṅka evokes the attacks of Meghamālin on Pārśva, he begins in prose the statement which is well-known to his audience (267.9–13) and then provokes their curiosity with a question and gives a sequence in verses (267.14–22) with specific

---

[41] As a matter of fact, there is an interesting parallel reminding of the theatre techniques between the introductory elements in the novels and the articulations which introduce the stanzas in the dramatized narrations of Central Asia, as noted by Bansat-Boudon (2007, pp. 60–61) and earlier by Pinault (Pinault 1991, p. 144 and Pinault 2000, p. 152).

[42] For instance in the CMPC: *padhiya* (12.31; 44.6; 44.16) or *gā* (13.6).

[43] Thus *thuṇium*: 40.1; 44.26.

alliterations and expressive words which depict the scaring attacks and also suggest a change in the declamation. Thus, the very form of the *campū* with its transition from prose to verses implies different ways of reciting and declaiming on various tones and with facial as well as body gestures.

The dramatised recitation of novels seems to be corroborated by subsequent testimonies of Jain writers. For instance, in the *Candappahacariya* dating from the twelfth century, it is stated that "among the entertainers, storytellers were also included. They told various kinds of stories with physical and facial gestures, so that people became wonderstruck".[44] Besides, it seems also to be attested by the ongoing tradition of the more or less sophisticated performance of narrative poems which has been preserved in several regions of India till today. For example, Bender reports how he experienced a performance of a *carita* in the tradition of the Gagaria Bhat of Gujarat in 1993:

> At the front of the hall, clothed and turbaned in white, the narrator sat cross-legged on a white clothed dais. The long necked, large metal pot, set before him, reached to the middle of his chest. All of a sudden, he struck the pot with his heavily ringed fingers. The musicians seated slightly behind him to his right began to tap softly on a tabla and the one in the left background joined in with his harmonium as the narrator chanted a stanza from the story. He followed this with a brief commentary. The performance proceeded to its conclusion with round after round of the clanging pot, joined by drum and harmonium with an occasional jingling of cymbals, backing the chant of the narrator

---

[44] *kahagā kahemṭi bahuviha kahāo taha vivihahāvabhāvehiṃ / jaha cittālihio iva uvauttamaṇojaṇo suṇai //* (ed. and tr. by Joshi 1998–1999, pp. 45, 47). However it ought to be noted that the edition of the text should probably be revised, since Joshi has worked on a manuscript preserved at Patan and attributed to Haribhadra, disciple of Candrasūri, without taking notice of another manuscript available at Jaisalmer and attributed to Jasadeva. The latter document has been used by Pagariya for editing the text in the collection of the L. D. Institute in 1999. The same passage reads as follows: *kahagā kahemṭi vivihā kahāo taha kaha vi hāvabhāvehiṃ | jaha akkhittā tāo loyālihiya va nisuṇaṃti ||* (v. 1727, p. 66).

who intermittently traded good-humoured remarks with the audience, which, as far as I could make out in the low light consisted of some fifty or sixty women[45].

Karine Schomer, who could attend the dramatised performance of *alha* in the Hindu tradition, gives an even more striking report.[46] One of the performances dealt with a sophisticated text in varied metres taken from medieval poetry. The narrator would flesh out the text by emphasising the narrative details and the emotional expression and by playing with the different rhythms of the verses. At the other end, the singer expressed with his voice and a considerable repertoire of gestures and facial expressions, a wide range of emotions (love, pathos, devotion, fear, anger, disgust, wonder and amusement). For instance, to express the emotion of righteous anger, he would sneer, roll his eyes, furrow his brow and make his nostrils flare. Besides, he would beat a drum as an emotional backup and punctuation, while the speed of the song served as yet another method of emotional underscoring.

Thus, the unity of composition of Śīlāṅka's work and the insertion of a whole play in it, serve to prove that the long Jain novels, having borrowed several features from classical theatre which could manifest themselves in their full bloom with the creation of the form of the *campū*, were presented in front of an audience as a dramatic performance combining the subtleties of the text, the rich language of gestures and facial expressions, as well as in varied musical modes. If the Jain authors chose to dramatise the narration in their long works, it was partly because they had to attract their audience, but partly also to serve their edification. Indeed, the visualization of a text contributes to conviction, since visual images are more trustworthy than mere words. Seeing leads to believing, even more than hearing, as is explicitly said by one of the protagonists in Śīlāṅka's novel: asked by his minister if he has heard the explanation of the cycle of existences, King Mahābala replies that he did not only hear it, but he saw it with his

[45] Cf. Bender 1995, p. 183.

[46] Cf. Schomer 2007 ([1]1992), pp. 47–88.

own eyes in an enacted play.[47] Such a role of the visual image is evoked by Singh, who writes:

> The bards who sing the Bagrawat or Pabu epics in front of their painted scrolls speak as though their phads confirm their words. When I laughed disbelievingly at the story of a man who ate a ton of opium, I was shown the pad and told: "If you don't believe me, see for yourself, it is shown here". [1998, p. 102.]

Thus, images accompanying narratives as well as physical interpretations act as an affirmation and almost as a proof of the fictive world.

The Genuine Use of a Rare Dramatic Genre

A study of the genre of Śīlāṅka's play could seem superfluous, since the *Vibudhānanda* is now considered by many scholars as a rare specimen of *utsṛṣṭikāṅka.*[48] However, given that the data supplied by both the play and the surrounding novel apparently lack coherence, they must be carefully investigated.

As is usual in Indian theatre, the text of the *Vibudhānanda* too begins with a prologue in which the stage-manager explains how he has been entrusted with the task of performing a play. He first recalls to himself the order he has just received from an assembly of monks: "Now you have to stage a work of the poet characterised by virtue, whose name is Vimalamati, the heroic drama (*nāṭaka*) entitled *Vibudhānanda*, a unique play of the genre (*rūpaka*) called act (*aṅka*)".[49] He then informs his wife that he has been ordered by monks to stage "the heroic drama (*nāṭaka*) entitled *Vibudhānanda*".[50] By mentioning it twice, Śīlāṅka has highlighted a title which, as we shall see later, could be a reference to earlier works. He has

---

[47] *tao laddhāvasareṇa bhaṇiyaṃ maṃtiṇā / mahārāya ṇisuyaṃ jamaṇeṇa saṃsāra-sarūvaṃ ṇiveiyaṃ / rāiṇā bhaṇiyaṃ kiṃ sueṇaṃ paccakkhaṃ ceva diṭṭham aṇuhavijjai ya /* (CMPC 28. 1–2)

[48] Warder 1988, §3132; Bhayani 1993, p. 113.

[49] *ādiṣṭo'ham adya sādhu-jana-parṣadā / yathā adya tvayā kaveḥ śīlāṅkasya vimalamaty-abhidhānasya kṛtiḥ vibudhānandaṃ nāma nāṭakaṃ ekam aṅkākhya-rūpakaṃ nāṭayitavyam iti /* (CMPC 17. 8).

[50] *ādiṣṭo'haṃ sādhu-janena / yathā adya tvayā vibudhānandaṃ nāma nāṭakaṃ nāṭayitavyam iti /* (CMPC 17. 19).

also succeeded in giving at the same time the names of both authors of the play, since the fictitious Vimalamati is qualified as a virtuous man in a compound which is nothing else than the name of the real Śīlāṅka.

The genre of the *Vibudhānanda*, however, remains uncertain: besides *rūpaka*, which broadly means dramatic form or genre, the director uses two other technical terms, *nāṭaka* and *aṅka*, which are apparently contradictory, as they both refer to varieties of *rūpaka*, respectively the heroic drama and the act or, more precisely, the one-act pathetic drama. It is not easy to determine which one is to be preferred: if *aṅka* seems to have a strong generic meaning inasmuch it appears in composition with *rūpaka*, *nāṭaka* is mentioned twice in the prologue, the first time along with *aṅka*, the second time alone. Besides, *nāṭaka* similarly appears alone in the narration preceding the play: the minister Vimalamati says that he will enlighten King Mahābala with a *nāṭaka* provoking the renunciation of the world.[51] And in the canonical sources Śīlāṅka has probably relied upon, it is also a *nāṭaka* which awakes Mahābala: "He has been enlightened by [his minister] Subuddhi, the mind attracted by the spectacle of a *nāṭaka*".[52]

However, if it were a heroic drama, the *Vibudhānanda* would appear to be irregular in many aspects. First, in contradiction with the rules of dramaturgy, its denouement is unhappy: the hero Lakṣmīdhara dies suddenly,[53] bitten by a black cobra, and the heroine Bandhumatī immolates herself on his funeral pyre. Bruhn tried to explain this tragic end as an appendix "only loosely connected with the rest of the piece", the happy denouement being secured by the performance of the marriage ceremony which takes place just before the accidental death of the hero,[54] but, as noticed by Warder[55]

---

[51] *tā veraggajaṇaeṇaṃ nāḍaeṇaṃ eyaṃ bohemi* (CMPC 16. 27).

[52] *tattha subuddhiṇā ṇāḍagapekkhāakkhittamaṇo saṃbohio [mahābalo]* (Bruhn 1961, p. 29).

[53] According to Bharata, the death of the character who is known as the triumphant hero must not be made, neither in an act, nor in an introductory scene: *aṅke praveśake ca prakaraṇam āśritya nāṭake vāpi / na vadhaḥ kartavyaḥ syād yo'bhyudayī nāyakaḥ khyātaḥ //* (NŚ XVIII. 39).

[54] Bruhn 1961, p. 29.

(and incidentally by Bruhn himself), the prologue[56] and the play[57] are interspersed with many allusions to the sad outcome of Lakṣmīdhara and Bandhumatī's love story. Even the inaugural benediction alludes to it through the legend of Rājīmatī who was abandoned by Nemi on the very day they were to get married.[58] The real denouement and the only one is thus without any doubt the death of the main characters, and not the marriage preceding it. Besides, the *Vibudhānanda* has only one act, whereas according to the *Nāṭyaśāstra* the number of acts in a *nāṭaka* ranges from five to ten.[59] It is unlikely that Śīlāṅka deviated so much from dramatic rules he proved to be acquainted with: later in the *Cauppaṇṇamahāpurisacariya*, he mentions the *Nāṭyaśāstra*, among other technical treatises,[60] and just before the insertion of the *Vibudhānanda*, he makes use of several terms referring either to aesthetic theory or dramatic performance. For instance, the actor Haragaṇa introduced by the minister Vimalamati to King Mahābala "knows perfectly the sentiments (*bhava*) and the aesthetic emotions (*rasa*), does well the dance steps (*karaṇa*), and is very skilled in the fourfold art of acting (*abhinaya*)". The

---

[55] Warder 1988, §3133, 3135, 3138–3139.

[56] The actress is weeping, because "a soothsayer has informed [her] of [her] family's ruin immediately after the marriage of [her] son" (*mujjha puṇa puttassa vivāhasamayāṇaṃtaram eva ṇemittieṇaṃ kuḍuṃbabhaṃgo samāiṭṭh*, CMPC 17. 21–22).

[57] The jester and the chamberlain foretell the death of the prince many times (see for instance CPMC 18. 16–18; 25. 12–13).

[58] *rājīmaty avadhāraya priyakathām ātmānam ālocaya kiṃ ko'pīha jagaty anindyacarite patyur viyoge mṛtaḥ | ity ākarṇya vaco'vadhārya ca tato mūrchāvinodas tayā cakre yasya k te sa pātu bhavataḥ śrīneminātho jinaḥ ||* (VĀ I. 1). Cf. Bruhn 1961, p. 27 n. 12; Warder 1988, §3133. The allusion to the plot is one of the functions assigned to the *nāndī* in treatises and commentaries (first attestations in the *Daśarūpaka*—wherein Dhanañjaya might have quoted an older commentator named Devapāṇi—and the *Abhinavabharatī*), and may be found in dramatic texts as ancient as Kālidāsa's *Abhijñānaśaluntalā* (Lévi 1963, pp. 132–135, appendix p. 25; Bansat-Boudon 2001, p. 61).

[59] *pañcāparā* [Gaekward Oriental Series: *pañcākṣarā* Parimal Sanskrit Series] *daśaparo hy aṅkāḥ syur nāṭake prakraṇe ca* (NŚ XVIII. 19); *prakaraṇanāṭakaviṣaye pañcādyā daśaparā bhavanty aṅkāḥ* (NŚ XVIII. 29).

[60] *taṃ ca kalā-lakkhaṇāiyaṃ bahuhā vibhajjantaṃ parigaliyasesaṃ saṃpai keṇāvi kiṃpi nibaddhaṃ taṃ jahā ṇaṭṭaṃ bharaheṇaṃ* (CMPC 38. 24).

king having consented to see the performance, "the stage (*raṅgabhūmi*) is prepared", and "the actors (*kuśīlava*) take their roles (*bhūmikā*) according to usage".[61] Henceforth, the word *nāṭaka* has been probably applied by Śīlāṅka to the *Vibudhānanda* with the broader meaning of drama, and not with the narrower one of heroic drama.[62]

The other word used by Śīlāṅka in the prologue, *aṅka*, means properly "act", and is more adapted to the dramatic text inserted in the novel, which consists, as stated before, in a single act, but it could be either an act taken from a broader play or an independent act. Among the ten *rūpaka* reckoned in the *Nāṭyaśāstra*, there are four kinds of play in one act, the *bhāṇa*, the *vyāyoga*, the *vīthī* and the *utsṛṣṭikāṅka* which could also be simply called *aṅka*. Since *aṅka* is associated in a compound with *rūpaka* in the prologue of the *Vibudhānanda*, it is very tempting to understand it in a generic sense. However, in the frame story of king Mahābala, it is said that, after the minister Vimalamati had invited an actor called Haragaṇa to enlighten his lord with a drama, "one *aṅka* liable to provoke the renouncement of the world was taken from a *nāṭaka* connected with ancient stories".[63] Here *aṅka* apparently designates a segment of a drama, and, as we know that in the traditional theatre of modern Kerala, "plays are performed not in whole, but in part",[64] we could surmise that a similar procedure existed in medieval Gujarat.[65] Thus, Śīlaṅka's *Vibu-*

[61] *viṇṇatto avasaraṃ lahiūṇa rāyā jahā deva samāgao accanta-rasa-bhāva-ṇṇū sukaya-karaṇo cauvvihāhiṇaya-pattaṭṭho haragaṇābhihāṇo ṇaḍo tao tad-daṃsaṇe-ṇaṃ kuṇau devo aṇuggahaṃ ti | rāiṇā bhaṇiyaṃ evaṃ kīrai tti | tao sajjiyā raṃga-bhūmī uvaviṭṭho mantisameo rāyā | gahiyāo jahā-joggaṃ bhūmiyāo kusilavehiṃ |* (CMPC 16. 29–31).

[62] Another instance of contradictory use of generic terms is provided by Rāmacandra's *Mallikāmakaranda* (12th c.). Though presented in its title and in its prologue as a *nāṭaka*, it is obviously a *prakaraṇa*, because its action is invented and its hero is the son of a merchant. Moreover, the author rightly calls it *prakaraṇa* in another work of his, the *Nāṭyadarpaṇa* (Trivedi 1966, p. 232).

[63] *lāhio tassa cirantaṇa-kahā-saṃbaṃdhassa ṇāḍayassa ya veragga-jaṇaṇo ekko aṃko |* (CMPC 16. 28–29).

[64] Richmond 2007, pp. 93, 106.

[65] The hypothesis of a tradition of performing single acts in Northern India is all the more likely since as early as the 8th c., the *Kuṭṭanīmata* relates

dhānanda might be nothing but a part of an unknown drama, as is the case with *Bālivadhāṅka* and *Torāṇayūdhāṅka*, which have almost become autonomous plays in the Kūṭiyāṭṭam repertoire, but are actually the first and the third acts of Bhāsa's *Abhiṣekanāṭaka.*[66] Furthermore, at the end of the play, the exit of the characters is followed by the stage direction "the first act is completed",[67] which suggests that this act was to be followed by other ones in the larger frame of a *nāṭaka*. In most of the extant one-act plays, either a *bhāṇa*[68] or *vyāyoga,*[69] the text ends with the mention of the author, its name and its genre, but not with any indication of the completion of the first act.[70] However, this piece of evidence is not decisive, since Rāmacandra, before signing his *vyāyoga* entitled *Nirbhayabhīma*, makes it clear that the "first act" of the play is

---

the enactment in Benares of the first act of Harṣa's *Ratnāvalī*. Similarly, other acts from famous plays, like the fourth act of Kālidāsa's *Vikramorvaśī*, were probably represented separately (Bansat-Boudon 1994, pp. 310–311).

[66] Similarly, each act of the *Vilāsavatī*, a play written in 12th c. Gujarat by the Jain monk Devacandra, bears its own title (Warder 2004, §6068). Since the circumstances of prince Lakṣmīdhara's coming to the court of King Rājaśekhara are merely alluded to at the beginning of the play (CMPC 18. 13; 20. 4–5), it could be surmised that the *Vibudhānanda* was integrated in a broader drama describing at length the exile of the hero from his father's kingdom.

[67] *prathamo'ṅkaḥ samāptaḥ* (CMPC 27. 14). There is another stage direction (*samāptam idaṃ vibudhānandaṃ nāma nāṭakam*), but as it appears in brackets, it must have been added by the editor.

[68] *iti kaver udīcyasya viśveśvaradatta-putrasyārya-śyāmilakasya kṛtiḥ pādatāḍitakaṃ nāma bhāṇaḥ samāptaḥ* (*Pādatāḍitaka*, I. 148+); *iti śrīmad-vararuci-muni-kṛtir ubhayābhisārikā nāma bhāṇaḥ samāptaḥ* (*Ubhayābhisārikā*, I. 35+); *iti śrī-śūdraka-viracitaḥ padmaprābh takaṃ nāma bhāṇaḥ samāptaḥ* (*Padmaprābhṛtaka*, I. 44+); *samāpto'yaṃ karpūracaritābhidhāno bhāṇaḥ* (*Karpūracarita*, I. 32+); *itīśvaradattasya kṛtir dhūrtaviṭasaṃvādo nāma bhāṇaḥ samāptaḥ* (*Dhūrtaviṭasaṃvāda*, I. 70+). See Dezső, Csaba and Vasudeva, Somadeva, (trs) 2009.

[69] *samāpto'yaṃ pārthaparākrama-nāmā vyāyogaḥ śrī-prahlādana-nirmitaś ca* (*Pārthaparākrama*, I. 61+); *kavi-sārvabhauma-mahopādhyāya-śrī-harihara-kṛtiḥ śaṅkhaparābhavo nāma vyāyogaḥ* (*Śaṅkhaparābhava*, I. 81+); *iti śrī-kirātārjunīyo nāma vyāyogaḥ kavi-vatsarāja-viracitaḥ samāptaḥ* (*Kirātārjunīyavyāyoga*, I. 61+).

[70] Even in the *Karuṇāvajrāyudha*, which is irregular in many other aspects, Bālacandra has directly concluded by saying that "here the drama entitled *Śrīkaruṇāvajrāyudha*, composed by the king of poets Śrībālacandra, is completed" (*iti śrī-bālacandra-kavīndreṇa viracitaṃ śrī-karuṇāvajrāyudha-nāma nāṭakaṃ samāptam* (*Karuṇāvajrāyudha* I. 135+).

finished.[71] Moreover, we could also understand that the single act of the *Vibudhānanda*, instead of being literally taken from an older heroic drama, is rather derived from or inspired by it.

In any case, even if the one act of the *Vibudhānanda* were originally the first part of a bigger drama, the form it has in the *Cauppaṇṇamahāpurisacariya* must be taken as a whole, because, like any drama, it is provided with an inaugural benediction, *nāndī*,[72] a prologue, *prastāvana*,[73] and also a final benediction addressed by the actor to the audience, *bharatavākya*.[74] It is not clearly evident that the last verse of the play is a *bharatavākya*, since it is not presented as such in a stage direction; besides, the verse still refers in its first half to the fiction of the play, while it should shift to the audience and the circumstances of the performance; nevertheless, the mention of the stage in the second half of the verse indicates that the actor no longer speaks as the character of the king, but in his proper name:

> May you be happy, Madam! May our son enjoy prosperity with the people, and may the theatre have good conduct! I shall myself strive for final emancipation.[75]

Therefore, *aṅka* can be rightly considered as referring to the genre of Śīlāṅka's *Vibudhānanda*. Besides the fact that it is a one-act play, it has most of the features of the genre as described by Bharata in the eighteenth chapter of the *Nāṭya-*

---

[71] "The first act [is finished]. Here ends the work of the great poet Śrīrāmacandra, Śrīhemacandrasūri's disciple, who is the author of a hundred compositions" (*prathamo'ṅkaḥ || iti prabandha-śata-kartur mahakaveḥ śrī-hema-candra-sūri-śiṣya-śrī-rāmacandrasya kṛtir iyam | Nirbhayabhīmavyāyoga*, I. 32+).

[72] *tataḥ praviśati nāndī parikramya ca* (CMPC 17. 1); *nāndy-ante* (CMPC 17. 6). The word *nandī*, which usually refers to the inaugural benediction, designates in the first occurrence to the stage-manager who is entrusted to recite it (cf. Warder 1988, §3133).

[73] The word appears in the text of the play, after the exit of the characters of the prologue (CMPC 18. 7).

[74] *Théâtre de l'Inde ancienne*, pp. LXIX–LXX.

[75] *bhadraṃ bhavatu bhavatyai śiśur api kalyāṇa-bhāk saha janena | sac-chīla-vāṃś ca raṅgo'py aham api mokṣaṃ prati yatiṣye ||* (VĀ I. 40).

śāstra.[76] It is "furnished with male characters other than divine ones", who are, in order of appearance, the chamberlain, the jester, the prince and the king. It is a play "wherein the violent blows of the fight have ceased",[77] since the hero, as soon as he comes onto the stage, alludes to a battle he seems to have launched and won alone.[78] It is "full of women's lamentations": Queen Citralekhā cries out,[79] calls herself an unfortunate one[80] and addresses her dead daughter in a pitiful way: "Ah! My daughter! Even though you have obtained a husband

---

[76] *vakṣyāmy ataḥ param ahaṃ lakṣaṇam utsṛṣṭikāṅkasya || prakhyāta-vastu-viṣayas tv aprakhyātaḥ kadācid eva syāt | divya-puruṣair viyuktaḥ śeṣair yukto bhavet puṃbhiḥ || karuṇa-rasa-prāya-kṛto nivṛtta-yuddhoddhata-prahāraś ca | strī-parivedita-bahulo nirvedita-bhāṣitaś caiva || nānā-vyākula-ceṣṭaḥ sāttvaty-ārabhaṭi-kaiśikī-hīnaḥ | kāryaḥ kāvya-vidhi-jñaiḥ satataṃ hy utsṛṣṭikāṅkas tu ||* (NŚ XVIII. 93–96). The criterion of the well-known plot has not been taken into account, since unknown subjects were occasionally permitted. However, we can remark that the story related in the *Vibudhānanda* may have been well-known, since it is connected with ancient stories.

[77] In his gloss Abhinavagupta analysed *nivṛtta-yuddhoddhata-prahāraś* as *nivṛtta-yuddhā uddhata-prahārāḥ puruṣā yasmin* (ABh ad NŚ XVIII. 95), which may be translated by "wherein men [giving] violent blows have ceased from fighting", whereas Ghosh understood that the action of such plays takes place "when battle and violent fighting have ceased". Warder translated the passage by adding a word, which does not seem to be satisfying ("fighting, (the arrogance of) proud heroes and blows have ceased", does not seem accurate, cf. Warder 2004, §7029).

[78] Indeed, the prince is upset because his father has reproached him for having gone alone without all the requisites, and we understand that he has struggled for a kingdom, since his father has added that "individuals cannot acquire and govern land alone" (*katham etat sandiṣṭaṃ tātena yathā ekākī tvaṃ nirgataṃ sāmagrī-vikalaḥ na caikākibhiḥ pṛthivī-lābha-pālane śakye vidhātumiti* | CMPC 20. 4–5). He then compares himself to a solitary lion able to break the tusks of elephants simply by slapping them with the tip of its claws (VĀ I. 12), and, after evoking great warriors from the epics (VĀ I. 13), turns back to his own victory: he says that "[he is] wandering the earth, [his] fore-arm callous because of drawing the string of [his] irresistible, after splitting asunder the glory of all [his] enemies dispersed by [his arrows]" (*durvāra-cāpa-guṇa-karṣa-kiṇi-prakoṣṭho bāṇāvaśīrṇa-ripu-cakra-vikīrṇa-tejāḥ* [...] *vasudhām aṭāmi* | VĀ I. 14). In Bhāsa's *Ūrubhaṅga*, the only other extant specimen of the genre, the fight between Bhīma and Duryodhana is described in the prelude by three soldiers.

[79] The interjection *hā* appears in almost all her replies (CMPC 26. 17–19; 27. 1).

[80] *hā haya mhi maṃdabhāiṇī* (CMPC 26. 17; 27. 1).

full of passion, extremely difficult to obtain in the triple world, our wishes have not been fulfilled. Ah! My daughter! You have made me share your pains";[81] she also sheds tears[82] when King Rājaśekhara decides to put their son on the throne; moreover, in conformity with Abhinavagupta's gloss on the word "lamentations" ("a lamentation is a sorrow consisting in blaming fate and reproaching one's self"),[83] she reviles destiny: "Ah! Wicked Fate! Pitiless [Fate]! It is not suitable for you to behave in such manner!"[84] The *Vibudhānanda* also fits Bharata's definition inasmuch it reports "desperate speeches":[85] after seeing the pitiful death of his daughter and son-in-law, King Rājaśekhara can no longer stay at home, and declares he will follow his duty by adopting the errant life adopted by his ancestors.[86] Lastly, the *Vibudhānanda* does depict "different kinds of confused gestures" if, by "confused gestures", we are to understand, as Abhinavagupta invites us to do so, "falling on the floor, the fact of turning round and so on":[87] Queen Citralekhā faints and falls on the floor twice.[88] There is only one feature of the *utsṛṣṭikāṅka* which has apparently not been respected by Śīlāṅka. The *Vibudhānanda* should have been "composed with the pathetic as the main emotion", but the erotic seems dominant, as the love affair between Lakṣmīdhara and Bandhumatī constitutes the largest

---

[81] *hā putta lahiūṇa aṇurāyaṇibbharaṃ tihuyaṇe vi aidullahaṃ bhattāraṃ na pūriyā amhāṇa maṇoharā | hā putta kayā haṃ tumae dukkhāṇa bhāiṇī* (CMPC 26. 17–19).

[82] *iti roditi* (CMPC 27. 4).

[83] *paridevitaṃ daivopālambhātmanindārūpam anuśocanaṃ* (ABh ad NŚ XVIII. 95).

[84] *hā hayāsa devva ṇikkaruṇa ṇa juttaṃ tuha erisaṃ vavahariuṃ* (CMPC 26. 17).

[85] We rely on Abhinavagupta's gloss for the translation of *nirveditabhāṣitaś*: "desperate: as soon as they are heard, despair arises: there are such speeches in the *utsṛṣṭikāṅka*" (*nirveditāni yeṣu śruteṣu nirvedo jāyate tādṛṃśi bhāṣitāni yatra* | ABh ad NŚ XVIII. 95 [GOS vol. II, p. 446; *yeṣu* missing in PSS vol. II p. 329].

[86] *na śaknomi ca īdṛśaṃ kāruṇyaṃ dṛṣṭvā kṣaṇam api gṛhe sthātum | [...] ahaṃ tu pūrvapuruṣagṛhīta-pravrajyāgraheṇa svakāryam anutiṣṭhāmi* (CMPC 27–29).

[87] *vyākulā ceṣṭā bhūminipātavivartitādyāḥ* (ABh ad NŚ XVIII. 96).

[88] *iti mūrchitā patati* (CMPC 26. 19; 27. 1).

part of the drama.[89] Nevertheless, since the pathetic is substituted in the denouement for the erotic in a particularly impressive way, Śīlāṅka's play can be considered as an almost regular *utsṛṣṭikāṅka*.

The question of the genre of the *Vibudhānanda* being thus ascertained, we may wonder why Śīlāṅka chose an almost obsolete one among the genres at his disposal—the only other extant specimen being Bhāsa's *Ūrubhaṅga*, of uncertain date. Besides the fact that a short play could be more easily inserted in a novel than a long one, it was probably for the author a means to differentiate himself from his illustrious predecessors. Indeed, Kālidāsa, Harṣa and other great dramatists had already composed masterpieces of Indian theatre, which Śīlāṅka did have in mind when by the ninth century he wrote his own work, as is proved by more or less evident allusions. First and foremost, the title of *Vibudhānanda* ("Joy for the Learned") sounds like a variation on the title of Candragomin's *Lokānanda* ("Joy for the World") and Harṣa's *Nāgānanda* ("Joy for the Snakes"). Moreover, in the text of the *Vibudhānanda* Warder has traced reminiscences of Harṣa's plays, not only in the *Nāgānanda* but also the *Ratnāvalī*.[90] The name of the actor invited by the minister Vimalamati to stage a play, Haragaṇa, may also be considered as a subtle reference to the two rival masters of dramatic art Haradatta and Gaṇadāsa who appear in Kālidāsa's *Mālavikāgnimitra*.[91] These plays being for the most part *nāṭaka*, the genre of *utsṛṣṭikāṅka* is in itself a mark of originality. Besides, Śīlāṅka insists in the prologue on the fact that the *Vibudhānanda* is "a unique play of the genre called act".[92] A few centuries later, other dramatists will be interested in the genre of *vyāyoga* for the same reason.[93]

---

[89] In Bhāsa's *Ūrubhaṅga*, the pathetic dominates in the main part focussed on the character of Duryodhana, whereas the prelude is based on the heroic (cf. *Théâtre de l'Inde ancienne*, p. 1233).

[90] Warder 1988: §3136, 3140.

[91] *Mālavikāgnimitra* I. 10.

[92] Cf. above, n. 49.

[93] These *vyāyoga* are Rāmacandra's *Nirbhayabhīmavyāyoga*, Prahlādana's *Pārthaparākrama*, Vatsarāja's *Kīrātārjunīya* (12th c.), Harihara's *Śaṅkhaparābhavavyāyoga* (13th c.), Viśvanātha's *Saugandhikāharaṇa*, Mokṣāditya's *Bhīmavikramavyāyoga* (14th c.). Nīlakaṇṭha's *Kalyāṇasaugandhikavyāyoga* is not

Śīlāṅka's choice may also have been motivated by religious considerations. As noticed by Warder, the genre of *utsṛṣṭikāṅka* is "very appropriately adapted to the Jaina theme of renunciation (*vairāgya*)".[94] Śīlāṅka himself explicitly refers to the religious doctrine in the surrounding narration: minister Vimalamati decides to enlighten his lord with a drama provoking the renouncement of the world,[95] and immediately after the performance King Mahābala feels deeply in his heart the inner turmoil (*saṃvega*) which precedes the renunciation.[96] According to the treatises on Jain doctrine, a human being becomes upset when "he penetrates the fact that every aspect of life is transitory and mortal" in the cycle of transmigration.[97] If the *utsṛṣṭikāṅka* is more suitable than the other genres for inspiring agitation, it is not because bad events occur in its plot and provoke the characteristic lamentations of women—the *nāṭaka* is not deprived of such incidents—but rather because, in an *utsṛṣṭikāṅka*, there is by rule no divine being who could cancel in the denouement the calamities that might have occurred. In the *Nāgānanda*, the hero Jīmūtavāhana is torn to pieces by Garuḍa, and then restored to life by the goddess Gaurī.[98] In the *Vibudhānanda*, on the contrary, the death of the hero and the heroine is irreversible, so that King Rājaśekhara, having perfectly understood the ineluctability of death[99] and the nature of the cycle of transmigration (*saṃsāra*),[100] can do nothing but leave home and strive for final emancipation by adopting the wandering life of a Jain monk (*pravrajyā*). Moreover, the disequilibrium in the structure of

---

included in the list, as the date of its composition is the 10th c. for some scholars, the 15th c. for others (cf. Leclère 2007, p. 32).

[94] Warder 1988, §3132.

[95] *tā veraggajaṇaeṇaṃ nāḍaeṇaṃ eyaṃ bohemi* (CMPC 16. 27).

[96] *tao rāiṇā garuyasaṃvegāvaṇṇahiyaeṇaṃ maṃtiṇo vimalamaissa muhaṃ paloiyaṃ* (CMPC 28. 1).

[97] Jaini 1998, p. 149. Cf. also Williams 1963, p. 42.

[98] *gaurī [...] nāyakam upasṛtya kamaṇḍalujalenābhyukṣya || nijena jīvitenāpi jagatām upakāriṇaḥ | parituṣṭāsmi te vatsa jīva jīmūtavāhana || nāyakaḥ || uttiṣṭhati ||* (*Nāgānanda*, p. 72).

[99] VĀ I. 35.

[100] VĀ I. 38.

the play between the long development of the love-affair between Lakṣmīdhara and Bandhumatī, culminating in a marriage and the brief and sad denouement, far from being a negligence towards the rules of dramaturgy, is probably intended to make the members of the audience feel surprised and realize that even in the happiest moments of life, unexpected suffering may happen. The mundane goal of *kāma* is thus discredited as being transient and fugitive, while the ideal of *mokṣa* is highlighted in the concluding verse.[101]

To sum up this section, Śīlāṅka's main purpose, when he elaborated the plot of the *Vibudhānanda*, was to give an insight into the unhappiness prevalent in worldly existence in accordance with the Jain doctrine. He gave it the shape of an *utsṛṣṭikāṅka*, because, among the dramatic genres, it was the most akin to the Jain stories of renunciation, and he appropriated it all the more easily since the *utsṛṣṭikāṅka*, as far as can be judged from the extant plays, was almost freed from any Hindu or Buddhist influence and thus liable to be transformed into a specifically Jain genre. Consequently, the Vibudhānanda represents a genuine and interesting attempt made by a Jain author to overcome ancient interdicts regarding theatre and to reconcile it with religion.

Conclusion

Both the novel and the play by Śīlāṅka show how Jains contributed to the development and the enrichment of Indian literature. In order to counteract the success of Hindu works and to promote their own faith, they made genuine use of different literary genres. Thus, by reviving the obsolete *utsṛṣṭikāṅka*, they could conclude the love-story as found in the *nāṭikā* by the tragic death of heroes without deviating from dramatic rules. Besides, they won over their audiences by displaying in the new genre of the *campū*, all the subtleties of *kāvya* heightened by the use of Prakrit. But above all, Jain writers understood what a lasting impression on the mind a visual representation of the stories could make about reincarnations and final emancipation, and that is probably the reason why, in spite of canonical interdictions, they finally

[101] Cf. above, n. 77.

turned to theatre and developed other kinds of expressive performance, like displaying painted scrolls or the enactment of narrative texts structurally akin to plays. The very genre of *campū*, wherein versified and prose passages alternate like in *nāṭya*, may even have stemmed from a Jain attempt at dramatising narration in order to make it more attractive. In any way, it was probably publicly performed with the help of techniques of acting, as suggested by the insertion of the *Vibudhānanda* into the larger frame of the *Caupaṇṇamahāpurisacariya*.

Abbreviations and Bibliography

ABh *Abhinavabhāratī*
CPMC *Cauppaṇṇamahāpurisacariaṃ*
KM *Kuvalayamālā*
NŚ *Nāṭyaśāstra*
VĀ *Vibudhānanda*

Balbir, N. et al. 2006, *Théâtre de l'Inde ancienne*, édition établie sous la direction de L. Bansat-Boudon, avec la collaboration de N. Balbir, S. Brocquet, Y. Codet, A. Couture, C. Malamoud et M.-C. Porcher, Gallimard.

Bansat-Boudon, L., 1992, *Poétique du theatre indien. Lectures du Nāṭyasāstra*. Paris: Ecole Française d'Extrême-Orient.

——— 1994, "Le texte accompli par la scène. Observations sur les versions de *Śakuntalā*", *Journal Asiatique* 278 n°2, pp.281–333.

——— 2007, "Sylvain Lévi et le théâtre indien. Une passion fixe", in Bansat-Boudon and Lardinois 2007, pp. 35–71.

Bansat-Boudon, Lyne and Lardinois, Roland (eds), 2007, *Sylvain Lévi (1863-1935), Etudes indiennes, histoire sociale,* sous la direction de Lyne Bansat-Boudon et Roland Lardinois, avec la collaboration d'Isabelle Ratié, Bibliothèque de l'Ecole des hautes études en sciences religieuses, Brepols: Turnhout.

Bender, E., 1995, "The Trials and Tribulations of a Text", *Journal of the American Oriental Society*, 115.1, pp. 181–192.

Bharata, *Nāṭyaśāstra with the commentary of Abhinavagupta*, ed. M. Ramakrishna Kavi in 4 volumes. Baroda: Oriental Institute, 1926–1964 (GOS 36, 68, 124, 145).

——— *Nāṭyaśāstra of Bharatamuni with the commentary Abhinavabhāratī*, ed. R. S. Nagar in 4 volumes. Delhi, etc.: Parimal Publications, 1981–1984 (PSS 4).

Bhayani, H. C., 1993, *Indological Studies. Literary and Performing Arts. Prakrit and Apabhraṁśa Studies.* Parshva Prakashan: Ahmedabad.

——— 1995–1996, "About Some Lost Prakrit *prakaraṇas*", *Bulletin d'Etudes Indiennes*, pp. 51–59.

Bruhn, K., see Śīlāṅka.

Chojnacki, C., 2008, *Kuvalayamālā. Roman jaina de 779 composé par Uddyotanasūri*, vol. I : études, vol. II : traduction et annotations. Marburg: Indica et Tibetica Verlag.

Covill, L., 2009, *A Metaphorical Study of the Saundarananda*, Delhi: Motilal Banarsidass.

Dehejia, Vidya, 1998, "Circumambulating the Bharhut Stupa: the Viewers' Narrative Experience" in Jain (ed.) 1998, pp. 22-31.

Dezső, Csaba and Vasudeva, Somadeva, (trs) 2009, *The Quartet of Causeries (Caturbhāṇī (Pādatāḍitaka, Ubhayābhisārikā, Padmaprābhṛtaka & Dhūrtaviṭasaṃvādaḥ))* by Śyāmilaka, Vararuci, Śūdraka & Īśvaradatta. New York University Press and JJC Foundation: The Clay Sanskrit Library.

Dundas, Paul, 2002, *The Jains*. London, etc.: Routledge, second revised ed. (first ed. 1992).

Erdman, Joan L. (ed.), 1992, *Art Patronage in India. Methods, Motives and Markets.* Delhi: South Asia Books (reprinted 2007).

Haribhadrasūri, *Pañcāśakaprakaraṇam*, ed., Sāgarmal Jain and Kamaleśkumār Jain, Varanasi: Parśvanāth Vidyāpīṭh, 1997.

Harṣa, 1991 ed., *The Recensions of the Nāgānandaby Harṣadeva vol. I. The North Indian Recension*, ed. Madhava Candra Ghoṣa, assisted by Kṛṣṇa Kamala Bhattācārya, with a general introduction by Michael Hahn.... New Delhi: Aditya Prakashan.

Jacobi, Hermann, 1884, Gai*na Sûtras*, volume 1. Oxford: Clarendon Press.

Jain, Jyotindra, 1998, "The Painted Scrolls of the Garoda Picture Showmen of Gujarat", in Jain (ed.), pp. 74–89.

——— (ed.), 1998, *Picture Showmen. Insights into the Narrative Tradition in Indian Art.* Mumbai: Marg Foundation.

Jaini, P. S., 1998, *The Jaina Path of Purification*. Delhi: Motilal Banarsidass.

Jha, D. N. and Vanina, Eugenia (eds), 2009, *Mind over Matter. Essays on Mentalities in Medieval India*. New Delhi: Tulika Books.

Jha, Vishva Mohan, 2009, "Medieval Sanskrit Drama as a Literate Medium for Non-Literate Communication". In: D. N. Jha, Eugenia Vanina (eds), *Mind over Matter.* Essays on Mentalities in Medieval India. New Delhi: Tulika Books, pp. 207–227.

Joshi, S. N., "Popular Sports and Pastimes in the 12th century Gujarat as Depicted in the *Candappahacariya*", *Sambodhi*, vol. XXII, 1998–1999, pp. 43–48.

Kapadia, Hiralal Rasikdas, 1941, *A History of the Canonical Literature of the Jainas*. Surat.

Karpūracarita bhāṇa of Amātya Vatsarāja. Text with English Translation and Critical Study by S. S. Janaki, 1989. Madras: The Kuppuswami Sastri Research Institute.

Karuṇāvajrāyudha. Karuṇāvajrāyudhaṃ nāṭakam by Bālacandra Sūri, ed. Muni Caturvijaya, 1916. Bhāvanagara: Ātmānanda-grantha-ratna-mālā.

Kinsley, David R., 1979, *The Divine Player: A Study of Krsna Lila*. Delhi: Motilal Banarsidass.

Kiratārjunīyavyāyoga, see Vatsarāja.

Leclère, Basile, 2007, "Le théâtre de l'Inde médiévale entre tradition et innovation : le Moharājaparājaya de Yaśaḥ-pāla", vol. I : étude, vol. II : traduction. Unpublished Ph. D. thesis, Université Jean Moulin Lyon 3.

Lévi, Sylvain, 1963, *Le théâtre indien*, Paris: Honoré Champion.

Malavikāgnimitra. The Malavikāgnimitra: a Sanskrit play by Kālidāsa. Ed. with notes by Shankar P. Pandit, 1869. Bombay: Government Central Book Depot.

Mittal, Jagdish, 1998, "The Painted Scrolls of the Deccani Picture Showmen: Seventeenth to Nineteenth Century", in Jain (ed.) 1998, pp. 56–65.

Nāgānanda, see Harṣa.

Nirbhayabhīmavyāyoga by Rāmacandrasūri, 1996, ed. Aśoka Kumāra Siṃha and translated into Hindi by Dhīrendra Miśra. Vārāṇasī: Pārśvanātha Vidyāpīṭha.

Pañcāśakaprakaraṇam, see Haribhadrasūri.

Pārthaparākrama Vyāyoga by Paramāra Prahlādanadeva,. Edited with an introduction by C. D. Dalal, 1917. Baroda: Central Library.

Pinault, G.-J., 1991, "Les manuscrits tokhariens et la littérature bouddhique en Asie Centrale", *Comptes rendus de l'Académie des Inscriptions et Belles Lettres*, pp. 227–251.

——— 2000, "Narration dramatisée et narration en peinture dans la région de Kucha", *La Sérinde, terre d'échanges. Art, religion, commerce du Ier au Xe siècle*. Actes du colloque international publiés sous la direction de J. P. Drège, Paris, pp. 149–168.

Pischel, R., 1999, *A Grammar of the Prākrit Languages*, translated from German by S. Jhā, Delhi: Motilal Banarsidass.

Richmond, Farley P. et al., 2007, *Kūṭiyāṭṭam. Indian Theatre: Traditions of Performance* (reprint of the 1993 ed.).

Salomon, R., 2009, "Aśvaghoṣa's Saundaranda IV–VI: A Study in the Poetic Structure of the Buddhist Kāvya", *IIJ* 52, pp. 179–196.

Śaṅkaparābhava vyāyoga 1965, by Harihara, ed. B. J. Sandesara. Baroda: Oriental Institute (Gaekward Oriental Series 148).

Schomer, Karine, 1992, "The Audience as Patron: Dramatization and Texture of a Hindi Oral Epic Performance", in Erdman 1992, pp. 47–88.

Shastri, Ajaya Mitra, 1975, *India as Seen in the Kuṭṭanī-Mata of Dāmodaragupta*. Delhi: Motilal Banarsidass.

Śīlāṅka, Ācārya Śrī, *Cauppannamahāpurisacariaṃ*. Edited by A. M. Bhojak, with an introduction by K. Bruhn, Ahmedabad, etc.: Prakrit Text Society, 1961.

Singh, Kavita, 1998 "To Show, To See, To Tell, To Know: Patuas, Bhopas and their Audiences", in Jain (ed.) 1998, pp. 100–115.

Steiner, R., 1997, *Untersuchungen zu Harṣadevas Nāgānanda und zum indische Schauspiel*. Indica et Tibetica: Swisttal-Odendorf.

Sylvain Lévi (1863-1935), Etudes indiennes, histoire sociale, see Bansat-Boudon and Lardinois, 2007.

Théâtre de l'Inde ancienne, see Balbir, N., et al.

Trivedi, K. H., 1966, *The Nāṭyadarpaṇa of Rāmacandra and Guṇacandra. A Critical Study*. Ahmedabad: L. D. Institute of Indology.

Vatsarāja, 1918, *Rūpakaṣatkam. A Collection of Six Dramas*, ed. Chimanlal D. Dalal. Baroda: Central Library.

Warder, A. K., 1988 and 2004, *Indian Kāvya Literature*, volumes 5 and 7, Delhi: Motilal Banarsidass.

Williams, R., 1963, *Jaina Yoga. A Survey of the Mediaeval Śrāvakācāras*. London: Oxford University Press.

How to Combine the *Bṛhatkathā* with Jain Universal History—Reflections on Saṅghadāsa's *Vasudevahiṇḍī* *

Anna Aurelia Esposito

Abstract
Like many works of Indian narrative literature, Saṅghadāsa's *Vasudevahiṇḍī* is based to a large extent on the *Bṛhatkathā* of Guṇāḍhya, a work that is no longer extant. The peculiarity of the *Vasudevahiṇḍī* is that here the Hindu oriented material of the *Bṛhatkathā* is in a unique way intertwined with the universal history (and so also with the system of values) of the Jains. The main questions I would like to pursue in my paper are: did the *Vasudevahiṇḍī* emerge out of Jain material that was integrated into the *Bṛhatkathā*, or on the contrary, was the *Bṛhatkathā* incorporated in the Jain universal history? How Jain is the *Vasudevahiṇḍī* really?

Keywords: *Vasudevahiṇḍī,* Saṅghadāsa, *Bṛhatkathā,* Guṇāḍhya, Jain Universal History

For many Indian authors the *Bṛhatkathā* of Guṇāḍhya has been a source of inspiration—and often also of borrowing. Although this famous work is now lost, we know approximately what its contents were because of surviving versions: three works written in Sanskrit, Buddhasvāmin's *Bṛhatkathāślokasaṃgraha* (8th or 9th cent. CE), probably closest to the *Bṛhatkathā,* Kṣemendra's *Bṛhatkathāmañjarī* (dated 1037 CE), and the well-known *Kathāsaritsāgara* of Somadeva (composed between 1063 and 1081 CE). Additional information comes from a work in Old Tamil, Koṅku Vēḷir's *Peruṅkatai* (tenth century CE), as well as the *Vasudevahiṇḍī* (about fifth century CE) of the Jain monk Saṅghadāsa, written in an old version of Jaina-Māhārāṣṭrī.[1]

---

* I thank Dr Lucinda Martin for checking my English.

[1] For further studies concerning the relationship between the above-mentioned works and the *Bṛhatkathā* see especially the following books and articles: Lacôte (1908) emphasized the importance of the *Bṛhatkathāślokasaṃgraha* in reconstructing the *Bṛhatkathā,* but did not yet know the *Vasudevahiṇḍī* and the *Peruṅkatai*; Alsdorf 1936 (34–40, 94–109) and 1938 pointed for the first time to the *Vasudevahiṇḍī* as an important Jain version of the *Bṛhatkathā.* Jain summarised previous research on the *Bṛhatkatā* with special focus on the *Vasudevahiṇḍī* (1973/74) and commented on some important episodes in the *Vasudevahiṇḍī* for the reconstruction of the *Bṛhatkathā* (1975). Furthermore, he tried to reconstruct parts of the *Bṛhatkathā* on the basis of the common episodes in the *Vasudevahiṇḍī* and the *Bṛhatkathāślokasaṃgraha* (1977: 39–155; see also 159–434 for a direct comparison of the text of both

The peculiarity of the *Vasudevahiṇḍī* (Vh) is, that here the Hinduistic material of the *Bṛhatkathā* is intertwined in a unique way with the universal history of the Jains—and thus also with their system of values. The main plot line of the *Bṛhatkathā* thereby serves as a kind of framework, which is not only overlaid by an abundance of secondary stories, but also wrapped in several narrative layers of pure Jain origin. It was not Saṅghadāsa's main interest to create a new version of the *Bṛhatkathā*. More important for him were doubtless the numerous secondary stories, leaving room not only for various narrations about the *śalākāpuruṣas*, the sixty-three "great men" of Jain universal history,[2] but also for the transmission of religious contents. Before commenting on this aspect of the *Vasudevahiṇḍī*, which contrasts in particular with the other works of the *Bṛhatkathā*-tradition, I would like to consider briefly the most significant differences between the main stories of both works. The principal plot of the *Bṛhatkathā* as we can reconstruct it from our above-mentioned sources must have run roughly as follows:[3]

---

works). Nelson ruminated on the problems of reconstructing an Ur-text of the *Bṛhatkathā* (1978) and investigated the possible relationship between the *Peruṅkatai* and the *Bṛhatkathā* (1980), as did Vijayalakshmy (1982). Vijayalakshmy (1985) also examined the Jaina elements in the different versions of the *Bṛhatkathā*, arguing that the *Bṛhatkathā* had an affinity to Jaina religious and mythological beliefs and hence served as a source for their narratives.

[2] In every world-period the mostly mythological sixty-three "great men" (*mahāpuruṣa* or *śalākāpuruṣa*) appear. Most important among them are the 24 *jina* or "ford-makers" (*tīrthaṃkara*), born consecutively at a time, when eternal wisdom, the *dharma*, had been forgotten, so that they might spread it again among mankind. Furthermore, there are the twelve *cakravartin*, the "universal monarchs," destined to rule over the whole of Bharata, and the nine triads of heroes, consisting of one *vāsudeva*, one *baladeva* and one *prativāsudeva* all of whom live simultaneously. The *vāsudeva* and the *baladeva* are half-brothers who fight together against their arch-enemy, the *prativāsudeva*. The well-known heroes from the Hindu epic *Rāmāyaṇa*, Rāma, Lakṣmaṇa and Rāvaṇa, form the eighth of these triads of heroes, Kṛṣṇa, the most famous incarnation of the Hindu god Viṣṇu, appears together with his half-brother Balarāma and their enemy Jarāsandha as the ninth category.

[3] I will leave out some parts irrelevant for my present study. For a more comprehensive and detailed reconstruction see Warder 1990: 121–127.

The emperor of the Vidyādharas,[4] Naravāhanadatta, relates how he became emperor. He begins with the romantic tale of his father, King Udayana, who fell in love with his enemy's daughter, Vāsavadattā, and continues with his own biography. His first love was Madanamañjukā, the daughter of a courtesan. Soon after their marriage she was abducted by the Vidyādhara Mānasavega. His sister Vegavatī sympathised with Madanamañjukā and promised to bring a message to Madanamañjukā's husband. However, as soon as she saw Naravāhanadatta, she fell in love with him and tricked him into a marriage. Some days later he was carried off through the air by her brother Mānasavega. Vegavatī intervened, and Naravāhanadatta was dropped while they fought. Through Vegavatīs magical science (*vidyā*) he floated down to earth unharmed. At this point, Naravāhanadatta begins his long wanderings. Through his handsome appearance, charm of character and manifold skills, he wins not only mistresses wherever he goes, but also numerous powerful allies. In the end he defeats his arch-enemy Mānasavega and, reunited with his beloved Madanamañjukā, conquers the whole world,[5] gaining the seven imperial emblems (the "gems") of a universal emperor.

The most obvious difference between the *Vasudevahiṇḍī* and the other works of the *Bṛhatkathā*-tradition is that Vasudeva takes the place of Naravāhanadatta. At first glance, it might be surprising that it is Vasudeva, of all people, who substitutes for Naravāhanadatta in the Jain version of the *Bṛhatkathā*, while in the Hindu and early Jain tradition he is only of peri-

---

[4] A Vidyādhara possesses certain magical powers, *vidyās*, which can be acquired through a combination of ascetic practices and magical spells. The "owner" of a certain *vidyā* can even pass her on or lend her to somebody (cf. Vh 92.20, where Kaṇagamālā gives the *vidyā* Paṇṇattī to her foster-son Pajjuṇṇa, or Vh 108.17 f., where Pajuṇṇa lends the same *vidyā* to his brother Samba). For this reason it is quite possible for a human being to become a Vidyādhara—as is the case with King Naravāhanadatta. For a comprehensive treatment of the Vidyādharas in classical Indian literature see Grafe 2001.

[5] Warder (1990: 127) states it more precisely, Naravāhanadatta had to renounce one region: Mount Meru, the home of the ancient Vedic gods, which appears to be ever beyond the reach of even a universal ruler. Naravāhanadatta is told the story of Ṛṣabha, a former universal emperor, who had attempted the military conquest of this northern region and had met his death at the hands of Indra.

pheral importance. But for just this reason Naravāhanadatta's adventures can easily be transferred to him. As Vasudeva is the father of *vāsudeva* Kaṇha (Skt Kṛṣṇa), it is possible to insert also the story of the ninth (and last) triad of heroes, consisting besides Kaṇha of his half-brother Rāma and their enemy Jarāsandha. Furthermore, the tale of the twenty-second *tīrthaṅkara* Ariṣṭanemi can also easily be included, as he is born to King Samudravijaya, Vasudeva's eldest brother.[6] Indeed, no one other than Vasudeva could have been more suitable for the transmission of the *Bṛhatkathā* into a Jain milieu![7] Like Naravāhanadatta, Vasudeva himself narrates to his audience the adventures he encountered while gaining his various wives. The role of the emperor is not impersonated by Vasudeva, however, but by his son Kaṇha as the ninth and last *vāsudeva* of this descending world period. The two story-lines that Naravāhanadatta combined—the amorous adventures and the militant undertakings—are thus assigned in the *Vasudevahiṇḍī* to two persons.

Contrary to all the other works of the *Bṛhatkathā*-tradition, the *Vasudevahiṇḍī* leaves the romantic narration about Udayana's love for Vāsavadattā, and the consequent birth of Naravāhanadatta. Nelson (1980: 232) considers the Udayana stories as very old already at the time of origin of the *Bṛhatkathā*. What might have been Saṅghadāsa's reason for abstaining from such a well-known and popular tale? Perhaps it was

---

[6] As the end of the *Vasudevahiṇḍī* is missing, we can only assume that the story of Kaṇha's cousin Ariṭṭhanemi would have been included. In the present form of the *Vasudevahiṇḍī* there are only two references on Ariṭṭhanemi: in the first passage, Nemi (= Ariṭṭhanemi) and Daḍhanemi are mentioned as sons of Vasudeva's eldest brother Samuddavijaya (Vh 77.17). The second passage shows, that Ariṭṭhanemi has already attained enlightenment: Kaṇha's son Pajjuṇṇa asks Ariṭṭhanemi's mother Sivā for the ornaments presented to her son by the gods (Vh 106.22–24).

[7] Jain (1977: 20, fn. 36) mentions an unpublished foreword of 77 pages prepared by Alsdorf for his intended book on the *Vasudevahiṇḍī*. In this foreword he offers a possible explanation as to why Vasudeva and not Kṛṣṇa himself has been chosen as the hero of the *Vasudevahiṇḍī*: according to Alsdorf, the universal history, dealing with the 63 *śalākāpuruṣas*, had already been developed into a fairly fixed form, hence there was little possibility to put the whole narration in the mouth of Kṛṣṇa or to add a new *cakravartin* to the list.

exactly their widespread popularity that made the borrowing of these tales firmly connected with Udayana nearly impossible, at least into a complete different context like that of the *Vasudevahiṇḍī*. The narration about Naravāhanadatta, however, according to Nelson (1980: 232) a new creation of Guṇāḍhya was far less known and could easily be inserted into the *Vasudevahiṇḍī*, substituting Guṇāḍhya's hero with Vasudeva. But Saṅghadāsa followed the original tale in so far as he also placed the story of the hero's father in front of the main narrative, in the *Vasudevahiṇḍī* Andhagavaṇhi, enriched by the former births of his youngest son Vasudeva.

Another alteration in the *Vasudevahiṇḍī* concerns the very beginning of the principal plot, the reason why the hero had to leave his home and take up his long wanderings. While Naravāhanadatta is carried off by his brother-in-law, the Vidyādhara Mānasavega, and starts his wandering in a foreign country, Vasudeva is placed under house arrest by his eldest brother, fakes his own suicide and secretly leaves his brother's kingdom. Contrary to Naravāhanadatta, Vasudeva is forced to take up his wanderings as a bachelor: the narration of Naravāhanadatta's love with Madanamañjukā, the daughter of a courtesan, is assigned in the *Vasudevahiṇḍī* to Vasudeva's grandson Samba (Vh 98.11–19; 100.28–104.14).[8] Was it perhaps too objectionable for the hero of a Jain work?[9]

The further story of Vasudeva after his elopement runs more or less parallel to Naravāhanadatta's adventures. In the end Vasudeva makes peace with his brothers and returns with his wives to his ancestral home. As already mentioned above, the militant undertakings are assigned to his son Kaṇha. The

---

[8] Strictly speaking, Madanamañjukā is split in the *Vasudevahiṇḍī* into two totally unrelated characters: Suhiraṇṇā, the daughter of the courtesan Kālindaseṇā and Samba's beloved, and Somasirī, just one of the many princesses Vasudeva marries during his long wanderings. It is Somasirī who is captured by the Vidyādhara Māṇasavega. Parallel to the *Bṛhatkathā*-tradition, her abductor's sister Vegavatī, who actually had consented to deliver a message from Somasirī, fell in love with Vasudeva and tricked him into a marriage. For a more detailed comparison of both versions see Jain 1975: 48 f.

[9] Jain (1975: 50) emphasizes that the story includes in all versions of the *Bṛhatkathā*-tradition a justifying "history" of courtesans.

Vasudevahiṇḍī is incomplete and unfortunately breaks off before Kaṇha's appearance as a *vāsudeva*. In the text, however, some references to Kaṇha as a *vāsudeva* do exist: the prediction that one of the girls Vasudeva is about to marry will gain the father of the future Lord over half of Bharaha[10] (Skt Bharata) as a husband is quite frequent in the *Vasudevahiṇḍī* (Vh 125.8f., 180.24f., 199.13f., 220.12, slightly differing 197.28f., 231.5f., 306.19, 358.17f.). Furthermore, Kaṇha's arch-enemy Jarāsandha tries to kill Vasudeva twice, as it is predicted that he will be the father of his future enemy (Vh 248.9–26, 350.2–23). In addition, Kaṇha's disk Sudarisaṇa with the Yakṣa presiding over it, a typical possession of a *vāsudeva*, is mentioned in Vh 96.22–25.

Besides these more obvious alterations, there are also some minor changes in the main narrative, in which the Jain author becomes visible. We meet with a Veda whose contents seem to be purely Jain;[11] a goat about to be slaughtered is instructed to mentally recite the salutation to the *Arahant*s and to remember the five vows;[12] and the main hero, Vasudeva, turns out to be a philosopher well-versed in the Jain faith.[13] Even more conspicuous is the importance of Jain monks and nuns in the *Vasudevahiṇḍī*. Those who have attained supernatural knowledge through their asceticism are the principal narrators of the secondary stories that interrupt the main plot. As

---

[10] In Jain mythology, a *vāsudeva* is the lord over half of Bharaha, while a *cakravartin* rules over the whole of Bharaha.

[11] To gain Somasirī, the daughter of the village-head Devadeva (not to be confused with Somasirī, daughter of King Somadeva, see above fn. 8), Vasudeva had to answer questions regarding the Vedas. Vasudeva's explanations reflect exclusively Jain philosophical thought (cf. Vh 194.9–19).

[12] Merchant Cārudatta instructed a goat before it was slaughtered, whereupon it was reborn as a god (Vh 149.15–23; 151.16–18). Equally, the minister of King Jiyasattu advised the buffalo Bhaddaga, who acquired after his death, a birth as a god (Vh 273.21–274.10). Monk Sīhacanda instructed the elephant Asaṇivega, who had been his own father in a former life (Vh 256.15–23). After a couple of alternating births as god and prince he obtained final emancipation.

[13] Vasudeva defeats a materialist in a discussion about the existence of the soul (Vh 202.13–203.8) and also corrects an ascetic in a discussion about the nature of *prākṛti* and *puruṣa* (Vh 360.20–361.21). For a more detailed investigation of the first mentioned passage, see Esposito 2011a.

omniscient[14] and thus absolutely reliable persons they are predestined to answer questions about former births or future husbands, about the reason for an intense enmity or a strong affection. In this way it is possible to deviate into many side stories that usually convey clear didactic messages. The frequent mention of Jain sanctuaries and holy *tīrthas* is employed for a similar reason: as an opportunity to insert stories about their mythical history. For example, Vasudeva meets two monks who come from the *tīrtha* of *jina* Santi. Asked to tell about this *jina*, the monks give a long account, running over thirty-eight pages (Vh 310.5–348.9) and including besides the previous births of the *jinas* Santi, Kunthu and Ara also the story of Tiviṭṭhu, Ayala and Āsaggīva, the first *vāsudeva*, *baladeva* and *prativāsudeva* of this world period.

The most obvious 'Jainisation,' however, is the wrapping of the old *Bṛhatkathā*-story in various narrative layers that belong exclusively to the Jain tradition.[15] In a frame story of the *Vasudevahiṇḍī* we meet Jambu, a merchant's son, who aspires to renounce the world. In the night before his renunciation, he encounters Pabhava, a prince who has gone astray and has just broken into Jambu's house. A didactical dialogue interrupted by numerous parables and tales evolves between the two, and at daybreak both Jambu and the prince renounce the world at the feet of the Jain monk Suhamma (Skt Sudharman), a pupil of the twenty-fourth and last *jina* of this world period, Vardhamāna Mahāvīra. One day King Koṇia visits Suhamma. During their conversation, Suhamma tells Koṇia about an earlier meeting between *jina* Mahāvīra and Koṇia's father, King Seṇia of Rāyagiha (Skt Rājagṛha).[16] Here we are in the second narrative layer. During that meeting, Mahāvīra told Seṇia the

[14] As Soni points out in his article in the present volume, there is a slight difference between the single stages of supernatural knowledge. Only somebody possessing *kevala-jñāna* is absolutely reliable; persons possessing *avadhi-* and *manaḥparyāya-jñāna* are still subject to errors. However, some of the Jain monks and nuns in the *Vasudevahiṇḍī* who answer questions posed by the audience have 'only' reached *avadhi-jñāna*.

[15] For the importance of the dialogue in creating the various narrative layers, see Esposito 2011b.

[16] Seṇia (Skt Śreṇika) is identical with King Bimbisāra of Buddhist sources, his son Koṇia (also Kūṇia, Skt Kūṇika) with Ajātasattu.

story of King Vasudeva's grandsons (third narrative layer). In the course of this narration, Vasudeva recounts his own adventures to his grandsons. Only in this fourth narrative layer of the *Vasudevahiṇḍī* does the main story borrowed from the *Bṛhatkathā*-tradition start. In other words, most of the numerous secondary stories are situated only on the fifth narrative layer or even lower—which often makes the narrative quite confusing. These tales are mostly connected somewhat loosely with the main story. In the following I will give a few examples of how the tales about the *śalākāpuruṣas* are embedded:

One day, an old, low-caste woman is offering Vasudeva her granddaughter in marriage. Vasudeva refuses, pointing at their difference in social status. The old woman responds with a long story, beginning with an explanation of the world ages, the emergence of the *kulakaras*, the birth of *jina* Usabha (Skt Ṛṣabha), his reign as the first king, his renunciation and his *kevalajñāna*. Embedded in this narration is a long, artfully intertwined tale about Usabha's former births, told by his grandson Sijjaṃsa (Skt Śreyāṃsa).[17] Why is the old woman narrating Vasudeva all these events, going on for over twenty-one pages (Vh 157.1–178.14)? Because a grandson of Usabha, Nami, mentioned only in the penultimate line of the whole story, is her ancestor, and hence her granddaughter is not inferior to Vasudeva. Besides, they were only disguised as low-castes. Yet if the old woman had revealed this crucial fact at the beginning, there would have been no opportunity for Saṅghadāsa to have inserted his long tale about *jina* Usabha.

We can find two further stories about the life of *jina* Usabha in the *Vasudevahiṇḍī*—both, interestingly enough, in the passage about the Aryan and the non-Aryan Veda (Vh 183.1–193.20): one day Vasudeva entered a village where he learnt that Somasirī, the beautiful daughter of the village chief, was to be married to the person who could answer questions regarding the Vedas. He decided to begin immediately with the study of the scriptures and approached the learned Bambhadatta. The latter asked Vasudeva which Veda he would like

[17] For a study of the narration about *jina* Usabha in the *Vasudevahiṇḍī* in comparison to other versions of the story, see Esposito 2011c.

to learn, the Aryan or the non-Aryan one? Asked about the difference, Bambhadatta explained the origin of both scriptures: Usabha reached the *parinirvāṇa* together with ten thousand ascetics on Mount Aṭṭhāvaya. During the reign of his son Bharaha, the Aryan Veda developed as a doctrine for laymen (Vh 183.1–185.22).

The non-Aryan Veda originated in an offended love: King Sagara wanted to marry Princess Sulasā, whose *svayaṃvara* had been announced. Through a spy, he learned about a conversation between Sulasā and her mother Ditī: the mother admonished her daughter to marry according to the family lore that came into being at the time of *jina* Usabha. Usabha had divided his realm between his hundred sons. Bharaha, his eldest son, was not content with what he had received and ordered his brothers to recognize him as sovereign. Only Bāhubali dared to revolt against him. As he saw it, Bharaha used unfair means to get what he wanted. Bāhubali was disgusted by the whole matter and renounced the world. The sons of Bharaha and Bāhubali, Āiccajasa and Somappabha, considered themselves to be the most powerful among all kings. They agreed to marry their daughters not to inferior kings, but only to the sons of the family of one another. For this reason, Queen Ditī concluded her tale, Princess Sulasā should choose her cousin, King Mahupiṅgala, in the *svayaṃvara*. Of course, King Sagara, who learned about this conversation, managed to bring his opponent into disrepute and to marry Sulasā himself. Mahupiṅgala did not forget his hatred even after death: he became a god by the name of Mahākāla and waited patiently for an opportunity to take revenge. Soon he found a proper tool in Pavvaya. Although Pavvaya had been instructed by his father Khīrakayaṃba, an able teacher, he remained a poor scholar. Mahākāla approached him, pretending to be a good old friend of his father, and offered to impart his wisdom to him—an offer Pavvaya accepted. Mahākāla secretly unleashed an epidemic in the kingdom of his archenemy Sagara. Pavvaya was asked for help and introduced on Mahākāla's advice various violent sacrifices to stop the epidemic.[18] These erroneous teachings, introduced by god Mahākāla, are known as the non-Aryan Veda (Vh 185.24–193.20).

The previous narration in particular makes clear just how loose the connection to the main story can be. Often a mere name is enough for Saṅghadāsa to connect Jain stories like those of the *śalākāpuruṣas* with the main story. What is more, artificial narratives are sometimes embedded into the main plot, as the next example demonstrates:

Vasudeva had just married Princess Mayaṇavegā, daughter of King Vijjuvega. Some days later her brother, Prince Dahimuha, wanted to ask him a favour. His explanations take up fifteen pages (Vh 230.26–245.28) of the *Vasudevahiṇḍī*: due to a prophecy a certain Princess Paümasirī will one day marry a *cakravartin*. Her father, King Mehaṇāya, asked some omniscient monks about the former lives of his daughter. Inter alia, she was the unloved wife of Saṇaṃkumāra, the fourth *cakravartin*, a fact that provided our author the possibility to 'incidentally' relate his story as well. Furthermore, Mehaṇāya asked the whereabouts of his daughter's future husband. The monks told him, how Jamadaggi, the son of King Aggisihara, practiced severe penance, but led astray by some gods, decided to take a wife. He managed to marry the young Princess Reṇuā and they had a son, Rāma, who became involved in combat with some kings and decided to kill all the Kṣatriyas on earth. Queen Tārā had managed to escape with her son Subhūma to a hermitage. This young prince will some day kill Jamadaggi and become a *cakravartin*—and the husband of Princess Paümasirī. Of course the prophecy was fulfilled. We witness the further life of Subhūma till his death and also his next rebirth: he went to the seventh hell. To the family of King Mehaṇāya, his father-in-law, belonged a certain Bali who had a fight with the sixth *vāsudeva* Purisapuṇḍarīya, and to the family of Bali belonged a King Sahassaggīva, whose great-great-great-grandson was Dassaggīva, also known as Rāmaṇa (the Rāvaṇa of Hindu mythology). Now the Jain Rāmāyaṇa is told, in which we encounter the eighth *vāsudeva*, *baladeva* and

---

[18] Among others he utilized the Aśvamedha. Queen Sulasā, who had been supposed to marry God Mahākāla in his former life, died out of sheer disgust during this sacrifice.

prativāsudeva, Rāma, Lakkhaṇa (Skt Lakṣmaṇa) and Rāmaṇa. As is well known, Vihīsaṇa (Skt Vibhīṣaṇa) and Suggīva (Skt Sugrīva) helped Rāma to conquer half of Bharaha. To the family of Vihīsaṇa belongs King Vijjuvega, who is the father of Dahimuha, the narrator of this story. All these preceding explanations are quite important to understand Dahimuha's final request: Could you, Vasudeva, please rescue your father-in-law Vijjuvega, who has been captured by a certain King Tisehara?

Conclusion

As we can see from these few examples, Saṅghadāsa connects his stories often quite loosely with each other and with the main narrative. Sometimes a mere name is enough to insert another tale, a further myth or an additional story. Saṅghadāsa put his main emphasis not on the central plot, borrowed from the *Bṛhatkathā*, but on the numerous secondary stories. His intent is obviously not to create a new version of the *Bṛhatkathā* with a Jain background, but instead to use the material from the popular *Bṛhatkathā* as a background for edifying stories, including the Jain universal history. The main focus of the *Vasudevahiṇḍī* is the transmission of doctrinal content, packaged in compelling stories—and *this* is what sets the *Vasudevahiṇḍī* apart from the other works of the *Bṛhatkathā*-tradition.

Bibliography

Alsdorf, Ludwig, 1936, *Harivaṃśapurāṇa. Ein Abschnitt aus der Apabhraṃśa-Welthistorie "Mahāpurāṇa Tisaṭṭhimahāpurisaguṇālaṃkāra" von Puṣpadnta. Als Beitrag zur Kenntninis des Apabhraṃśa und der Universalgeschichte der Jainas herausgegeben.* Hamburg: Friedrichsen, De Gruyter & Co., Alt- und Neuindische Studien 5.

——— 1938, "Eine neue Version der verlorenen Bṛhatkathā des Guṇāḍhya." *Atti del XIX Congresso Internationale degli Orientaisti, Roma*, pp. 344–349 [= *Kleine Schriften* pp. 101–106].

——— 1974, *Kleine Schriften.* Hrsg. von Albrecht Wezler. Wiesbaden: Franz Steiner Verlag (Glasenapp-Stiftung 10).

Esposito, Anna Aurelia, 2011a [Forthcoming], "Vasudeva the Philosopher—Soul and Body in Saṅghadāsa's *Vasudevahiṇḍī*." In: Peter Flügel (ed.), *Jaina Scriptures and Philosophy*.

——— 2011b [forthcoming], "Didactic Dialogues: Communication of Doctrine and Strategies of Narrative in Jain Literature." In: Brian Black, Laurie Patton (eds), *Dialogue and Early South Asian Religions: Reading the Sources* (Dialogues in South Asian Traditions: Religion, Philosophy, Literature, and History 1).

——— 2011c [forthcoming], "Life before Life before Life—an Exceptional Perspective on Jina Usabha's Biography." In: *International Journal of Jaina Studies* 11.

Grafe, Jörg, 2001, *Vidyādharas. Früheste Zeit bis zur Kaschmirischen Bṛhatkathā*. Frankfurt a. M.: Peter Lang (Europäische Hochschulschriften, Reihe XXVII, 82).

Jain, Jagdish Chandra. 1973/74. "Is Vasudevahiṇḍī a Jain version of the Bṛhatkathā?" In: *Journal of the Oriental Institute* (Baroda) 23, pp. 59–63.

——— 1975, "Some important episodes in Vasudevahiṇḍi and the reconstruction of the Bṛhatkathā". In: *Sambodhi* 3.4, pp. 47–60.

——— 1977, *The Vasudevahiṇḍi. An authentic Jain version of the Bṛhatkathā. With selected translations compared to the Bṛhatkathāślokasaṅgraha, Kathāsaritsāgara, Bṛhatkathāmañjarī and some important Jaina works, including the unpublished Majjhimakhaṇḍa and with extensive notes, introduction and appendices*. Ahmedabad: L. D. Institute of Indology (L. D. Series 59).

Lacôte, Félix, 1908, *Essai sur Guṇāḍhya et la Bṛhatkathā suivi du texte inédit des chapitres XXVII a XXX du Nepāla-Māhātmya*. Paris: Ernest Leroux (Contribution a l'historie des contes Indiens).

Nelson, Donald, 1978, "Bṛhatkathā Studies: The Problem of an Urtext." *The Journal of Asian Studies* 37.4, pp. 663–676.

——— 1980. "Bṛhatkathā Studies: The Tamil version of the Bṛhatkathā." *Indo-Iranian Journal* 22.3, pp. 221–235.

Vijayalakshmy, R. 1982. "The Tamil Peruṅkatai and its relationship to the *Bṛhatkathā*. 1. The viricikai episode." *Indo-Iranian Journal* 24.1, pp. 27–36.

——— 1985, "The Jaina Elements in the Versions of the *Bṛhatkathā*." In: R. N. Dandekar, P. D. Navathe (eds), *Proceedings of the Fifth World Sanskrit Conference. Varanasi, India: October 21–26, 1981*. New Delhi: Rashtriya Sanskrit Sansthan, pp. 868–878.

Warder, A. K. [1974] ²1990, *Indian Kāvya Literature. Vol. II: The Origins and Formation of Classical Kāvya*. Delhi: Motilal Banarsidass.

Jinabhadra's *Bṛhatsaṃgrahaṇī* and Malayagiri's Commentary on it

Shin Fujinaga

Abstract

Jinabhadra's *Bṛhtsaṃgrhaṇī* along with Malayagiri's commentary are important for the details they contain about Jaina cosmology in particular and specific aspects of Jainism in general. The aim of this paper is to evaluate both works by analysing selected aspects of their content.

Keywords: Jinabhadra, Malayagiri, *Bṛhatsaṃgrhaṇī*, cosmology, Jaina *Āgamas*

Jinabhadra occupies a unique position in the history of Jainism. Firstly, and something that is quite unusual in the case of matters concerning ancient India, his exact dates can be reliably determined based on the available data. This means that we can arrive at relative dates of other ancient Jaina thinkers by using those of Jinabhadra as the criterion. Malvania has proved beyond doubt, on the basis of available historical material, that Jinabhadra lived between fifth and sixth centuries.[1] Thus, we are in a position to say that the works whose titles Jinabhadra mentions, or portions of them he quotes or alludes to in his writings, were obviously composed before his time. In the same manner, authors quoting his works must be senior to him.[2]

Another point which makes a study on Jinabhadra unique is that he wrote his works utilising material from the Jaina *Āgamas* at a very early time. Several works including two auto-commentaries are attributed to him and one of the most important in this regard is the *Viśeṣāvāvaśyakabhāṣa* (VĀBh), with an incomplete auto-commentary.[3] It is regarded as his

---

[1] See Malvaniya 1966, p.3.

[2] For example, Haribhadra quotes some portions of Jinabhadra's VĀBh in his *Anuyogadvāra vivṛtti*.

[3] See Wiles 1997, pp. 178–9 for available editions. Other works by Jinabhadra are *Bṛhatsaṃgrhaṇī* (see the bibliography), *Bṛhatkṣetrasamāsa* (published in 1920 with Malayagiri's commentary),*Viśeṣanavatī*, *Jītakalpasūtra* (with an auto-commentary, see Wiles again, pp. 224–5) and the *Dhyānaśataka* which does not seem have been published yet. Here I wish to thank Ms Hiroko Matsuoka, PhD candidate of Hiroshima University, for kindly sending me copies of the BS and other works.

magnum opus, and studied especially for the many *Āgamic* ideas contained in them, with discussions on Jaina moral doctrines and other topics.[4] His other works also have the same tendencies in different topics. Hence, many ideas scattered in the various *Āgamas* are combined together in specific contexts, and Jinabhadra helps us in this way to better grasp their intent.

This is also the case with Jinabhadra's *Bṛhatsaṃgrahaṇī* (BS), which will be dealt with here. This work exclusively concerns the Jaina view of cosmology or the structure of the universe. Its significance lies in being a compact treatise on living beings in this universe. It is well known that the Jainas maintain that the universe consists of three elemental parts: *uttara loka* or the upper world, *tiryak loka* or the middle world in which we human beings lives, and the *adhas loka* or the hells. Jinabhadra's interests in the BS are on the first and the last worlds, because the middle world is intensively dealt with in his other work, the *Bhṛhatkṣetrasamāsa*. His way of description seems rather unique to us; what the author shows in this book are mainly attributes of the living beings in each world, such as the duration of life, the size of the body and the colour of their soul or *leśyā*. Only in few stanzas does he refer to the size of the respective portions of the universe. In his *Tattvārthasūtra* chapters three and four, Umāsvāti too describes the shape of the universe in a similar way as does Jinabhadra.

As mentioned above, and Jinabhadra himself clearly says so in the last verse of BS,[5] the material out of which he of his own free will chose to compose this work, are the Jaina *Āgamas* or works written by Jaina monks senior to him. In order to adequately compare cosmological ideas in the BS and the *Āgamas*, we would first have to study the cosmology in the *Āgamas* and in works composed before the time of Jinabhadra. Such a task would be beyond the scope of an essay such as this. However, it is clear that Jinabhadra utilized such works because some stanzas in the BS are exactly the same as those in *Āgama* works. Malvania shows that seven verses of the BS have been

---

[4] For the quotation in this work, see VĀBh vol. III, pp. 927-929.

[5] *Jaṃ uddhiyaṃ suyaō puvvāyariyakayamahava samaīē/ khmiyavvaṃ suyheriṃ taheva suyadevyaē ya* //376//.

composed by others.[6] Of these, the stanzas 68, 69 and 72 are quoted from *Sūryaprajñapti* 19.22–8, 9, 10 respectively. The remaining four verses have not been identified. Besides this, the stanzas 44–47 in the BS are the same as those in *Prajñapanā.* Both the *Sūryaprajñapti* and the *Prajñapanā* belong to the *upāṅga* class of the Jaina *Āgamas.* Moreover, the stanzas 197–199 can be identified as the *Sūryaprajñaptiniryukti* stanzas 171–173. And we shall point out that four stanzas are quoted from the *Āvaśyakaniryukti* as stanzas 222, 223, 224 and 226. These two works are not a part of the *Āgamas,* but are traditionally regarded as having been composed by Bhadrabāhu. Hence, Bhadrabāhu would be one of the Jaina monks senior to Jinabhadra or, if we use his word, *puvvāyariyas.*[7]

It is rather strange that Jinabhadra does not systematically mention the names of the seven hells which are clearly given in *Tattvārthasūtra* 3, 1, where the author describes the hells in six (or seven) *sūtras.*[8] This does not mean, however, that Jinabhadra had no or very little knowledge of the hells. In fact, he explains the details of each and every layer of the seven hells. The same can be said about his attitude towards the gods. Jinabhadra shows the attributes of gods, their dwelling places and other aspects related to them in detail, but he does not give us a clear idea of the shape of the entire upper world. This means that in the BS we do not have a complete description of the hells nor of the world of gods, so naturally the idea to show the concrete shape of the universe as a human being standing with legs slightly apart and akimbo does not appear in the BS. At the end of the BS, Jinabhadra refers to several types of *gati* or course of reincarnation of a *jīva.* The idea of *gati* leads us to the concept of *lokanāḍī* which runs from the top of the universe to the bottom, straight like a spine, so to speak, of the *lokapuruṣa.* The *lokanāḍī* is a concept unique to Jaina cosmology. But neither the *lokapuruṣa* nor the *lokanāḍī* is clearly mentioned in the Śvetāmbara canon. Although Jinabhadra does not mention *lokapuruṣa,* however he seems to imply it: in BS stanza 222 he shows which gods have *avadhi-*

---

[6] Malvania 1985, p. 36, note 3.

[7] Cf. v. 376 quoted in note 4.

[8] The Digambara recension contains six and the Śvetāmbara seven *sūtras.*

knowledge, and to which extent it operates. It reads:

> *chaṭṭhi hiṭṭhima majjhima gevijjā sattaṃmi ca uvarillā/*
> *saṃbhinnaloga nāliṃ pāsaṃti aṇuttarā devā//*
>
> The *graiveyaka* gods in the lower and middle worlds can see as far as the sixth hell and those in the upper part to the seventh hell, while gods in the uppermost part see the *lokanāḍī*, which is somehow not deeper than the hells.

Two points are noteworthy with regard to this stanza. Firstly, the reference to *lokanāḍī* here must be the oldest to be found in the Śvetāmbara tradition. And from this we know that *lokanāḍī* does not extend to the very bottom of the universe, that is, the seventh hell. The other point is the reference to *graiveyaka*. Here, this group of gods is used as a criterion of measurement while the term referring to them means a necklace. The part of the body below the necklace is the trunk and upper parts are the neck and head. As we have seen previously, this verse is not original to Jinabhadra but belongs to the *Āvaśyakaniryukti*. In order to understand this point clearly and in detail, one would have to study the commentaries on this stanza of the *Āvaśyakaniryukti*. However, our point is that although Jinabhadra does not refer to *lokapuruṣa* explicitly, he implies it in the way just suggested. For the time being, we may assume that both Bhadrabāhu, the author of *Āvaśyakaniryukti*, and Jinabhadra must have known the word and concept of *lokanāḍī*, but may have not been familiar with it in the context of cosmology, or that they must have been interested in the scope of *avadhijñāna*, but not with the shape of the universe.

It may be noted in this context that Umāsvāti's *Tattvārthasūtra* also lacks an explicit reference to the shape of whole universe. Therefore, it seems that both works belong to the medieval period in the history of Jaina cosmology.[9]

Malayagiri, a contemporary of *ācārya* Hemacandra, is

[9] The so-called auto-commentary on the *Tattvārthasūtra* refers to the *lokapuruṣa* when it comments on chapter 3, *sūtra* 20. This author does not admit that Umāsvāti wrote the commentary. In any case, the point is that Umāsvāti does not mention the shape of the universe explicitly.

known as an author of commentaries, and not of independent works.[10] Some twenty works by him are available today.[11] He wrote commentaries on *Āgamas*, Jinabhadra's works, etc. A commentary on the *Nandīsūtra* by Malayagiri is well known to scholars on Buddhist logic because he quotes many works of that field, as Muni Jambuvijaya has already pointed out.[12] Here I would like to discuss two characteristic points in Malayagiri's commentary (*vṛtti*) on the BS (referred to as Mv here). The first point concerns the number of stanzas in the BS and the second point is about the richness of the Mv as a treatise on Jaina cosmology.

We have two recensions of the BS: one withs 367 stanzas and one with 500 stanzas.[13] Modern Jaina scholars such as Pandit Malvania regard the former as authentic,[14] and Muni Jambuvijaya says that the stanzas contained only in the latter are inserted by the someone later than Jinabhadra[15] (we shall call these the inserted stanzas). Malayagiri seems to be of the same opinion because he explains only the stanzas of the former. In the Mv, however, Malayagiri quotes almost all the stanzas which he does not admit as having been written by Jinabhadra. When he quotes the inserted stanzas, Malayagiri usually uses the words *uktaṃ ca* before them. It is difficult to understand what he intends with these words. But we can say that he does not know the origin of the inserted stanzas because when he quotes sentences from other works (except in the explanation of grammatical rules), he mentions the name of the author or the title of works. For example, commenting on stanzas 1–3, he quotes a sentence from the so-called auto-commentary of *Tattvārthasūtra* 2, 16, with the words: *tathā cāha tattvārthabhāṣyakṛt*.[16] So it must be said that when he began writing the Mv he may have had two recensions in the front of him and he may have regarded the BS

---

[10] For the date and works of Malayagiri, see Doshi 1967, pp. 3-8.

[11] See Mehta 1967, p. 417.

[12] Jambuvijaya 1994.

[13] Velankar 1944, p. 285 says that the BS is in 419 Gāthās.

[14] Malvania 1985.

[15] In a private discussion, in August 2009 at Nakoda, Rājasthān, India.

[16] P. 4b.

which contains fewer stanzas as the original. However, he did not deny the authenticity of the other recension, and so incorporated them in the commentary. The authenticity of the inserted stanzas can be testified in another way. In chapter 29 of *Syādvādamañjarī*, the author Malliṣeṇa discusses the topic of *nigoda* and quotes two stanzas from the inserted stanzas to support his view. [17]

As a commentary, the Mv has two aspects: a commentary to understand the meaning of the BS and a commentary to enlarge its contents. Malayagiri glosses the words of almost all the stanzas of the BS, by giving a Sanskrit equivalent of the original Prakrit word first, and after that by providing a synonym of the Sanskrit. This is the usual way that an author of a Sanskrit commentary on a Prakrit work takes. Even then, the Mv is very helpful in understanding the meaning of the BS.

The second aspect of the Mv, however, is what makes it even more valuable. Paṇḍit Malvania clearly says that this BS is an encyclopaedic work for Jaina thought on *jīva* and the universe, because Malayagiri wrote a commentary on it in an excellent way.[18] The manner in which he succeeded in achieving this can be classified again into two categories: quoting sentences from various sources and then explaining ideas in his own words. In the Mv, Malayagiri quotes more than two hundred sentences from various kinds of works so as to explain the original text by Jinabhadra; it seems that Malayagiri might have also known different recensions of the BS. Some of the quoted sentences are easily identified when Malayagiri mentions the name of an author or a title of a work. Quotations from a few other original works may not be very difficult to determine. But many other quotations have to remain as unidentified because they are from unknown works. Malayagiri's main sources of his quotations are works belonging to the *Āgamas*, such as the *Jīvābhigama, Sūryaprajñapti* and *Aupapātika.* We also find sentences from the Jaina *Aṅga* such as *Uttarādhyāyanasūtra.* Besides these canonical works, he often refers to and quotes stanzas or prose of authors senior to him. References are sometimes made to the *Niryukti.* Stanzas

---

[17] *Syādvādamañjarī* p. 171, lines 65–68.

[18] Malvania 1985, p. 36.

written by Jinabhadra also appear in the Mv. For example, VĀBh and *Viśeṣaṇavatī* are quoted in various places. The *Tattvārthasūtra* and its so-called auto-commentary are also referred to by Malayagiri. It is interesting that he uses a simple word *Tattvārtha* not *Tattvārthādhigma* when he quotes from this work.

Haribhadra's commentaries on the *Āgamas* such as the *Anuyogadvāra,* and *Āvaśyakasūtra*, seem to be the main sources for discussions by Jinabhadra. But the most important reference to Haribhadra must be the one to his *mūlaṭīkā*. In the Mv, Haribhadra is called *mūlaṭīkākāra* and Malayagiri quotes a few Prakrit sentences from the *mūlaṭīkā* without mentioning any person. This means that the first person who wrote a commentary on the BS would be Haribhadra. Bu who is this Haribhadra? One possible person is the Haribhadra who composed the *Munipaticaritra* in V. Sam. 1172 and who is said to have written a *vṛtti* on the BS.[19] But before him, in V. Sam. 1139 Śālibhadra wrote a commentary on the BS,[20] so this Haribhadra cannot be the *mūlaṭīkākāra*. The other possibility could be that Yākinī-mahattarāsunu Haribhadra wrote this *mūlaṭīkā*. He is known as a commentator of various works including the *Anuyogadvārasūtra*. In the Mv also, Malayagiri refers to and quotes Haribhadra's commentary on the *Anuyogadvārasūtra*.[21] But so far as our knowledge goes, no tradition tells us that this Haribhadra commented on the BS. Moreover, all the commentaries by this Haribhadra are written in Sanskrit, whereas our *mūlaṭīkā* is in Prakrit. All this means that this *mūlaṭīkā* problem still requires further research and study.

Now let us have a brief look at Malayagiri's explanation in his own words, in the Mv. As mentioned above, Jinabhadra's description in the BS is generally very simple. Malayagiri, on the other hand, explains the respective portions in more detail. Let us take the cd *pādas* of stanza 4 as an example. Here, Jinabhadra says just that we have to understand the maximum (life span) of the *vyantara* (gods) as being one *palyopama (paliovamamukkosaṃ vaṃtarāṇaṃ vijāṇijjā*). To this sen-

[19] See Velankar 1944, pp. 286 and 311.

[20] Velankar 1944, p. 285.

[21] Mv on BS 111a.

tence Malayagiri first gives the Sanskrit forms of each Prakrit word, and then supplies a few more words to make their meaning clearer. But still, the sentence remains some how vague, because the word *palyopama* is unfamiliar to us. So Malayagiri explains it in his own words. We come across numerous such explanations in the Mv.

Although the BS and the Mv cannot be ignored in any study concerning Jaina cosmology, very few studies have been done on them. It is hoped that the two works will at some point be edited, just as the late Jaina Muni Jambuvijaya did with many canonical works and their commentaries.

Bibliography

Original Sources

Anuyogadvāra-viṛtti, by Haribhadra. See *Anuyogadvāra Sūtram.*

Anuyogadvāra Sūtram cūrṇi-viṛtti-vṛttivibhūsitam. Edited by Jambuvijaya Bumbai: Jaina-Āgama-Granthamālā (18-1) 1999.

Ācārya Jinabhadra's Viśeṣāvaśyakabhāṣya *with Auto-commentary Parts I, II, III.* Ahmedabad : Lalbhai Dalpatbhai Series (Nos. 10,14, 21) ,1966–68.

Tattvārthādhigamasūtra by Umāsvāti being in the original Sanskrit with the Bhāshya by the author himself. Edited by Mody Keshavlal Premchand. (Bibliotheca Indica New Series No. 1044) Calcutta 1903.

Trailokyadīpikā yāne Bṛhatsaṃghrahaṇī mūla. Edited by by M. V. Shah. Surat V.S. 1972.

Bṛtatsaṃgrhaṇī with Malayagiri's vṛtti. Edited by Pannyāsa-dānavijaya, Bhavnagar: Śrī Jaina Ātmānanda Granthamālā (47) V.S. 1973.

Syādvādamañjarī of Malliṣeṇa with the Anuyoga-Vyavaccheda-Dvātriṃśikā of Hemacandra. Edited by A. B. Dhurva. Bombay: Bombay Sanskrit and Prakrit Series (No. 83) 1933.

Secondary Sources

Doshi, B. J. 1967, *Ācārya Malayagiri's* Śabdānuśasana *with Auto-commentary.* Ahmedabad: Lalbhai Dalpatbhai Series (No. 13).

Jambuvijaya 1994. "Quotations in Malayagiri's Commentary on the Nandisūtra". In: *Wiener Zeitschrift für die Kunde Süd-sasiens* 38, pp. 384–401.

Malvania, D., 1966, see Ācārya Jinabhadra's *Viśeṣāvaśyakabhāṣya*, volume I.

——— 1985, *Ācārya Jinabhadra-kṛt Gaṇadharvād nāṃ saṃvādātmak anuvād, ṭippaṇ ane prastāvnā*. Ahmedabad: Śeṭh Pūnamcaṃd Karamcaṃd Koṭāvālā Graṃthmālā (40), second edition.

Mehta, M., 1967, *Jain Sāhityaka Bṛhat Itihās*, Volume 3, Varanasi: Pārśvanāth Vidyālay Granthamālā (11).

Velankar, H. R., 1944, *Jinaratnakośa, an Alphabetical Register of Jain Works and Authors*. Volume 1, Poona: Government Oriental Series (Class C, No. 4).

Wiles, Royce, 1997, *The Śvetāmbara Canon. A Descriptive Listing of Text Editions, Commentaries, Studies and Indexes*. Canberra: Australian National University.